FALLING CHIPS

FALLING CHIPS

A deconstruction of the single-bullet theory of the JFK assassination

RODGER A. REMINGTON

To order additional copies of this book, contact:
Xlibris Corporation
1-888-795-4274
www.Xlibris.com
Orders@Xlibris.com
26739

CONTENTS

INTRODUCTION

One of the more fascinating books published in the year 2000 was titled *Passion for Truth*. It was written by United States Senator, Honorable Arlen Specter, with Charles Robbins, identified as the Senator's communications director in his Senate office and on his presidential campaign. The book's dust jacket tells readers that Robbins is a graduate of Princeton University and Columbia University Graduate School of Journalism.

The book jacket also identifies Arlen Specter's career as having "encompassed such milestones as originating the Single-Bullet Theory for the Warren Commission; derailing Judge Robert Bork's Supreme Court nomination; interrogating Anita Hill; and playing an important role in President Clinton's impeachment proceedings. A 2001 edition features "a New Epilogue on the 2000 Presidential Election, the Clinton Pardons, and Jeffords' Historic Switch." Both editions include an enticing blurb paragraph which reads in part:

> In this brutally honest book, Senator Specter analyzes these and other controversies, assessing each through both a legal and a historical lens. Throughout he tells the truth, naming names, identifying where the system worked and where it failed—and even admitting to his own mistakes.

Another blurb—this from *Publisher's Weekly*—reads: "Specter brings to each episode a prosecutor's dogged pursuit of truth . . . . An informative and enjoyable read."

I thoroughly enjoyed reading both the first edition and the New Epilogue. And as well I found each episode informative.

I was particularly interested in reading, studying and analyzing Part Two of Senator Specter's book, an 82-page section divided into ten chapters, each concerned with aspects of the Warren Commission's investigation of and *Report* on the assassination of President John F. Kennedy. The chapters are titled:

The Warren Commission

> Truth Is the Client
> Quick Reflexes
> Governor Connally
> Bullet 399
> The Biggest Mistake
> The Magic Bullet
> Bedlam
> The Sheriff's Kitchen
> Truth and Lies

My background is that of an academic historian who taught undergraduate history courses in the setting of a small private liberal arts college between 1963-1997. I had little personal interest, and virtually no academic interest, in that assassination until 1992 when I attended, as a guest, a course taught by a colleague, whose dynamic teaching style matched the exciting drama of the assassination itself. Following my retirement in 1997, I developed an active interest which led to self-publication of two books: *The People v. The Warren Report: Suggestions for Historians* (2002) and *The Warren Report's Evidence v. "Conclusions"* (2003).

With that background, I was excited by the Specter book's dust jacket allusion to his assessing controversies through a "historical lens". Though my memory is not as quick as it once ve no recollection of having seen or heard of the term at usage. Be that as it may, I presume that a "historical es a genuine commitment to a historical methodology intellectual honesty and informed common sense, e to the heart of pedagogical historians.

Conversely, and more warily, I was less confident in my understanding of the allusion to a "legal lens" assessment of controversy. As a layman uninitiated in the mysteries of the legal profession, I eagerly looked forward to an explanation of both the term and its methodology in the context of Arlen Specter's experiences while employed as an Assistant Counsel to the Warren Commission.

There is another term that both interested and puzzled me when I saw it in the dust jacket blurb: "This illuminating *memoir* is vintage Specter: thoughtful, provocative, and deeply informative." What, I asked myself, does "memoir" mean in a writing that undertakes to analyze controversy through a historical lens? Not confident of personal presumptive answers, I sought advice from both literature professors and dictionaries. None of the professors could provide a definitive answer, and none of the dictionaries gave a definition that seemed to fit the example at hand—a controversy viewed through a historical lens.

Thus there seemed to me at the outset a circular problem in any attempt by me to evaluate Senator Arlen Specter's *Passion for Truth*. And I note at this point my disinterest, and incompetence, to evaluate any part of Senator Specter's book other than Part Two, which is concerned with the assassination of President John F. Kennedy. That disclaimer aside, my problem lay with the term, "memoir". If by memoir, his writing is intended to be that which is encompassed by the third definition (applicable to the plural "memoirs") in *Webster's New World College Dictionary*, Fourth Edition, c1999, 898: "a report or record of important events based on the writer's personal observation or knowledge," there is no real problem in understanding a memoir as a record of personal observations. Conversely, if by historical lens is intended to be that which utilizes the historical method of investigation—intellectual honesty and informed common sense in the use of authentic and credible data—I assumed the writing may be appropriately evaluated on the basis of references and citations. The problem appears when an attempt is made to combine the two notions: personal observations not supported by appropriate references and citations.

This then is the thesis of my present writing: Senator Arlen Specter's Part Two of his *Passion for Truth* is vulnerable to critical review based on canons of historical methodology. The style of my review is to examine each of the ten chapters in Part Two for evaluation consistent with those canons.

In this examination, it is important to remember that there is a close relationship between/among Arlen Specter/David W. Belin/Gerald R. Ford as evidenced by their mutual dependence and support for each other's contributions to the literature on behalf of the work of the Warren Commission's 1964 *Report*. A remembered awareness of that relationship will assist in understanding the significance of the following data:

- U. S. Congressman Gerald R. Ford, a member of the Warren Commission, wrote a feature article in *Life* magazine as early as October 2, 1964—the week following release of the Warren *Report*—in which he identified Howard L. Brennan as "the most important witness" to appear before the Commission. In 1965, in collaboration with John R. Stiles, his special assistant during work of the Warren Commission, he wrote a book, *Portrait of the Assassin,* which focused exclusively on Lee Harvey Oswald as the guilty party.

- David W. Belin was an Assistant Counsel of the Commission. He conducted the testimony examination of Howard L. Brennan, given on March 24, 1964. In 1973, he published a book titled *November 22, 1963: You Are the Jury*, in which he utilized a literary device of using the book's readers as endorsers of the findings and conclusions of the Warren Commission.

- In 1975, Belin served as Executive Director of the Rockefeller Commission, appointed by then U.S. President Gerald R. Ford, charged with investigating the role of the CIA in alleged clandestine assassination operations on behalf of the United States Government.

- On March 12, 1992 the *Grand Rapids* [Michigan] *Press* printed a newswire article written by Gerald R. Ford and David W. Belin. It was titled "THE KENNEDY ASSASSINATION: HOW ABOUT THE TRUTH?"
- Part Two of Senator Arlen Specter's *Passion for Truth*— 85 printed pages—published in 2000, contains 25 notes of reference/ citations, including six each for Gerald R. Ford and David W. Belin.

Moreover, the relationship between Assistant Counsel colleagues Specter and Belin is particularly significant in terms of both substantive and procedural understandings negotiated between them in areas of investigation undertaken on behalf of their work for the Warren Commission. Lest there be possible misunderstanding concerning this observation, I declare at this point: There is nothing sinister intended or implied. Both men were experienced professional lawyers who shared a genuine enthusiasm for their task at hand. Understandably they developed a close personal relationship in the exercise of their responsibilities. They shared many common perspectives.

The point I wish to make is important: Senator Specter's *Passion for Truth* covers 542 printed pages, 82 of which are devoted to his service on the Warren Commission; Belin's book, *November 22, 1963: You are the Jury*, has 475 pages of text, all of which are related to his service on the Warren Commission. Because of circumstances not of his making and beyond his control, Arlen Specter was forced to work without a Senior lawyer partner in performing his services; David Belin was the beneficiary of the assistance and support of a Senior lawyer partner, Joseph A. Ball, in performing his services. Thus, in recounting their experiences, Belin had the opportunity in his book to explore, sometimes at great length, legal concepts, strategies and tactics that governed his experiences. Whether Specter would endorse each of the comments and arguments in Belin's book is irrelevant to the self-imposed limitations mandated by space in his, Specter's, *Passion for Truth*.

My present writing is concerned with just one of the controversies included in Senator Specter's book, *Passion for Truth*. That subject is the role of Arlen Specter in developing the Single-Bullet Theory for the Warren Commission. My particular interest is his exposition on behalf of a relationship between the two prominent topics, "truth", as in Specter's "Passion for" and "theory", as in his Single-Bullet creation. Indeed, in a book that is dramatically emphatic—"passionately" so—in its concern for "the truth", it is a remarkable intellectual journey by way of a progression of thought from, in his words, "theory" through "conclusion" to "fact."

Senator Specter began his book with an introductory section titled "Prologue:The Single-Bullet Conclusion." Therein he relates an incident that occurred in July 1995, when he appeared at a Dallas Convention Center media session as one of a panel of nine candidates seeking the 1996 Republican Party nomination for the Presidency. He relates the following as his introduction to a discussion of that theory he made famous:

> Then one newspaper reporter hollered a question, an accusation really, that stilled the others. 'Cynicism in America,' the reporter said, 'all began with your Single-Bullet Theory and was fanned by Watergate.'
>
> It was a heavy charge. I had developed the Single-Bullet Theory more than thirty years earlier as a staff lawyer on the President's Commission on the Assassination of President John F. Kennedy, more commonly known as the Warren Commission. I now call it the Single-Bullet Conclusion. It began as a theory, but when a theory is established by the facts, it deserves to be called a conclusion. The conclusion is that the same bullet sliced through President John F. Kennedy's neck and then tore through Texas Governor John Connally's chest and wrist, finally lodging in the governor's thigh, as the presidential motorcade wound through downtown Dallas on November 22, 1963. The Warren Commission

adopted the Single-Bullet Conclusion as its official explanation. Essentially, the reporter was accusing me of bringing cynicism to American government, with Richard Nixon as an accomplice years after the fact. (1-2)

Such being so, there should be no petty criticism of *Passion for Truth*'s dust jacket reference to Specter's "originating the Single-Bullet Theory" for the Commission as one of the milestones of his remarkable public career. Indeed, it is difficult for any John Kennedy assassination writer to think of Arlen Specter apart from that role.

However, there is another reality that cannot be ignored. Arlen Specter's work in writing the Warren *Report*'s crucial Chapter III—"The Shots From the Texas School Book Depository"— generated the three essential findings posited by the Warren Commission in the *Report*'s Chapter I: "Conclusions":

1. Lee Harvey *Oswald* was the
2. *lone assassin* who fired
3. *three shots* from the southeast corner window of the sixth floor in the Texas School Book Depository Building.

The issue—indeed the nagging unanswered question of 40+ years—is whether those findings constitute "the truth" upon which must be based *each* and *all* of the three steps entailed in Specter's thought progression: Single-Bullet Theory to Single-Bullet Conclusion to Single-Bullet Fact. And it seems at the outset that this particular search for "the truth" is something of a secular Grail quest as it relates to the phenomenon of the assassination of John F. Kennedy. It is most unfortunate that there is little if anything by way of guidelines in Senator Specter's *Passion for Truth* that constitutes an undisputed pathway to *that* elusive commodity.

In the context of Senator Specter's justifiable annoyance with the 1995 reporter's accusatory brashness in charging cynicism in America to Specter's personal account, he offered in his book's introductory remarks some personal observations concerning problems as he perceived them in the 1990s:

> A central problem in America today is distrust of government. It goes beyond cynicism. Many Americans believe their elected representatives are for sale and that their government lies to them. When momentous historical events occur, such as the assassination of President Kennedy, the popular reaction is that government deceives and covers up through an explanation like the Single-Bullet Theory. (2)

Without parsing any distinction between cynicism and that which goes beyond cynicism, it is well to remember that any cynicism generated by the momentous event—the assassination of President Kennedy—was *really* cynicism (or that which goes beyond cynicism) with the work of the Warren Commission and the *Report* it generated in 1964. But it also should be remembered that the same year, 1964, generated another momentous historical event—the Vietnam War via the Gulf of Tonkin Resolution—the justifiable cynicism (or that which goes beyond it) for which has not yet been fully calculated.

A further introductory comment is in order concerning another declaration made in the dust jacket of Senator Specter's *Passion for Truth*: "Throughout he tells the truth . . . . This illuminating memoir is vintage Specter: thoughtful, provocative, and deeply informative." This reviewer has no quarrel with the adjectives. When, however, the noun—"truth"—is reflected upon in the context of the "historical lens" claimed for this memoir, the claim seems problematical. Certainly I have no trouble with the proposition that the writing of historians constitutes a *search* for the truth. But that is a step or two away from any claim that writers of history *tell* the truth. Such being so, what is missing from the "Prologue" in Senator Specter's *Passion for Truth* is any working definition of the existence of, or his version of, *the* truth. Absent such data, "the truth" becomes what I suspect is has been all along—a matter of beliefs about belief.

Finally, no introduction to an evaluation of the Single-Bullet Theory would be complete without mention of a strangely circular genesis associated with its evolution. The various points on the circle include the following claims:

- In his "Prologue" to *Passion for Truth*, Senator Specter wrote in 2000:

    I had developed the Single-Bullet Theory more than thirty years earlier as a staff lawyer on . . . the Warren Commission. I now call it the Single-Bullet Conclusion. It began as a theory, but when a theory is established by the facts, it deserves to be called a conclusion. The conclusion is that the same bullet sliced through President John F. Kennedy's neck and then tore through Texas Governor's chest and wrist, finally lodging in the governor's thigh . . . . The Warren Commission adopted the Single-Bullet Conclusion as its official explanation. . . . (1-2)

- In his *November 22, 1963: You Are the Jury*, David Belin wrote in 1973:

    The 'single bullet theory' is the conclusion in our Report that the first bullet that struck President Kennedy exited from the front of his neck and then struck Governor Connally. However, what is not generally known is that the beginning of the single bullet theory was an attempt on my part to prove that a second gunman was involved in the assassination. (302)
    . . . .
    If I were to prove that there was another rifle involved, one means of proving this was to show that less than 2.25 seconds elapsed between the first and second shots or between the second and third shots. (303)
    . . . .
    . . . You should have this frame of reference: Almost everyone had assumed up to this point that the first shot

struck President Kennedy, the second shot struck Governor Connally, the third shot struck President Kennedy, and all three shots had been fired from one weapon. The FBI had reached this conclusion, as had the Secret Service. No physical evidence had been found up to that point that would prove otherwise. On the other hand, here was one independent person, a lawyer from Des Moines, Iowa, who was trying to prove—in the face of the FBI and the Secret Service—that this theory was wrong.

And I succeeded. According to the FBI photographic laboratory experts, Governor Connally was not in the position reconstructed by his doctors at any time after frame 240. (306)

At this point I interrupt Belin's narrative to invite his readers to note the phenomenon of conjecture, as exemplified by his use of the conjunction "if" in his argument. Belin continues:

If Governor Connally could not have been hit after frame No. 240, and *if* President Kennedy was hit between frames 210 and 226, then there would be a maximum of 30 frames between the time President Kennedy was first hit and the time Governor Connally was hit. *If* the film speed was 18.3 frames per second, this meant that the elapsed time from President Kennedy's first wound to Governor Connally's wounds was less than two seconds. *If* the rifle could be operated no faster than 2.25 seconds, there were only two possibilities: (1) The first shot that struck President Kennedy also struck Governor Connally; (2) another rifle was involved in addition to the one that fired the bullet fragments found in the Presidential limousine. This, in turn, would mean a conspiracy involving at least two different riflemen.

These two possibilities were reinforced when we received from *Life* Magazine the 35 mm. slides. Governor

Connally clearly shows signs of reacting before frame 250. The key question then became how long it took Governor Connally to react after he was struck. Our research disclosed that the reaction time could range from tenths of a second to several seconds or more.

We ultimately concluded that the same bullet that struck President Kennedy in the neck also struck Governor Connally. The evidence supporting this conclusion was overwhelming.

In the controversy that has followed the publication of the Warren Commission Report, most of the analysis pertaining to the single-bullet theory relates to the testimony of Governor Connally, Mrs. Connally, their physicians, and the physicians who performed the autopsy. Arlen Specter, who is now the District Attorney of Philadelphia, handled all of this interrogation. Specter had the rare combination of academic brilliance and down-to-earth common sense and judgment. A native of Kansas, he was a champion debater and a Phi Beta Kappa graduate of the University of Pennsylvania. At the Yale Law School he served as an editor of the Yale Law Journal. Methodically, he took all the witnesses through the salient facts.

Members of the jury, let us turn to the testimony of Governor Connally and his attending physicians. (306-307)

- In Senator Specter's account in *Passion for Truth* he credits the lead autopsy surgeon, Dr. James J. Humes, with an important role in the evolution of the Single-Bullet Theory. In the context of an interview on March 13, and Humes's testimony on March 16, he wrote:

Our Friday interview with Humes and Boswell produced a revelation. The bullet that passed through Kennedy's neck proceeded in a straight line, struck nothing solid, and exited with great velocity. The doctors had not mentioned this in their autopsy report. 'The missile struck no bony structures in traversing the body of the late president,' Humes testified when I questioned him the following Monday. 'Therefore, I believe it was moving at its exit from the president's body at only very slightly less than that velocity, so it was still traveling at great speed.

Humes then referred [in his testimony] to Commission Exhibit 398, a frame of the Zapruder film that showed Kennedy raising his hands to his neck, presumably after being shot there. 'I believe in looking at Exhibit 398, which purports to be at approximately the time the president was struck,' Humes said, 'I see that the Governor is sitting directly in front of the late president, and suggest the possibility that this missile, having traversed the low neck of the late president, in fact traversed the chest of Governor Connally.' (80)

A key importance of Dr. Humes's testimony was then established by Senator Arlen Specter in his *Passion for Truth* memoir written 36 years later:

> There was a real question whether Humes should be asked at all about matters beyond his immediate personal knowledge, such as his view on the trajectory of the bullets or the metallic flakes in Governor Connally's wrist. Under the technical rules of evidence that apply in court, such testimony might be barred. But the commission made the commonsense decision to ask Humes and other witnesses for their views, impressions, and opinions on a variety of issues. Questions about outside subjects might produce answers about inside subjects. For example, by asking Humes—who had never examined Connally— about damage Connally might have suffered, we were probing at the same time about resistance the bullet met in passing through Kennedy's neck, an area within

Humes's sphere. From this freewheeling questioning, the Single-Bullet Conclusion developed naturally. (81)

. . . .

While I later put the pieces together, Humes laid them out, even if he did not think the bullet went through Connally's wrist. I have always been willing to take on the mantle of authorship . . . , mostly because I have always been confident that the Single-Bullet Conclusion is correct. I have also had a sense that if the conclusion turned out to be incorrect, that would be okay, too, because if was an honest, good-faith, soundly reasoned judgment. Let the chips fall where they may. (82)

• Interestingly, despite the time and effort Arlen Specter expended to develop his Single-Bullet Conclusion, that term does not appear in the list of conclusions found in Chapter II of the Warren *Report*. Rather No. 3 in the list of 12 entries found under the section titled "Conclusions" is that which reads:

Although it is not necessary to any essential findings of the Commission to determine just which shot hit Governor Connally, there is very persuasive evidence from the experts to indicate that the same bullet which pierced the President's throat also caused Governor Connally's wounds. However, Governor Connally's testimony and certain other factors have given rise to some difference of opinion as to this probability but there is no question in the mind of any member of the Commission that all the shots which caused the President and Governor Connally's wounds were fired from the sixth floor of the Texas School Book Depository. (19)

• The most recent judgment, of which I am aware, concerning the Single-Bullet saga was offered by Senator Arlen Specter on November 22, 2003—the fortieth anniversary of the assassination of President Kennedy. In a formal presentation on the campus of Duquesne University, in Pittsburgh, Pennsylvania, he declared that he then regarded his former Single-Bullet Conclusion as having become the Single-Bullet Fact.

If by "fact" is meant a statement that is empirically verifiable within the framework of a conceptual scheme, it but remains to be seen whether Senator Specter's *Passion for Truth* establishes whether his Single Bullet Conclusion warrants promotion to the rank of Single-Bullet Fact, or whether the chips may have fallen in a somewhat different pattern. Be that as it may, Specter indicates at the outset that facts are very important in his writing, as evidenced by his observation on page xii: "In my precarious profession, every effort must be made to make this book totally accurate because my potential adversaries will read it with a microscope. Only time will tell." And while I do not regard myself as being in any way an adversary of Arlen Specter in his professional life, I am very interested, and believe that each of his readers should be very interested, in the accuracy of the historical facts upon which he formulates his theories and conclusions.

Two years ago I wrote a book titled *The Warren Report: Suggestions for Historians*. Therein I included the concept of "Mr. Everyman," who had been created by Carl L. Becker, an American professional historian of prominence in the 1930s. His Mr. Everyman dramatized the conviction that the average person lives a life molded by history, which he held to be the memory of what has been said and done. Accordingly, he believed that any average person willing to use the methodology of intellectual honesty and informed common sense can be his own historian. My own training and experience as an academic historian has been strongly influenced by Professor Becker, and I commend his ideas and writing to any serious student of history—regardless of whether he is a professional or Mr. Everyman.

Within that personal framework, I tend to regard the Single-Bullet Theory/Conclusion/Fact/Whatever as riddled with errors. And if such be so, then the Warren *Report*—so much of which is based on that Theory developed by Arlen Specter—is simply an account of the President Kennedy assassination that cannot have happened the way the report says it happened. Senator Specter believes it happened the way he recounts in his *Passion for Truth*. And that belief is unequivocal: "I have always been confident that the Single-Bullet Conclusion is correct. I have also had a sense that if the conclusion turned out to be incorrect, that would be okay, too, because if was an honest, good-faith, soundly reasoned judgment. Let the chips fall where they may." (82) I submit for the judgment of the future historians—professional and Mr. Everyman alike—that my present writing generates falling chips in a pattern much different from that provided by Senator Specter.

CHAPTER I

WARREN COMMISSION

Senator Arlen Specter's memoir of his work for the Warren Commission begins with an account of a telephone call he received on December 31, 1963 from Howard Willens, a former law school classmate then working in the U.S. Department of Justice. The thrust of the call, we are told, was a query whether Specter "was interested in joining the staff of a commission to be chaired by Chief Justice Earl Warren, that would investigate the assassination of President John F. Kennedy." (43) At this point, I note that Specter is inclined to blur the distinctions between/ among three separate but related entities: (1) The Warren Commission; (2) "Counsel" to the Commission; and (3) "Staff" of the Commission. It is noted and will be remembered that Arlen Specter was never a member of the Warren Commission appointed by President Lyndon Johnson; nor was he asked to join the "Staff". He was invited to serve as one of 14 lawyers recruited as "Assistant Counsel" under General Counsel J. Lee Rankin, who had been selected by Commission Chairman Earl Warren. That distinction aside, Specter indicates that he accepted Rankin's January 8 request that he join the work of the Commission.

It is also noted that the Specter memory of facts includes the assertion in *Passion for Truth* that Howard Willens' telephone call of December 31 indicated that the Warren Commission "would investigate the assassination of President John F. Kennedy." (43) Assuming the accuracy of that assertion, there is an obvious inference that may be drawn: Somewhere between November 29, when the Commission was created by President Johnson, and the December 31 telephone call from Willens, an unnamed decision maker must have perceived the need for a Commission investigation.

Two questions arise: (1) When was it decided that the Warren Commission would undertake its own investigation? and (2) Who would undertake that investigation?

Regarding the first question, there is a reasonably clear chronology between November 29—when the Warren Commission was created—and Willens' call to Specter on December 31, by which time the Commission had determined the need for its own investigation.

- November 29: The Executive Order appointing President Johnson's Commission to Report Upon the Assassination of President John F. Kennedy—and it was the *President's Commission* despite popular usage that has memorialized Chief Justice Earl Warren. The Order specified that:

> the purposes of the Commission are *to examine the evidence developed by the Federal Bureau of Investigation and any additional evidence that may hereafter come to light or be uncovered by federal or state authorities; to make such further investigation as the Commission may find desirable*; to evaluate all the facts and circumstances surrounding such assassination, including the violent death of the man charged with the assassination, and to report to me its findings and conclusions. (WR 471) [Emphases added]

The Office of the White House Press Secretary also released a statement on November 29, indicating that

> The President stated that the Special Commission is to be instructed to evaluate all available information concerning the subject of the inquiry. *The Federal Bureau*

of Investigation, pursuant to an earlier directive of the
President, is making complete investigation of the facts.
An inquiry is also scheduled by a Texas Court of Inquiry
convened by the Attorney General of Texas under Texas
law. (WR 472) [Emphases added]

• December 5: In its September 1964 formal report to
President Johnson, the Warren Commission included
a "Foreword", which included the following: "From
its first meeting on December 5, 1963, the Commission
viewed the Executive Order as an unequivocal mandate
to conduct a thorough and independent investigation."
(WR x)

The FBI, which as early as November 25 had been directed
by President Johnson to investigate the assassination, submitted
its Summary Report to him.

• December 9, the Warren Commission received from the
FBI a five-volume Summary Report of its investigation
of the assassination of President Kennedy and the murder
of Lee Harvey Oswald.

After reviewing this report, the Commission requested the
Federal Bureau of Investigation to furnish the underlying investigative
materials relied upon in the summary report. (WR xi)

• December 16: J. Lee Rankin, former Solicitor General
of the United States, was sworn in as General Counsel
for the Warren Commission on December 16. (WR xi)
Note! This data from the Warren *Report* is immediately
followed by a declaration of relevance to the present
analysis:

The Commission has been aided by 14 counsel with
high professional qualifications, selected by it from widely

separated parts of the United States. This staff undertook
the work of the Commission with a wealth of legal and
investigative experience and a total dedication to the
determination of the truth. (xi)

Without challenging at this point the accuracy of those vague
claims in the *Report*, nevertheless the reality is this: Nowhere in
the *Report*'s Appendix IV—Biographical Information and
Acknowledgments—is there specific data detailing the specifics
of the "wealth of . . . investigative experience" of the 14 Assistant
Counsel. Certainly it was not a common practice for law schools
in the 1950s to teach required courses in "Investigations." Two
of the fourteen may have had relevant practical experience: Francis
Adams, who had served in 1954-1955 as New York City Police
Commissioner; and Arlen Specter who relates on page 3 of *Passion
for Truth*: "My efforts at truth-seeking began right out of college,
as a second lieutenant in the Air Force Office of Special
Investigations stateside during the Korean War."

- December 20: The first investigative reports submitted
  in response to the Commission request were delivered
  by the FBI to the Commission. (WR xii)
- December 31: Howard Willens' call to Arlen Specter
  "would investigate the assassination of President John F.
  Kennedy."

Regarding the second question posed above—Who would
undertake that Commission investigation?—the Warren *Report*
includes an extraordinary procedure:

Because of the diligence, cooperation, and facilities
of Federal investigative agencies, *it was unnecessary for
the Commission to employ investigators other than the
members of the Commission's legal staff. The
Commission, recognized, however, that special measures
were required whenever the facts or rumors called for*

an appraisal of the acts of the agencies themselves. The staff reviewed in detail the actions of several Federal agencies, particularly the Federal Bureau of Investigation, the Secret Service, the Central Intelligence Agency, and the Department of State. Initially the Commission requested the agencies to furnish all their reports relating to the assassination and their relationships with Oswald or Ruby. On the basis of these reports, the Commission submitted specific questions to the agency involved. Members of the staff followed up the answers by reviewing the relevant files of each agency for additional information. In some instances, members of the Commission also reviewed the files in person. Finally, the responsible officials of these agencies were called to testify under oath. Dean Rusk, Secretary of State; C. Douglas Dillon, Secretary of the Treasury; John A. McCone, Director of the Central Intelligence Agency; J. Edgar Hoover, Director of the Federal Bureau of Investigation; and James J. Rowley, Chief of the Secret Service, appeared as witnesses and testified fully regarding their agencies' participation in the matters under scrutiny by the Commission. (WR xiii)

COMMENT

1. Regarding "Because of the diligence, cooperation, and facilities of Federal investigative agencies, it was unnecessary for the Commission to employ investigators other than the members of the Commission's legal staff": There is no way of conclusively answering the question whether it was the FBI or the Warren Commission who had primary authority for the investigation of the John F. Kennedy assassination.

    a. Isolated documentary declarations suggest a strong case can be made for answering, as of December 5, the question in favor of the FBI.

- The minutes of the first Executive Session of the Commission, held on December 5—four days prior its receipt of the FBI Report from an investigation ordered by President Johnson— establish clearly, as of that date, the thinking of Chief Justice Warren and three Commissioners:

Chairman Warren: Now I think our job here is essentially one for the evaluation of evidence as distinguished from being one of gathering evidence, and I believe that at the outset at least we can start with the premise that we can rely upon the various agencies that have been engaged in investigating the matter, the FBI, the Secret Service, and others that I may not know of at the present time.

I believe that the development of the evidence in this way should not call for a staff of investigators. I don't see any reason why we should duplicate the facilities of the F.B.I. or the Secret Service or any of the other agencies.

If we should find some special need for a particular phase of it I think that would be time enough after to have the Commission consider it. But at the present time I do not feel that it would be necessary for us to have any staff of investigators. . . . [Alluding to the investigative agencies] If we can't rely on them I couldn't think of any investigators we can get to do it anyway. . . . (1-2)

Senator Russell: Mr. Chairman, of course I think I am in general agreement with your statement that our principal duty is to evaluate all of those various reports and undertake to reconcile them if we can, any conflict or differences.

Now you didn't mention anything about a staff. I don't think we ought to have any investigators but we are going to have to have somebody. (35-36)

Senator Cooper: [In the context of Senator Russell's opposition to public hearings under any circumstances] Mr. Chairman. If they come to us we could simply say to them to write the Commission staff, then the Commission staff could refer them to the FBI and other agencies perhaps to evaluate all the testimony that has been taken anyway, which had been taken before and will be taken in the future. (41)

Mr. McCloy: [in the context of the anticipated FBI report—which was subsequently received four days later—McCloy does not even seem interested in having the Commissioners functioning as evaluators of evidence.] We ought to get somebody, not a general counsel, but get a good reader, good young lawyer, for example, and go through the report and maybe summarize it so you could have some analysis of it. Maybe there are a lot of individual statements and you don't have to read every one of them. (63)

(Note! Commissioners Boggs, Ford and Dulles did not commit themselves in this December 5 meeting as to the Commission's role as an investigator.)

b. Conversely, there is a contradictory claim in the Warren *Report* of September, 1964 :

From its first meeting on December 5, 1963, the Commission viewed the Executive Order [of November 29] as an unequivocal Presidential

> mandate to conduct a thorough and independent
> investigation. (x)

It is noted that there is no reference/citation for this claim. As demonstrated immediately above the claim, four Commissioners—Warren/Russell/Cooper/McCloy—had reservations about the Commission conducting an investigation. And as may be inferred from their silence, the other three Commissioners—Boggs/Ford/Dulles—do not support any claim that as of December 5 the Commission regarded Johnson's Executive Order of November 29 as "an unequivocal Presidential mandate to conduct a thorough and independent investigation". Thus the claim appears as a conspicuous absurdity.

Independently of that, however, the paragraph from page x of the *Report* continues:

> Because of the numerous rumors and theories, the
> Commission concluded that the public interest in insuring
> that the truth was ascertained could not be met by merely
> accepting the reports or analyses of Federal or State
> agencies. Not only were the premises and conclusions of
> those reports critically reassessed, but all assertions or
> rumors relating to a possible conspiracy, or the complicity
> of others than Oswald, which have come to the attention
> of the Commission, have been investigated.

Again it is noted that there is no reference/citation for either of these two sentences.

That point aside, those two sentences exemplify a chronic Warren *Report* problem of vagueness in a matter of relevant chronology. *When* did the Commission conclude that the public interest could not be met by merely accepting the reports or analyses of Federal or State agencies? Inasmuch as the Commission did not receive the FBI Report until December

9, it seems reasonable to assume that the Commission conclusion—"the public interest . . . could not be met by merely accepting the reports or analyses of Federal . . . agencies"—must have been reached after having read the FBI Report received on December 9.

Working from that assumption, it may be possible to narrow the time frame a bit by noting two subsequent developments:

- Appendix III of the Warren *Report* established December 13 as the date on which Congress enacted Senate Joint Resolution 137 (Public Law 88-202) bearing the following language: "Authorizing the Commission established to report upon the assassination of President John F. Kennedy to compel the attendance and testimony of witnesses and the production of evidence."

- Page xi of the *Report* includes this: "On December 16 J. Lee Rankin, former Solicitor General of the United States, was sworn in as general counsel for the Commission. Additional members of the legal staff were selected during the next few weeks."

Beyond these skimpy chronological details, there is nothing in the Warren *Report* that sheds light on the process and rationale for the recruitment of a "legal staff." In this context, it is noted that Appendix IV of the *Report*—Biographical Information on Members of the Commission, General Counsel, Assistant Counsel, Staff Members—discloses that 8 of the 12 Staff Members were lawyers. The Appendix also includes a section titled "Acknowledgments," in which 57 persons—"lawyers, secretaries, and clerks" were thanked for their "unstinting efforts on behalf of the Commission." (475-482)

One of the key members of the legal staff was Howard P. Willens, mentioned earlier as a classmate of Arlen Specter at Yale Law School, who recruited Specter on behalf of General Counsel J. Lee Rankin. Willens' biographical data includes service with a

Washington D.C. law firm following his graduation from Yale in 1956. In 1961 he was appointed Second Assistant in the Criminal Division of the U.S. Department of Justice. (479) Apparently he worked very closely with General Counsel Rankin, and served the Commission as liaison with the Department of Justice. Beyond that singular mention of Willens' recruitment of Specter, I am unaware of other details in the process whereby the Commission acquired its Assistant Counsel.

The second inquiry relating to the Commission's acquisition of legal counsel addresses the question: What was the Commission's perceived need for a separate "legal staff"? If, on the basis of the FBI Summary Report, it was determined there was a need for a separate investigation as of December 9, then the hiring of Rankin as General Counsel was a logical consequence as of December 16. And that step in turn was followed just as logically by recruitment of Assistant Counsel as early as December 31, when Willens contacted Arlen Specter. (I isolate Arlen Specter for example simply because he is the focal point of my present writing.) And it is interesting to speculate on Specter's own judgment—undisclosed in *Passion for Truth*—concerning what he was hired to do. He does tell us on pages 50-51: "The commission decided not to hire its own investigators. Beyond the question of cost, we faced the problem of finding and recruiting investigators." This observation generates interesting, but seemingly incongruent realities as of December 31:

- The Commission is unwilling to rely upon the report of the FBI's investigation of the assassination of President John Kennedy, so it will undertake its own investigation authorized by the mandate of President Johnson's Executive Order of November 29;
- The Commission is recruiting special legal counsel to undertake an investigation of its own;
- The Commission *Report*'s biographical sketches of the 15 special legal counsel hired by the Commission make no reference to their previous investigative experience.

By implication, two of them—Francis Adams and Arlen Specter—have professional experiences that parallel the role of investigators: Adams with the New York City Police Department, and Specter with the Philadelphia District Attorney's Office.

The seemingly inescapable inference to be drawn is that by December 31 the Warren Commission is determined to conduct an investigation to be undertaken by persons whose qualifications do not necessarily include experience as investigators. Despite that inference, and *its* implications, the Warren *Report* was nevertheless willing to claim this reality: "Because of the diligence, cooperation, and facilities of Federal investigative agencies, it was unnecessary for the Commission to employ investigators other than the members of the Commission's legal staff."

If the need for a Commission investigation was indeed prompted by an uneasiness with the quality of the investigation reflected in the FBI's Summary Report in December 1963, there is no indication that such uneasiness was generated by the central conclusions in that report. Those conclusions are essentially the same as those submitted nine months later by the Warren Commission in its *Report* on September 24, 1964:

- Three shots, fired from the sixth floor window at the southeast corner of the Texas School Book Depository, killed President Kennedy and wounded Governor Connally.
- The shots which killed President Kennedy and wounded Governor Connally were fired by Lee Harvey Oswald. (18-19)

The one critical difference between the two reports is this:

- Whereas the FBI Report reads "Two bullets struck President Kennedy, and one wounded Governor Connally" (1)

- The Warren *Report* reads "Although it is not necessary to any essential findings of the Commission to determine just which shot hit Governor Connally, there is very persuasive evidence from the experts to indicate that the same shot which pierced the President's throat also caused Governor Connally's wounds. (18-19)

* * *

Regarding the "Commission investigation," assuming (a) "the staff" to be "the legal staff" and (b) there is a sequence involving four successive steps:

- "The staff reviewed in detail [dealing with things item by item] the actions of several Federal agencies, particularly the Federal Bureau of Investigation, the Secret Service, the Central Intelligence Agency, and the Department of State;
- "Initially the Commission requested the agencies to furnish all their reports relating to the assassination and their relationships with Oswald or Ruby;
- "On the basis of these reports, the Commission submitted specific questions to the agency involved; and
- "Members of the staff followed up the answers by reviewing by reviewing the relevant files of each agency for additional information." (xiii)

Recalling the earlier observation that Francis W. Adams and Arlen Specter were the only Assistant Counsel who brought with them to the Warren Commission a background of investigative experience, it is not surprising that they were paired, as "Area 1" by Rankin, as Senior and Junior Counsel. In his memoir, Senator Specter relates that following his reporting for work on January 20, he was joined a few days later by Adams. Apparently on the same day—January 23— Specter drafted a Memorandum to Rankin, in which he graciously, if incorrectly, identified "From" as being "Mr. Francis W. H. Adams and Mr. Arlen Specter." Harold Weisberg, in his 1975 publication, *Post Mortem*, included as an attachment to it a second memo, titled "MEMORANDUM OF THINGS TO BE DONE AND SOME OF THE PROBLEMS INVOLVED." There are 18 entries which read on pages 490-491 as follows:

(a) Prepare a detailed chronology.

(b) Prepare a working index of the evidentiary material.

(c) Secure from the FBI and consider the underlying documents and reports related to rifle and shells. Since Mr. Ball and Mr. Belin are also covering this aspect, we shall work with them.

(d) Secure the survey of the scene made by the Secret Service, and arrange for additional surveys, including probably a contour map of the area.

(e) Consider the various reports on the reconstructions made by both the FBI and the Secret Service.

(f) Further viewing and analysis of the moving pictures of the actual happening and of the reconstructions.

(g) There would seem to be a considerable amount of confusion as to the actual path of the bullets which hit President Kennedy, particularly the one which entered the right side of his back.

(h) It will be necessary to examine the windshield and try to determine whether the shots did any damage to the windshield.

(i) Consideration should be given to taking the sworn testimony of the bystander witnesses.

(j) Consideration should also be given to obtaining statements from Mrs. Kennedy, Governor and Mrs. Connally, Senator Yarborough, and Mr. and Mrs. Johnson. A decision should be made by the Commission as to whether those individuals should be requested to give testimony, under oath.

(k) The Secret Service agents involved have all made statements of which we have copies. Consideration should be given to having each of those agents make such statements under oath.

(l) We are considering examining the scene of the shooting ourselves. If it is determined that statements should be taken from Governor Connally, perhaps this could be done at the same time.

(m) Consideration should be given to obtaining the camera to determine if the speed of the vehicles can be ascertained and the timing between shots from a review of the film.

(n) The FBI should obtain statements from certain bystanders, identified in prior reports, who have not been interviewed.

(o) Newspaper reports of November 22nd through the next few days should be reviewed to consider questions in the public mind and to determine whether there is any competent evidentiary basis for allegations of fact which differ from the Secret Service or FBI reports.

(p) Obtain expert opinions from medical personnel and professionals in weaponry field to explain the path of the bullet in President Kennedy's body.

(q) Obtain the transcript of the television interview by the doctors at Parkland Hospital on the evening of November 22nd.

(r) Ascertain whether the President was wearing a brace and undershirt.

Keeping in mind that these 18 entries appear in a memorandum titled "Things to be Done and Some of the Problems Involved", there are relevant matters to be considered. They include the following:

- Regarding (a) "Prepare a detailed chronology": If this was done, it is strange that there are so many "whens" that are not explored in testimony of witnesses interrogated by

Arlen Specter. Specifics of this claim are deferred for further consideration below.

- Regarding (c) "Secure from the FBI and consider the underlying documents and records related to rifle and shells. Since Mr. Ball and Mr. Belin are also working this aspect, we shall work with them": This point will be addressed presently.

- Regarding (g) "There would seem to be a considerable confusion as to the actual path of the bullets which hit President Kennedy, particularly the one which entered the right side of his back": It will be seen below that the crux of the problem with the Single-Bullet Theory/ Conclusion/Fact is the vertical location of the entry wound as being in the "back," or the "neck," or the "base of the neck," or the "upper back," or the "lower neck," or wherever else may be necessary to proceed with the theory/ conclusion/fact.

- Regarding (p) "Obtain expert opinions from medical personnel and professionals in weaponry field to explain the path of the bullet in President Kennedy's body": As will be explored below, a critical issue is selectivity in acceptance or rejection of evidence from the same witness.

- Regarding (q) "Obtain the transcript of the television interview by the doctors at Parkland Hospital on the evening of November 22nd": Given the controversy concerning the nature of the anterior throat wound— entry or exit—the failure of the Warren Commission to issue a subpoena for this transcript is both inexcusable and indefensible. Note! Assuming "the evening of November 22" should read "the afternoon of November 22," this is a harmless oversight of the editing process.

Item (c) in Specter's memorandum of January 23 to Rankin is deserving of extended analysis because of its mention of Messrs Ball and Belin. The context for such a discussion involves chronological backtracking to Senator Specter's indication in *Passion for Truth* that his initial meeting with General Counsel Rankin was in Washington, D.C., on Monday, January 13. At that time "Rankin asked me for details on my background and explained the commission's approach." (45)

The choice of the word "approach" was masterful. Of the five meanings for that noun provided by *Webster's New World College Dictionary*, c1999, page 69, certainly the most appropriate for Specter's contextual usage is this: "a means of attaining a goal or purpose." The phenomenological utility of this meaning for "approach" is seen clearly in Specter's account provided in the paragraph immediately following the word.

> The commission had divided the investigation into six major areas. At that time the senior lawyers had been assigned to areas, but the younger lawyers had not. As one of the first junior lawyers to check in, if not *the* [emphasis in the original] first, I found that the field was pretty much open. Area 1 covered President Kennedy's activities from the departure by helicopter from the White House lawn on November 21, to his body's return to the White House in the morning of November 23, after the autopsy. Area 2 covered the identity of the assassin. The Area 2 team would treat it as an open question, despite Oswald's arrest. Area 3 covered the life and background of Lee Harvey Oswald, except for his foreign travel and his activities on the day of Kennedy's assassination. Area 4 picked up Oswald's foreign travel. Area 5 covered the background and activities of Jack Ruby, who shot Oswald to death in the basement of Dallas Police Headquarters on Sunday morning, November 24, 1963, two days after the Kennedy assassination. Area 6 covered presidential protection for the future. (45-46)

It is a welcome learning experience to read Senator Specter's rationale for his appointment to Area 1, where he was paired with the senior lawyer, Francis W.H. Adams, the former Police Commissioner in New York City, then currently a senior partner in a major New York law firm. The account reads:

> In my preliminary discussions with Rankin and Willens, we eliminated Areas 2 and 4 as possible assignments for me. They didn't want to assign me to area 2 because my background as an assistant DA suggested I might be too prosecution-oriented to tackle the question of the assassin's identity objectively. They didn't want to assign me to area 4 because Bill Coleman, a partner at the Philadelphia-based Dilworth firm, had been assigned as the senior lawyer in Area 4, and they didn't want two lawyers from the same city working in one area. I immediately agreed that I should avoid Areas 2 and 4.
>
> After some thought and discussion . . . I chose Area 1, the president's activities. It seemed the most compelling. Obviously, John F. Kennedy was the focal point of the entire event. I had no idea at that point the turns the medical evidence would take or where Area 1 would lead. Lee Rankin said that placing me in area 1 would work well from the commission's point of view, and he made the assignment. (46)

Attention is called to Senator Specter's unexplained linking of two separate notions in his January 13 allusion to the Commission's division of labor for the upcoming investigation: (1) "Area 2 covered the identity of the assassin"; and (2) "The Area 2 team would treat it as an open question, despite Oswald's arrest." Inasmuch as the FBI Summary Report of December 5 had declared, without qualification, Oswald to be the assassin, and the claim that Area 2 would treat the identity of the assassin as "an open question", it is a fair inference to assume that Area 2 was obligated to consider an alternative to that FBI declaration. And if such be so, there are several questions that beg for answers:

1. Did General Counsel Rankin specify in his January 13 explanation to Specter that the "*commission's* approach" included Area 2's treating the identity of the assassin as an "open question"? If so, it is difficult to understand the rationale for a virtually exclusive focus on Oswald in the Commission's division of labors for Areas 3-5: Area 3 covering the life and background of Lee Harvey Oswald; Area 4 concerned with Oswald's foreign travel; and Area 5's concern with Jack Ruby's killing of Oswald? Does this "approach" suggest that the six lawyers in Areas 3-5 are to mark time pending Area 2's resolution of the "open question"?

2. Or did the Area 2 lawyers—Joseph A. Ball (senior lawyer) and David W. Belin (junior lawyer)—*themselves* decide to treat the identity of the assassin as an open question? In consideration of this possibility, attention is called to David Belin's 1973 book, *November 22, 1963: You Are the Jury*, in which he writes of his experiences while serving as an assistant counsel for the Warren Commission. Despite diligent search of the 504 pages of text in that writing, I was unable to learn the details of either consideration or resolution of any "open question" concerning the identity of the assassin on November 22, 1963.

3. Or does Senator Specter's memoir *editorially assign* that "open question" treatment to the Area 2 team? If so, an equally diligent search of *Passion for Truth* failed to disclose any genuine evidence that the Area 2 team did in fact treat the identity of the assassin as an "open question".

In the happening, 30 pages following his memoir's mention of the "open question", Senator Specter details an additional division of labor in a working relationship between Areas 1 and 2:

> The line between area 1, the activities of President Kennedy, and Area 2, the identity of the assassin, had not been sharply drawn. Since the moment of the assassination brought together the president and his killer, the witnesses at the scene could have been placed in either area. There would always be some overlap.
>
> In early March, I worked out an agreement with Joe Ball and Dave Belin for dividing the witnesses: They would handle all witnesses at the assassination scene except for those in the presidential motorcade, whom I would handle. Even that split could not be made precisely. The wounds on the president's body fell naturally, into Area 1, Kennedy's activities, but the source of the bullets fell into Area 2, the assassin's identity. We decided that the bullet in flight was the dividing point between Areas 1 and 2. Before the bullet left the rifle barrel, it was the responsibility of Ball and Belin. After striking the president, it was my responsibility. Ball, Belin, and I continued to work closely and never fought over turf. (70)

This much seems clear as of "early March": Arlen Specter, a 34-year-old Assistant District Attorney from Philadelphia, ostensibly the Junior Counsel in Area 1, was solely responsible for making decisions on behalf of Area 1. His remark that "I worked out an agreement with Area 2" is a subtle disclosure of the reality that his nominal partner, Senior Counsel Francis W. Adams, had simply abandoned participation in the work of Area 1. Indeed, the explanation of the reason(s) for Adams's distancing himself from the work of Area 1 has/have never been clearly explained.

*   *   *

Pursuing the theme of an "open question" introduced by Senator Specter, but using David Belin's 1973 book, *November 22, 1963: You Are the Jury* as the reference, it is a short-lived search of its pages for convincing evidence in support of Arlen Specter's January 13, 1964 claim that "Area 2 would treat the identity of the assassin as an open question." In five pages, David Belin undertakes to present what reads as a tenuous example on behalf of that claim when he writes of himself and his partner, Joseph Ball:

> We started with no 'foregone conclusions'; in fact, I subconsciously wanted to find evidence to prove that Lee Harvey Oswald was **not** [emphasis in original] the assassin.
>
> After a month of reading, theorizing, cross-examining each other and writing, Joe Ball and I prepared a 248-page first report, primarily for our own use in making further investigation. We set forth our framework in the beginning:
>
>> At no time have we assumed that Lee Harvey Oswald was the assassin of President Kennedy. Rather, our entire study has been based on an independent examination of all the evidence in an effort to determine who was the assassin of President Kennedy.
>
> The initial 'assume nothing' standard established by Lee Rankin constituted an important part of the basic framework of our investigation. How important can be illustrated by one example—there were many others— the paraffin test. In our first report Joe Ball and I commented on material we had received on the paraffin test. This portion of our report we had received from the

FBI and the Dallas Police Department, which included diagrams of the palm and the back of Lee Harvey Oswald's hands. The FBI material stated that the report of the paraffin test showed the test results on Oswald were 'consistent with a person who had handled and/or fired a firearm.'

This is the discussion of the paraffin test in our first report:

> The report of the paraffin test, together with the drawings thereof, appears in Document #5 at pages 146-149. The paraffin test on the cheek is negative. The paraffin test on the left hand is positive on the palm of the hand, particularly the area below the middle finger and the fourth finger and on the side of the thumb. Also, on the center of the back of the left hand, there are nitrate positive [sic] marks showing. On the right hand on the palm side, there are positive nitrate marks on all fingers and the thumb—the marks on the fingers being around one-third to one-fourth from the end. Also, on the palm and the left portion thereof, not too far from the wrist, there is a positive nitrate showing. On the back of the hand, near the juncture of the thumb and the index finger, there are also nitrate positive marks. The three paraffin casts which were made from the right cheek, right hand and left hand were delivered by Captain George Doughty of the Dallas Police Department to laboratory technician, Al Anderson, and the Dallas City County Criminal Investigation Laboratory and Parkland Hospital; and Anderson assisted Dr. M. F. Mason in processing the nitrate tests and Anderson made the drawings as to where the nitrates were found. The report of Dr. Mason said that in the paraffin tests of the right and left

hands, he found 'punctuate traces of nitrate, which would be consistent with a person who had handled and/or fired a firearm,' (Document #5, page 147.)

The complete significance of the paraffin test must be determined. Messrs. Redlich and Eisenberg [two of the other assistant counsel] are working in this area and their findings will be carefully studied by counsel in area II, particularly since our entire efforts are based on an independent determination of who was the assassin, rather than from the viewpoint of a prosecutor. If anyone firing a rifle within a few hours prior to the submission of a paraffin test on the right cheek with a high degree of certainty would have nitrates on his right cheek which could not be easily removed, this is a factor in weighing against the conclusion that Lee Harvey Oswald was the assassin.

. . . .

Although the Dallas Police Department used the paraffin test in an effort to determine if Oswald fired a weapon, we found that the *paraffin test is wholly unreliable in determining whether a person has recently fired a weapon.* [Emphasis in original]

Therefore, a *positive* reaction to the paraffin test is worthless in determining whether a suspect has recently fired a weapon.

The only question that remained was whether a *negative reaction* on the paraffin test would be evidence that a person had *not* fired a weapon. We found that it made a great difference if the weapon was a revolver on the one hand or a rifle or an automatic pistol on the other. . . .

. . . By the time the chamber of a bolt-action rifle would be open for the next bullet to be inserted, the gases already would have gone down the barrel and there would be no pressure that would cause them to be expelled upon the hands (or, for that matter, upon the cheek) of the person who fired the weapon.

None of these facts appeared in the investigation file of the Dallas Police Department, which had performed the paraffin test. *Moreover, there was nothing concerning the paraffin test furnished independently by the FBI that would have shown its unreliability.* Rather, it was only after we had interviewed the personnel in the FBI laboratory that we found that the FBI itself, prior to the assassination, had demonstrated the unreliability of the paraffin test. . . .

. . . .

Thus, we had the other side of the coin: A negative reaction from the paraffin test did not prove that a person had not fired a rifle.

With this information, we were interested in why any law enforcement agency would give a paraffin test. The question was raised by [Warren Commissioner] Representative Ford: 'Why are paraffin tests conducted and how extensive are they?'

FBI expert Courtland Cunningham, in testimony before the Commission, replied:

> Many local enforcement agencies do conduct these tests, and at their request, the FBI will process them. They take the casts and we will process them. However, in reporting we give them qualified results since we frequently will get some reaction. Numerous reactions or a few reactions will be found on the casts. However, in no way does this indicate that a person has recently fired a weapon. Then we list a few of the oxidizing agents, the common ones, such as urine and tobacco and cosmetics and a few others that one may come in contact with. Even Clorox would give you a positive reaction.

Representative Ford. Is this a test that has been
conducted by law enforcement agencies for some
time? Is this a new test?

Mr. Cunningham. No, sir; the first tests that
I reported on here were conducted in 1935. There
may be some law enforcement agencies which use
the test for psychological reasons.

Mr. Dulles. Explain that.

Mr. Cunningham. Yes, sir; what they do is
they ask, say, 'We are going to run a paraffin test
on you, you might as well confess now . . .'

Cunningham then testified that the FBI, when
conducting its own investigations, does not use the
paraffin test because 'it is definitely not reliable as to
determining whether or not a person has fired a
weapon . . .' (15-19)

Thus far Mr. Belin's example of Area 2 treating the identity
of the assassin as an "open question" consists of rejecting the Dallas
Police Department's paraffin test of Lee Harvey Oswald because
the FBI demonstrated that it was a useless test. But there is more
to this exhaustive examination of the "open question" conducted
by Belin.

Continuing with his account in *November 22, 1963: You
Are the Jury*:

Now that you jurors have the facts, you might be
interested in how the paraffin test was handled in one
internationally distributed film about the assassination.
This film, 'Rush to Judgment,' was distributed by its
coproducers, Emile de Antonio and Mark Lane, as a 'brief
for the defense' of Lee Harvey Oswald.

Every experienced trial lawyer knows that when he
presents a brief, he generally starts with his strongest point.

The starting point in the moving-picture 'brief for the defense' is the paraffin test.

After an opening attack on the Warren Commission as 'insensibly and progressively' having 'emphasized the evidence which seemed to support Oswald's sole guilt and insensibly and progressively attenuating the evidence which pointed away from it,' the film turns to the paraffin test and the producers strawmen, the Dallas Police Department and the District Attorney, Henry Wade.

The movie first shows a film clip from a news conference after the assassination with the Dallas Police Chief, Jesse E. Curry. A reporter asks, 'Chief, we understand you have the results of the paraffin tests which were made to determine whether Oswald had fired a weapon. Can you tell us if . . . ?'

Chief Curry replies before the question is completed: 'I understand that it was positive.'

Asked what that means, Chief Curry replies, 'It only means that he fired a gun.'

Then there is another film clip—Dallas District Attorney Henry Wade. 'The paraffin test showed that he had recently fired a gun; it was on both hands.'

From the film clip taken of Wade shortly after the assassination, the camera then turns to coproducer Mark Lane, who reads:

> Gordon Shanklin, the FBI agent in charge of Dallas, added, quote: A paraffin test used to determine whether a person had fired a weapon recently was administered to Oswald shortly after he was apprehended on Friday, one hour after the assassination, which showed particles of gunpowder from a weapon, probably a rifle, remained on Oswald's cheek and hands, close quotes.

Lane then concludes:

> The test, however, showed no gunpowder on
> either hands or cheek and no nitrates on Oswald's
> face. Confronted with but one possible
> interpretation that the paraffin test results were
> consistent with innocence, the Commission
> concluded that the test, formerly presented as a
> cornerstone in the case against Oswald, was, quote:
> completely unreliable.

Note carefully the language of Lane. He does not say
that there were no *nitrates* on Oswald's hands. Rather, he
asserts that the test 'showed no gunpowder' on either
hands or cheek.

You jurors now know that Chief Curry, District
Attorney Wade and Mark Lane, are all wrong. What the
paraffin test showed was nitrates on Oswald's hands—
which could have come from gunpowder, but which also
could have come from many other substances, such as
tobacco, urine, or household cleansers. Although the
Dallas Police Department used the paraffin test as part of
its case against Oswald, we threw out the test because we
found on the basis of our independent investigation that
the test's showing of nitrates on Oswald's hands did not
prove those nitrates were gunpowder. By the same token
it could not be said that the nitrates were not gunpowder.
Therefore Lane is wrong when he asserts that the test
showed 'no gunpowder.' You also know that because a
rifle has a 'sealed chamber' one would not necessarily find
nitrates on the person who had just fired a rifle.

The misrepresentation by Lane in the film is not
innocent, for the film was produced after the Warren
Commission Report was published. Pages 560-562 of
the Warren Commission Report summarize the FBI

experiments with the test to show why we concluded that the paraffin test was unreliable.

But Lane's film confounds this confusion with a smear; he asserts that the tests were rejected because there was just 'one possible interpretation,' that the tests 'were consistent with innocence.' You now know that this statement by Lane is fallacious. The Commission rejected the results of the paraffin test for one reason only: The test had been shown to be an unreliable indicator of whether a person had fired a weapon. You also know that Lane selected this as the opening proposition in his brief. This typifies the attacks on the Warren Commission by assassination sensationalists.

An epilogue in this area turned up in our investigation and was confirmed by Joseph Nicol, whom the Commission retained as an independent expert witness, Mr. Nicol, superintendent of the Bureau of Criminal Identification and Investigation of the State of Illinois, said there were cases where people had been convicted of murder in which the paraffin test was part of the evidence.

Why the FBI processes paraffin tests for other law enforcement agencies remains an unanswered question. [All emphases in the original]

Stripped of these fascinating, if tedious, details in Belin's account, Area 2's commitment—the "open question" of the identity of the assassin—seems very superficial at best. I offer this for the judgment of the future historians: Belin's essential contribution to the commitment is that found on page 20 of his book, which reads:

Although the Dallas Police Department used the paraffin test as part of its case against Oswald, we threw out the test because we found on the basis of our independent investigation that the test's showing of nitrates on Oswald's hands did not prove that those nitrates were gunpowder.

The irony is too obvious to be overlooked: The Warren Commission's investigation was called into being in December, 1963 for unstated reasons following the submission of the FBI's five-volume report of its investigation which declared Oswald to be the lone assassin. But the Warren Commission Area 2's "open question" investigation concerning the identity of the assassin merely endorsed the FBI's rejection of the Dallas Police Department's use of the paraffin test in building its case against Oswald.

It is recalled that David Belin indicated the paraffin test was but "one example—there were many others"—of Area 2's investigative response to "the initial 'assume nothing' standard established by Lee Rankin." Unchallenged by Area' 2's "investigation" are any of the dimensions of the other parts of the Dallas Police Department's case against Oswald.

In the happening, the chronology of events establishes clearly that Area 2's commitment to the "open question" was abandoned within two months of its existence. Assuming that David Belin was hired as an assistant counsel sometime near January 13 when Arlen Specter was hired, Belin's account of his time includes the following sequence detailed in *November 22, 1963: You are the Jury*:

- He and his partner, Joseph Ball, spent "a month of reading, cross-examining each other and writing" which accounts for time until the middle of February;
- Following that month, Belin and Ball wrote a 248-page report—"primarily for our own use in making further investigation."
- However much undisclosed time it took to write that report, the "many other examples" demonstrating Belin's

"subconsciously want[ing] to find evidence to prove that Lee Harvey Oswald was *not* the assassin must have surfaced and been discarded by March 20, when he "prepared" the Commission's key witnesses for testimony relating to the designation of Lee Harvey Oswald as the lone assassin.

• As of March 24, Area 2's legal team of David Belin and Joseph Ball conducted the questioning of the key witnesses—Howard Brennan/ Harold Norman/James Jarman, Jr./Bonnie Ray Williams—in developing the case against Oswald as the lone assassin.

*   *   *

In closing this discussion of the short-lived "open question" of Area 2"s investigation in February-March 1964, it but remains to mention the practice of "preparation" of Warren Commission witnesses favored by Assistant Counsel David Belin, Joseph Ball, and Arlen Specter. Belin explains this practice on page 49 in his book, *November 22, 1963: You are the Jury*:

Most experienced trial lawyers, when they present a case, 'prepare' their key witnesses. I do not mean by this that they try to get a witness to change their testimony or perjure himself. Rather, they review the major facts with the witness in great detail. If there are inconsistencies, the attorney will often point these out to a prospective witness and give him an opportunity to resolve them. On preparing a witness for direct examination, the attorney may ask a witness leading questions to help him—the kinds of questions that are used in cross-examination.

. . . The questions Joe Ball and I asked were not leading ones in which we sought to have the witness arrive at any preconceived conclusion. Moreover, in interviewing these witnesses prior to their formal testimony, our pattern was merely to ask general questions and have the witnesses relate the story in their own words.

Unmentioned is whether the search for "the truth, the whole truth, and nothing but the truth" was enhanced or impeded by the reality that the person asking the questions—or interrupting an answer—was in complete control of the process that determined whether a specific area of inquiry, or comment, could be bypassed at his pleasure.

I note in passing that Arlen Specter indicates a sharp difference of opinion among the Commission lawyers concerning preparation of witnesses. He write in pages 80-81 of *Passion for Truth*:

> When the time came to take testimony, a battle erupted among the staff lawyers as to whether we should interview witnesses in advance. Joe Ball, by far the most experienced trial lawyer on our staff, Dave Belin, and I argued that we had to. Norman Redlich [assistant to General Counsel Rankin] led the opposition.
>
> Redlich said we might be accused of leading witnesses one way or another if we talked to them before they testified. Ball, Belin, and I countered that the witnesses had already been interviewed by other agencies, that they were adults, and that we would have to be trusted not to push them. We also argued that it was necessary to talk to witnesses before they testified, to get a general idea of what they would say. Otherwise, it would be impossible to present their testimony in any orderly way.

Specter's dismissal of Redlich's concern seems irrelevant to the validity of Redlich's point. The thrust of the dismissal seems to involve three notions: (1) Interviews by "other agencies" constitute record answers by the prospective witnesses; (2) If the witnesses are adults there is no need for protection of them; and

(3) Ball, Belin, and Specter must be trusted to lead witnesses. However reasonable may be this third point, it necessarily entails a generous measure of blind faith in the conduct of an off the record proceeding.

Left unasked is the core question: Is the practice of "witness preparation" ethically appropriate in anything other than an adversarial proceeding with its provision for cross-examination of the witness? The implication in Senator Arlen Specter's *Passion for Truth* is an affirmative answer for that question.

Be that as it may, further exploration of this practice is deferred until consideration is given Arlen Specter's preparation of autopsy doctors prior to their testimony.

*   *   *

Continuing with comment on the "Adams/Specter" Memorandum—"Things to be Done and Some of the Problems Involved—of January 23, it is recalled that item (g) reads: "There would seem to be a considerable confusion as to the actual path of the bullets which hit President Kennedy, particularly the one which entered the right side of his back." There are two points to be noted:

- As of January 23, Assistant Counsel Arlen Specter appears troubled by any prospective claim that the autopsy of November 22 conclusively determined the path of the bullet what will eventually achieve prominence in the Single-Bullet Theory/Conclusion/Fact.
- As of January 23, Specter appears to favor the location of a bullet entry on the "right side of the back" as opposed to a different location required by his future Single-Bullet Theory/Conclusion/Fact.

Regarding (p) "Obtain expert opinions from medical personnel and professionals in weaponry field to explain the path of the bullet in President Kennedy's body": This merely confirms that Specter appears troubled by a potential conflict between expert opinions in any attempt to "explain the path of the bullet in President Kennedy's body." Moreover, it will be demonstrated below that Assistant Counsel Arlen Specter's style of interrogation in proceedings of the Warren Commission utilizes an extraordinary accommodation for testimony outside the professional expertise of the witness.

CHAPTER II

TRUTH IS THE CLIENT

Senator Specter begins this chapter of his memoir as follows:

The Warren Commission's duty, as set forth in the presidential executive order forming the investigation of the Kennedy assassination, was to 'evaluate all the facts and circumstances concerning such assassination' . . . . (53)

Recalling his awareness of the importance of accuracy—"every effort must be made to make this book totally accurate because my potential adversaries will read it with a microscope"—it is surprising to learn that his language is not exactly that of the Executive Order issued by President Lyndon Johnson on November 29, 1963. That order reads:

The *purposes* of this Commission are to examine the evidence developed by the Federal Bureau of Investigation and any additional evidence that may hereafter come to light or be uncovered by federal or state agencies; to make such further investigation as the Commission finds desirable; to evaluate all the facts and circumstances surrounding such assassination, including the subsequent violent death of the man charged with the assassination, and to report to me its findings and conclusions. (WR 471)

One need not read very much of Arlen Specter's *Passion for Truth* to realize that as a trained lawyer, an experienced prosecutor, a key interrogator for the Warren Commission and a 20-year veteran United States Senator, he was a virtual wordsmith. Moreover, in his construction of the Single-Bullet Theory, he sometimes conveyed an attraction for language precision that is truly impressive (although sometimes suspect, as for example when he relates how the May 24 reenactment of the assassination established a shooting angle of 17°43'30"). Such being so, it is surprising to read his substitution of a word, "duty," for the term, "purpose," used in the executive order to which he alludes.

Assuming the conventional meaning of *purposes* as being assigned intentions (and independently of Specter's ignoring the plural to focus on a selected singular), it may of course be argued that such was or was not in the mind of the Executive Order issued by President Johnson. That aside, there is simply no way that Johnson himself could realistically insure that an appointed commission could or would "evaluate all the facts and circumstances surrounding such assassination, including the subsequent violent death of the man charged with the assassination."

Conversely, for Specter to substitute "duty"—obligation—for Johnson's "purpose" suggests that the Warren Commission itself undertook a self-imposed, practically impossible obligation to "evaluate *all* the facts and circumstances surrounding such assassination, including the subsequent violent death of the man charged with the assassination . . ."

It may be argued that the semantics of "purpose" v. "duty" is much ado about nothing. And the point is certainly as well taken as is the observation that a book titled *Passion for Truth* alludes to a "duty" claimed in an Executive Order which never uses that term—truth—in the context of "purpose" "duty" or anything else.

More important than the semantics of "purpose" v. "duty" of the Warren Commission, however, there is room for warranted apprehension for any reader of Senator's follow-up observation:

"We all had enough experience to know that news reports and the preliminary conclusions did not end the need for a thorough investigation." The first question is obvious: Experience in what? Certainly in this instance the answer cannot be "Experience in conducting a thorough investigation of an assassination of a President of the United States." Such being so, the question becomes: What *is* the experience to which he alludes? Limiting the question to Arlen Specter's relevant experience as of 1963, the answer from his account in *Passion for Truth* includes the following:

- His first employment following law school was with the Philadelphia law firm of Barnes, Dechert, Price, Myers and Rhoads, where he was one of a twenty-member trial team between 1956-1959. (12-13)
- Between October 1959 and December 1963, when he was recruited by Howard Willens to serve on the legal staff of the Warren Commission, he had served as an Assistant District Attorney in Philadelphia. The highlight of that service as a prosecutor was a ten-week criminal trial between March-June 1963, which ended with convictions of top Philadelphia Teamster Union leaders, a case in which United States Attorney General Robert F. Kennedy had taken great interest in Specter's work. (37)

It is noteworthy to mention that in the dust jacket of Specter's book there is an eye-catching allusion to this trial, which had generated a personal acquaintanceship between these two men. It reads:

Specter opens *Passion for Truth* in 1959, recounting his beginnings as a newly minted assistant district attorney prosecuting union racketeers—and earning the recognition and respect of Attorney General Robert Kennedy, who would later call on Specter to serve on the Warren Commission.

If the account of such a call is accurate, one can but wonder why Robert Kennedy was interested in having the Warren Commission secure the services of such a top-notch prosecutor as Arlen Specter was in 1963, to serve a commission ostensibly investigating the murder of his brother. The question arises automatically: Why was the Commission undertaking an investigation that required a high-profile prosecutor?

Whatever the answer to that hypothetical, my particular interest in Arlen Specter's account of that complex Teamsters case is his concerned with his comments on a vigorous courtroom exchange between Specter's boss, District Attorney Vic Blanc, functioning as a witness, who was being interrogated by Morton Witkin, identified by Specter as "the top gun in the Teamsters' legal arsenal." It reads:

> In City Hall Courtroom 602, Morton Witkin's cross- examination of Victor Blanc was rough and tough, but fair. In a sense, that approach captures the essence of the American trial system. The basic theory of the adversary system is that the clash of opposite interests will produce the truth. The keystone is cross-examination, in which the witness is forced by his opponent's lawyer to justify his position. Mort Witkin aimed, characteristically, for the gut. (23)

*   *   *

It is recalled that Arlen Specter and David Belin are the only Assistant Counsel to the Warren Commission who have written books in which they recounted their experiences in that role. Each mentions a legal staff meeting at which Chief Justice Warren delivered an orientation lecture to the fourteen members of that legal staff. It is surprising to realize how little of their respective book chapters focus on the subject of "truth" as a topic in the lecture. Comparing their accounts in chronological order, Belin's book, *November 22, 1963: You are the Jury* was published in

1973. Therein a four-page Chapter 2 is titled "**TRUTH IS OUR ONLY GOAL.**" He wrote:

> . . . This Commission was created on November 29, 1963, in recognition of the right of people everywhere to full and truthful knowledge concerning these events. . . .

> Our frame of reference was established in our first meeting with our chairman, Chief Justice Warren. Regardless of what we found, regardless of how the chips might fall, the Chief Justice said, our only concern was for the truth. We took him at his word. 'Truth is our only goal,' he said. The key word was 'only.' To be sure, in a trial, when examining or cross-examining a witness, I was always concerned with the truth—'the whole truth, and nothing but the truth, so help you God.' But my concern was never merely for the sake of the truth itself. There were always other considerations, principally: How does this affect my client? What further steps must be taken in the light of the facts to win the lawsuit?

> But here there was no lawsuit to win, no special client to serve. We were 14 lawyers selected from across the country. Our only goal was to find the truth, the whole truth, and nothing but the truth—for the sake of finding the truth.

> For us lawyers, in contrast to the commissioners, there were no outside influences that might affect our work. We had no government position to protect, no political ax to grind. We were not concerned with judicial precedent. We had no special client paying our fee. If we had any client, it was 190 million Americans who wanted to know the whole truth about the murder of their President. Beyond our shores, people throughout the world also wanted the facts.

Earl Warren spoke with great warmth and sincerity in that first meeting in January. He told us why the Commission had been established. After Lee Harvey Oswald was killed by Jack Ruby, the normal procedures of a trial of the alleged assassin were no longer available. . . . (9-10)

. . . .

. . . President Johnson convinced Chief Justice Warren that an extensive investigation under his leadership would be the most fair and impartial way of finding the truth and would also be accepted and trusted by Americans and by the other peoples of the world.

The President stated that without such a fair and impartial investigation, the increasing speculation could affect the ultimate issues of war or peace. Earl Warren put it simply: When President Johnson said that the assassination of President Kennedy could have an effect on whether there would be war or peace, 'I could not turn him down.' (10)

. . . .

The [legal] staff directed the investigation of the assassination of President Kennedy and wrote the report. And I know from first-hand experience that the work of the staff was performed with 'a total dedication to the determination of the truth." Truth was our only goal.

Before getting to the eyewitness evidence directly related to the two murders, you jurors should have a look inside the Warren Commission to see how far we went in the pursuit of the truth. To give you a typical example, let us explore the subject of the paraffin test performed by the Dallas Police Department on the alleged assassin, Lee Harvey Oswald. (12)

And that ends Belin's chapter titled "**TRUTH IS OUR ONLY GOAL**." Excluding the title, and two references to the Warren *Report*, the "truth" word appears 15 times, including two instances of the judicial mantra—"the truth, the whole truth, and nothing but the truth"—used in allusion to a non-judicial proceeding.

Basically, Arlen Specter's account of Warren's orientation lecture parallels that of Belin, but there are interesting differences. His 11-page chapter if titled **"TRUTH IS THE CLIENT."** His opening paragraph reads in part:

> Chief Justice Warren delivered our charge at an early [legal] staff meeting. All the lawyers gathered around the conference table in the commission hearing room to receive an indoctrination message from the chief justice. Earl Warren had tremendous presence, but even more so on this occasion, when he spoke of duty. . . . (53)
>
> At the outset of his indoctrination talk, the chief justice explained his reasons for serving on the commission. He addressed the question that had troubled many, about the propriety of s Supreme Court justice's undertaking such an assignment. . . . (53)

Warren then relates how the solicitor general, Archibald Cox, indicated he had been instructed to ask Warren to serve as the chairman of a commission to investigate the assassination, an invitation that was declined; the same mission was undertaken by Attorney General Nicholas Katzenbach, with the same result. (54)

Specter continues with Warren's account:

> . . . The next call came from the White House, less than two hours later. 'And then, President Johnson asked me to come to the Oval Office, and asked me to do it. . . . and I said no.' . . . The president persisted. He told Chief Justice Warren that only he could lend the credibility the country and the world so desperately needed as the people tried to understand why their heroic young president had been slain. Conspiracy theories involving communists, the U.S.S.R., Cuba, the military-industrial

complex, and even the new president were already swirling. The Kennedy assassination could lead America into a nuclear war that could kill 40 million people, the president warned. President Johnson stressed that it was crucial to have men of prestige and ability to reassure the people that the whole truth was being aired. 'Then the president said to me, "Chief Justice Warren, would you refuse to put on the uniform of your country in time of national emergency, if requested by the commander in chief?"'

'Of course not,' the chief justice said. Well, the president said, that was the situation they now faced. 'I could hardly refuse that,' Warren told us. 'So I accepted.' (54)

Specter then digresses to recount former President Gerald Ford's similar experience being recruited by Lyndon Johnson to serve on the same Commission.

Returning to the account of Warren's orientation meeting, Specter continues:

At the staff meeting, Warren stressed that our mission, and our obligation, was to find the truth and report it. From the very start, the commission understood that we should not be advocates out to prove a case but must act as independent, disinterested professionals with a duty to find and disclose all the facts, regardless of their implications. 'Your client is the truth,' the chief justice told us. (55)

The "truth" word tally for Specter's 11-page chapter, including the title, is four, one of which is attributed to Lyndon Johnson's usage in his sales pitch to Warren. Thus, in Specter's *Passion for Truth* account, a reader learns that "truth" appears two times in isolated sentences in the same paragraph on page 55:

- "At the staff meeting, Warren stressed that our mission, and our obligation, was to find the truth and report it. . . .
- "'Your client is the truth,' the chief justice told us."

*   *   *

One of the realities in any analysis of the work of the Warren Commission is the frustration that accompanies the awareness that none of the key players, or the Commission's *Report* is on record of identifying the meaning of that commonly used term, "truth."

- Lyndon Johnson exhorts Earl Warren concerning a necessity "to reassure the people that the whole truth was being aired" but he offers nothing by way of defining his term;
- Earl Warren exhorts the Commission's legal staff: "Your client is the truth" but offers nothing by way of defining Johnson's and his term;
- David Belin infers from Earl Warren's orientation lecture that the Commission's legal staff was "14 lawyers [whose] only goal was to find the truth, the whole truth, and nothing but the truth—for the sake of finding the truth," but offers nothing by way of defining Johnson's and Warren's term;
- Arlen Specter writes a book detailing his *Passion for Truth*, but does not identify any meaning behind his use of the term;
- The Warren Commission in its *Report* of September, 1964, included on page xi of its Foreword:

The Commission took steps immediately to obtain the necessary staff to fulfill its assignment. . . . This staff immediately undertook the work of the Commission with a wealth of legal and investigative experience and a total dedication to the determination of the truth."

Arlen Specter's book includes two eye-catching numbers:

> In the end we would publish seventeen thousand
> pages of Warren Commission proceedings in twenty-six
> volumes. While those seventeen thousand pages provided
> grist for critical book's mills, they also showed our
> willingness to put the evidence and exhibits on the public
> record. Years later, in 1992, I co-sponsored legislation to
> declassify and publish as much as possible. (59-60)

I am unaware of any reference/citation for locating any
definition of "truth" which may be found in those seventeen
thousand pages. Moreover, as a consequence of the legislation
which Senator Specter co-sponsored in 1992, it is estimated that
4½ million pages of documentary materials relating to the John
F. Kennedy assassination have been declassified and made available
to the public. I am unaware of any reference/citation which offers
therein a definition of "truth" applicable to the findings of the
Warren Commission.

And when Senator Specter speaks of those seventeen thousand
pages having "provided grist for critical book's mills," he
presumably is including the work of Edward Jay Epstein, who
published a work titled *Inquest* in 1967. Therein he raised critically
important questions involving difficulties in Chapter IV of the
Report, which he identified as setting forth "the case against
Oswald." (142) In that vein, it is educational to read the title of
Epstein's Chapter 9 being "**The Selection Process.**" As his
introduction he uses a point developed by Dwight Macdonald
in his article which appeared in *Esquire* Magazine in March 1965.
It reads:

> Americans often assume that facts are solid, concrete
> (and discrete) objects like marbles, but they are very much
> not. Rather they are subtle essences, full of mystery and
> metaphysics, that change their color and shape, their
> meaning, according to the context in which they are

presented. They must always be treated with skepticism and the standard of judgment should not be how many facts one can mobilize in support of a position but how skillfully one discriminates between them, how objectively one uses them to arrive at Truth, which is something different from, though not unrelated to, the Facts. (141)

And it is always to be remembered that facts are merely statements. They may become *historical* facts when they are empirically verifiable within a conceptual scheme. In such a context, Epstein tells us: "The major problem in the writing of the [Warren] Report was the selection of evidence. From the tens of thousands of pages of evidence, which facts were to be included, and which facts excluded?

Of course, the question becomes: What was the conceptual scheme of the Warren Commission's investigation? Though never stated by the Commission, it is difficult to escape the suspicion that it was essentially the conclusions reached by the FBI in its Summary Report of December 1963—and virtually repeated in its own *Report* of September 1964—Oswald was the lone assassin who fired three shots from the sixth floor's southeast window of the Texas School Book Depository Building. There is only one essential difference between the two reports: There is no Single-Bullet Theory in the FBI Report; Arlen Specter's Single-Bullet Theory is the cornerstone of the Commission *Report*. If such be so, then the path to the Commission's "truth" lay in selecting the facts which supported the Single-Bullet Theory necessary to close successfully its investigation.

Epstein is very perceptive in his recognition of the Commission's problem with "facts" when he writes on page 142:

. . . [T]he writers of the [Warren] Report quite obviously could not simply select the evidence that supported their case, or the Report would have been of no more value than a prosecution's brief which was not tested or challenged by a defense counsel. Norman Redlich thought the problem could be solved by the 'impartial selection of facts.'[2] but [Wesley] Liebeler [an Assistant Counsel colleague] told him, 'I suggest, Norman, that you start to make an argument the minute you select a fact.'[3]

*   *   *

It is recalled that Arlen Specter and the Area 2 lawyers, David Belin and Joseph Ball, had reached an agreement concerning a chronological division of responsibilities for witnesses in relation to the gunshots in the assassination. Despite that agreement, Specter was forced to give way to the wishes of Chief Justice Warren in the matter of testimony to be taken from the two most prominent witnesses, Jacqueline Kennedy, the widow of President Kennedy, and President Kennedy's successor, Lyndon B. Johnson. Specter's account reads:

> The logical lead-off witnesses for my area were the people closest to the president when he was shot. Former First Lady Jacqueline Kennedy would have made an appropriate beginning. But the Commission resisted questioning her. The chief justice had taken a protective stance toward Mrs. Kennedy. It was, of course, natural for him to want to spare the widow the anguish of reliving her husband's murder. . . . My efforts to bring Mrs. Kennedy to testify before the commission were unsuccessful. (61)

In the happening, Mrs. Kennedy did give testimony on June 5 in an extraordinary deposition proceeding held in her own home in Washington, D.C. Joined by her brother-in-law Robert F. Kennedy, the Attorney General, Jacqueline Kennedy gave her testimony before Chief Justice Warren, General Counsel Rankin, and a court reporter. Understandably, Arlen Specter did not provide any indication in his memoir of the type questions *he* would have asked Mrs. Kennedy had he been the interrogator. He did, however, convey a reaction of resentment upon learning after the fact that Rankin had taken her testimony. In his words, "He braced for my response. I didn't say anything. I didn't have to. Rankin knew I was livid." (106)

Thirty-six years later, Senator Specter's tone in his memoir gives indication that his feelings had not mellowed very much. He writes:

> I had been pressing for an interview with Jacqueline Kennedy because she fell within my area and because her deposition would obviously be a key moment in the investigation. Warren had not wanted to subject Mrs. Kennedy to formal questioning before the commission. . . .
>
> The word, unconfirmed to this day, was that Commissioner John McCloy confronted Warren and insisted that the commission take Mrs. Kennedy's testimony. The chief justice reportedly, flatly told McCloy that Mrs. Kennedy's testimony would not be taken. McCloy, the former World Bank president and U.S. military governor of Germany, pressed the chief justice for Mrs. Kennedy's deposition. . . .
>
> In the end, Warren decided to take Mrs. Kennedy's deposition at her apartment. But he was not going to subject her to my detailed, protracted questioning—which he found so painful. I wound up questioning twenty-eight of the ninety-three witnesses who testified before the commission—but not Jacqueline Kennedy. The record on Mrs. Kennedy's deposition shows an abbreviated, nine minute session. The interview omitted most of the lines of questioning I had proposed. It was almost worthless. (107)

Left unmentioned in Senator Specter's account is an unexplained deletion in Mrs. Kennedy's testimony. The context is her reaction immediately following the shooting:

Mrs. Kennedy. . . . I remember I was shouting. And just being down in the car with his head in my lap. And it seemed just an eternity.

You know, then, there were pictures of me climbing out the back. But I don't remember that at all.

Mr. Rankin. Do you remember Mr. Hill [Secret Service] trying to help on the car?

Mrs. Kennedy. I don't remember anything. I was just down like that.

And finally I remember a voice behind me, or something, and then I remember the people in the front seat, or somebody, finally knew something was wrong, and a voice yelling, ... I was just down and holding him. [*Reference to wounds deleted.*] (5H 180) [Emphases added]

It is disappointing that Senator Specter ignores the deletion of what may have been a genuinely important contribution to understanding crucially important details—the wounds!—relevant to Assistant Counsel Specter's formulation of the Single-Bullet Theory. It may of course be argued that this is unwarranted speculation. Perhaps, depending on who says so. But these realities remain a part of the record:

- The closest witness to the wounds was Jacqueline Kennedy.
- Jacqueline Kennedy had the best opportunity of *any* witness to observe for approximately five minutes on the way to the hospital the wounds of President Kennedy, whose head she was holding on her lap.
- Jacqueline Kennedy's testimony concerning those wounds was withheld from the *Report* of the investigative commission which heard that testimony.
- Arlen Specter, the author of the Single-Bullet Theory— is not on record of the Warren Commission as offering any objection to, or criticism of, the deletion of Jacqueline

Kennedy's testimony concerning the wounds at issue in that theory.

*   *   *

Arlen Specter and his colleague, David Belin, were both critical of the decision not to have President Lyndon B. Johnson testify before the Warren Commission. In his memoir, Specter writes:

> I also wanted to question President Johnson, who would under other circumstances have been considered a prime suspect. I had been asked to prepare a list of questions for the new president. I composed seventy-eight questions, including many alternatives, depending on how the president responded to a previous question. I didn't think Lyndon Johnson was complicit in the assassination, but no self-respecting investigator would omit a thorough investigation of the slain president's successor. I strenuously objected when the commission would not question Johnson either, letting him submit a seven-page affidavit instead. 'It was very important to have Johnson questioned, to the extent there were rumors,' agreed fellow commission lawyer David Belin. 'Also, he was a witness. He was in the motorcade.'[5] Belin also dismissed Johnson's seven-page affidavit, which the president sent us several months before [on July 10] his 1964 election. President Johnson was not asked to expand that brief affidavit, and on the verge of the election he obviously was not inclined to say more than required. (61)

While the data in David Belin's account closely parallels the factors mentioned by Arlen Specter, he concludes in his *November 22, 1963: You Are the Jury* by way of a somewhat prescient observation that may or may not have been implied in the above account:

One of the basic lessons of the Warren Commission investigation is the ramifications that arise when special treatment is given to a favored few. The reverberations from the decision to withhold publication of the autopsy photographs and X-rays will be felt for many decades as a part of the overall diminution of the confidence that the American people have felt in the integrity of their elected officials. (348)

In closing this commentary on the contribution of President Lyndon Johnson to the record of the Warren Commission, both Specter and Belin use a term of questionable accuracy for me as a legal layman. Each refers to President Johnson as providing an affidavit, a term which a lay dictionary will identify as a written statement made on oath before a notary public or other person authorized to administer oaths. In the happening, President Johnson's written statement is dated July 10, 1964. It is printed in Volume 5 of the Commission Hearings, at pages 561-564, without any indication that it is given under oath administered by a notary public or anyone else. If such be so, it is difficult for this layman to understand why Specter and Belin refer to the statement as an affidavit. This distinction becomes curiously interesting when reading David Belin's judgment that ". . . President Johnson was wrong in some of his observations." (347)

CHAPTER III

QUICK REFLEXES

Senator Arlen Specter's third chapter in Part 2 of his *Passion for Truth* is a seven-page account that introduces one of the unusual elements factored into his Single-Bullet Theory. It is the seemingly simple question: What is the location of the entry wound that generated the theory? Disagreement over the answer has resulted in a long-running argument that has assumed the style of a sometimes meanspirited "could have" v. "could not have" debate usually encompassing both the location and nature of that wound.

The chapter begins with this paragraph:

> There were many Secret Service agents involved in the activities the day of Kennedy's assassination who could have been called as witnesses. There were agents in the lead car that preceded the presidential limousine, in the president's follow-up car, with the vice presidential limousine, and the car that followed the vice presidential limousine. Statements had been obtained from each of the agents and were included in the Secret Service report. The two agents who demanded attention in addition to Roy Kellerman and William Greer, who had been riding in Kennedy's Lincoln, were Clint Hill and Rufus Youngblood.

My present interest in this seven-page chapter is on Arlen Specter's focus of his historical lens on Agents Kellerman and

Greer. However, in a book which is highly critical of Senator Specter's memoir of his service on the Warren Commission, admiring candor prompts recognition of an example of his generous capacity for sympathetic evaluation of the role of Clint Hill in the hectic moments of that tragic day. Specter writes in *Passion for Truth*:

> Hill had jumped from the left running board of the president's follow-up car after the shooting and caught up with the Lincoln. I was amazed every time I watched the Zapruder film and saw Hill dash to the limousine, barely grasp the handle on the left rear fender and leap on the small running board at the left rear just as the car accelerated. Hill was one of the agents who went out on the town the night before the assassination. According to his own signed statement, Hill left his hotel shortly before 1:30 a.m., drank a Scotch and water at the Press Club of Fort Worth, then had part of a nonalcoholic fruit drink at a nightspot called The Cellar, leaving about 2:45 a.m. to return to his hotel. But Clint Hill's reflexes could hardly have been quicker later that day.[1] (64)
>
> In the instant after the assassination, Clint Hill saved Jacqueline Kennedy's life. The first lady had inexplicably climbed onto the trunk of the moving limousine. Clint Hill pushed her back into the car. If he had not, Mrs. Kennedy would have tumbled into the street when the Lincoln accelerated, into the path of the speeding backup car. (64)

Senator Specter's memoir-style of writing is perhaps at its best when he writes about the role of Agent Youngblood:

> I did interview Secret Service Agent Rufus Youngblood. According to preliminary reports, 'Rufe' Youngblood had scrambled to protect the life of Vice

President Johnson. Youngblood was sitting on the right front seat of the vice presidential limousine. Johnson was sitting in the rear on the extreme right, ...

When I spoke briefly with Youngblood before he was called to testify formally before the Commission [on March 9], he was sheepish about his speed in bounding from the front seat to the vice president. At the time of the shooting, Youngblood had jumped over the front seat and shielded the vice president with his own body. Johnson had said that Youngblood was on top of him after the first shot and before the second. Youngblood deferred to President Johnson's version, for at least two obvious reasons: First, who wants to contradict his boss? And, second, it would not harm Youngblood's reputation to be considered so quick.

In reconstructing the assassination, it seemed unlikely that Youngblood could have moved fast enough to vault the front seat and land on Johnson between the first and second shots. But it sounded great. Some of the commission lawyers, jesting among ourselves, made it an even more spectacular story: Shortly *before* [emphasis in original] the first shot, Youngblood leaped over the front seat to shield the vice president with his own body. Several lawyers thought that sequence was almost as plausible as Johnson's version.

Be those things as they may, there is only one other Specter comment that I find significantly relevant for the present review of Senator Specter's *Passion for Truth*. It reads: "When Hill and Youngblood testified, they were in much better spirits than Kellerman and Greer, the other two Secret Service agents we interviewed early." (66) This comment I take to mean that Specter "prepared"—by way of preliminary interviews—all four of these agents before he took their formal testimony on March 9. This is a point to be recalled when attention is given below to the testimony of Roy Kellerman.

*   *   *

Senator Specter's memoir relates that "[i]n his informal interview, Secret service Agent William Greer seemed shaken by the shooting. He clearly felt deep affection for Kennedy, which I sensed had been reciprocal." Specter then goes on to say that "Greer told a touching story that he later repeated in part in his formal testimony before the commission." (67) Essentially the story concerns a question that was of serious concern to Specter: Was President Kennedy wearing an undershirt at the time he was assassinated? In the happening, Greer answered the question in the negative by way of an inference from personal experience that Kennedy wore an undershirt only when the weather was cold. And since it was not cold in Dallas the day of the assassination, he was not wearing an undershirt that day. (67-68)

Of relevance to the present writing, I am interested in Specter's account of why he was interested in the question he asked Greer. He writes in *Passion for Truth*:

> I was interested to know whether President Kennedy wore an undershirt, because his clothes could indicate the direction and location of the bullet. Fibers from the back of the president's jacket and shirt had been pressed forward, indicating that the bullet had come from the rear. The president's garments were also important, given the controversy over the location of the hole in his body versus the locations of the holes in his clothing. Some critics have seized on the locations of the holes in the suit jacket and shirt to argue that the hole was lower on the president's back than the reports asserted. This concern had been aggravated by the withholding of the autopsy photographs and X rays.
> *President Kennedy's activities, dress, and physique indicate that his shirt and jacket rode up on his body.*

During the ride from Love Field to downtown Dallas, the president had twice ordered the limousine stopped so he could stand up and greet watchers. When Kennedy sat down in the open controvertible, his contact with the seat would tend to move his clothing up. Waving with his right hand, as shown on the Zapruder film, would also tend to lift the president's jacket and shirt on his body. Kennedy's back brace and muscular build would further hike up his garments. To nail down the direction and the location of the bullet that struck the president's back, we wanted all possible indicators. One of those was an undershirt, if in fact Kennedy had been wearing one that day. The simplest approach would have been to ask Mrs. Kennedy, but the commission was reluctant to make that inquiry. Instead, I asked every witness I questioned whether the president was wearing an undershirt in Dallas. Generally, I got nowhere. Then, to my surprise, Agent Greer said, 'Oh, no, we wasn't wearing an undershirt.'

. . . .

    When Secret Service Agents Kellerman, Greer, Hill, and Youngblood testified [March 9], I questioned them about minute details of the assassination. I knew they could not give precise answers to all my questions, but I believed that those questions should be asked. To draw a composite picture of the shooting, we needed to gather and weigh evidence from all the vantage points. (67-68) [Emphases added]

Specter was well aware that his style of questioning tested the patience of the Chairman: "When I questioned witnesses, Warren frequently tapped his fingers. His annoyance at my prolonged questioning was obvious." Then follows an example of the style, followed by Warren's reaction, and the rationale defended by Specter:

The day the Secret service agents testified, we began at 9:10 a.m. and didn't finish until 6:20 p.m. Shortly after the morning session began, Warren left to sit with the Supreme Court. He returned for the afternoon session, when the questioning of Agent Kellerman continued. At one point during my questioning, when the chief justice's fingertapping reached a crescendo, he took me aside and asked me to speed it up. He said it was unrealistic to expect meaningful answers to questions about elapsed time between the first and second shots and between the second and third shots, or about the distance traveled between the first and second shots or the speed of the car at the time of the first shot, at the time of the second shot, and at the time of the third shot.

I said I thought the questions were essential. I knew it was difficult for witnesses to give precise answers, I told the chief justice, but I thought we had to ask those questions and get the most precise answers possible—this might produce some valuable information that could otherwise elude us. *And people would read and reread this record for years, if not decades or perhaps even centuries.* Even at that stage, on the basis of my experience reading records on appeals cases, I was concerned that the commission record be as professional as possible. The chief justice appeared dissatisfied with my answer, but he didn't order me to change my approach. Aside from drumming his fingers, Warren did not interfere with the examination. (68-69) [Emphases added}

COMMENT I.

Regarding "I was interested to know whether President Kennedy wore an undershirt, because his clothes could indicate the direction and location of the bullet": It is not clear how the presence or absence of an undershirt could indicate the "location of the bullet". Specter's interest should more properly be concerned with the location of "the wound", rather than the bullet which the government version of things claims was found outside the body.

COMMENT II.

Regarding "Fibers from the back of the president's jacket and shirt had been pressed forward, indicating that the bullet had come from the rear": It is not clear how the presence or absence of an undershirt could affect the direction in which the fibers of the jacket and shirt were pressed. Stated differently, it seems impossible to believe that an undershirt's fibers could have been pressed in a direction different from that of the jacket and shirt.

COMMENT III.

Regarding "The president's garments were also important, given the controversy over the location of the hole in his body versus the locations of the holes in his clothing": It seems more accurate to suggest that the controversy is really over the location of the hole in the body. If such be so, it makes absolutely no difference whether he did or did not wear an undershirt. The issue is whether the hole in the body is aligned with the holes in the clothing—suit jacket and shirt.

COMMENT IV.

Regarding "Some critics have seized on the locations of the holes in the suit jacket and shirt to argue that the hole was lower on the president's back than the reports asserted": Absent an identification of "the reports", the claim is equally valid that defenders of the Single-Bullet Theory have argued that the hole on the "president's back" was higher than the measurements of the corresponding holes in the clothing. The absence of reference/citation for the defenders' location of the "hole on the president's back" reduces their argument to an unsupported claim in conflict with the depiction of the hole on Commission Exhibit 397, the Autopsy Description Sheet on file in the National Archives.

COMMENT V.

Regarding "This concern has been aggravated by the withholding of the autopsy photographs and X rays": The simple reality is that the critics of the Single-Bullet Theory are not responsible for the withholding of either the photographs or the X-rays. If the defenders of the Theory have a sustainable argument concerning the location of the wound at issue, it is not supported by the refusal of the Warren Commission to publish the photographs and X-rays in either its *Report* or the 26 volumes of data upon which is it ostensibly based.

Senator Specter's memoir account continues with another conjecture-oriented paragraph devoid of references/citations:

> President Kennedy's activities, dress, and physique indicate that his shirt and jacket rode up on his body. During the ride from Love Field to downtown Dallas, the president had twice ordered the limousine stopped so he could stand up and greet watchers. When Kennedy sat down in an open convertible, his contact with the seat would tend to move his clothing up. Waving with his right hand, as shown on the Zapruder film, would also tend to lift the president's jacket and shirt on his body. Kennedy's back brace and muscular build would further hike up his garments. (67-68)

COMMENT VI.

Regarding President Kennedy's activities: "During the ride from Love Field to downtown Dallas, the president had twice ordered the limousine stopped so he could stand up and greet watchers. When Kennedy sat down in an open convertible, his contact with the seat would tend to move his clothing up":

1. This argument is important for acceptance of the claim that the holes in the jacket/shirt are misleading because "his contact with the seat would tend to move his clothing up." It is regrettable that Senator Specter does not provide reference/citation for this "activity". It is so important that a side trip to try finding a reference/citation is in order at this time.

2. The Warren *Report* provides uncontested data on the two limousine stops ordered by President Kennedy:

   The motorcade left Love Field shortly after 11:50 a.m. and drove at speeds up to 25 to 30 miles an hour through thinly populated areas on the outskirts of Dallas.[127] At the President's direction, his automobile stopped twice, the first time to permit him to respond to a sign asking him to shake hands.[128] During this brief stop, agents in the front positions on the running boards of the Presidential followup car came forward and stood beside the President's car, looking out toward the crowd, and Special Agent Kellerman assumed his position next to the car.[129] On the other occasion, the President halted the motorcade to speak to a Catholic nun and a group of small children.[130] (46)

3. The relevant references/citations are these:

   [128] 4H 132 (Connally); 2H 135 (Hill); 2H 70 (Kellerman).
   [129] Ibid.
   [130] 4H 132 (Connally).

A careful reading of the relevant portions of these citations is in order:

- [128] and [129]

Mr. Specter. Did the automobile stop at any point during this procession?

Governor Connally. Yes; it did. There were at least two occasions on which the automobile stopped in Dallas and, perhaps, a third. There was one little girl, I believe it was, who was carrying a sign saying, 'Mr. President, will you please stop and shake hands with me,' or some— that was the import of the sign, and he just told the driver to stop, and he did stop and shook hands, and, of course, he was immediately mobbed by a bunch of youngsters, and the Secret Service men from the car following us had to immediately stop and come up and wedge themselves between the crowd and the car to keep them back away from the automobile, and it was a very short stop.

At another point along the route, a Sister, a Catholic nun, was there, obviously from a Catholic school, with a bunch of little children, and he stopped and spoke to her and the children; and I think there was one other stop on the way downtown, but I don't recall the precise occasion. But I know there were two, but I think there was still another one.

Mr. Specter. Are there any other events prior to the time of the shooting which stand out in your mind on the motorcade trip through Dallas?

Governor Connally. No; not that have any particular significance. (4H 132)

• Mr. Specter. What is your best estimate of the maximum speed of the automobile from the time you left Love Field until the time you arrived at downtown Dallas?

Mr. [Clint] Hill. I would say we never ran any faster than 25 to 30 miles per hour.

Mr. Specter. What is your best estimate of the minimum speed during this same interval?

Mr. Hill. Twelve to fifteen miles per hour. We did stop.

Mr. Specter. On what occasion did you stop?

Mr. Hill. Between Love Field and Main Street, downtown Dallas, on the right-hand side of the street there were a group of people with a long banner which said, 'Please, Mr. President, stop and shake our hands.' And the President requested the motorcade to stop, and he beckoned to the people and asked them to come and shake his hand, which they did.

Mr. Specter. Did the President disembark from his automobile at that time?

Mr. Hill. No; he remained in his seat. (2H 135)

• Mr. Specter. Were there any unusual occurrences en route from Love Field until, say, you got to the downtown area of dallas, Tex.

Mr. [Roy] Kellerman. As we were on the outskirts of this town and apparently reaching a crowded area there were a group of youngsters on the right side of the car curb-line-wise, that had a large sign, oh, perhaps the width of the two windows there, that said, 'Please, Mr. President, stop and shake our hands,' and he saw this and called to the driver and said, 'Stop,' he said, 'call these people over and I will shake their hands,' which he did. The entire motorcade stopped. I got out of the car and stood alongside it while these people were right up on me. The agents who were on the followup car, all around it. And then after a few seconds, he said, 'All right; let's travel on.'

Mr. Specter. You say the agents in the followup car moved up at the stopping?

Mr. Kellerman, Always, sir.

Mr. Specter. Specifically, what did they do on that occasion?

Mr. Kellerman. They crowded right in between the President, the car, and the people.

[71] Mr. Specter. Did the President actually leave the car?

Mr. Kellerman. No.

Mr. Specter. And how long did that stop last?

Mr. Kellerman. A matter of seconds.

Mr. Specter. Was there any other unusual occurrence en route to the downtown area itself?

Mr. Kellerman. No; I can recall, however, one small affair. I think we were in the heart of Dallas on this street when a small boy jumped off the curb and apparently he was thinking of running over to the President's car and shaking his hands when one of our people left the followup car and put him back on the curb, and all that happened in motion so there was nothing out of the way.

Mr. Specter. I show you a photograph marked Commission Exhibit No. 347 and ask you if you are able to tell us what that photograph represents.

. . . .

Mr. Kellerman. This is an aerial photo of the downtown parade. (2H 70-71)

• [129] 4H 132 (Connally).

This much is clear from a search of these references/citations from the Warren *Report*: There is no basis therein for Senator Specter's memoir claim that "*the president had twice ordered the limousine stopped so he could stand up and greet watchers.*"

It is recalled that this claim was followed by another: "When Kennedy sat down in the open controvertible, his contact with the seat would tend to move his clothing up." Accepting this claim for a moment, the inference is clear: When Kennedy sat down in the open convertible at Love Field, "his contact with the seat would tend to move his clothing up," Such being the case, his clothing must have remained "up" until he was struck by the bullet which is the object of attention in Specter's Single-Bullet Theory.

Certainly that is possible. But it is difficult to imagine that immobility as a probability when it is remembered that the testimony evidence of Governor Connally is that he shook hands with at least one person whom he recalled as a "little girl". It simply tests the limit of common sense adult courtesy to believe that the President of the United States would halt his limousine to enable a child to reach in for a handshake while he remained immobilized with his "up" clothing pinned against the back seat. Assuming *that* reality, and in the absence of evidence that he stood before resuming a seated position would return his clothing to an "up" position, Senator Specter's memoir claim requires an incredible act of faith in the accuracy of his 37-year old recollection.

The claim, however, is functionally understandable as support for the more important Specter claim generally known as the "bunching" theory, which insists there is no contradiction between the location of the holes in the president's clothing and the entrance wound of the bullet necessary for the Single-Bullet Theory.

COMMENT VII.

Continuing with Senator Specter's memoir claims that President Kennedy's activities/dress/physique indicating that "his shirt and jacket rode up on his body"—the "bunching theory"—the next point to be evaluated reads: "Waving with his right hand, as shown on the Zapruder film, would also tend to lift the president's jacket and shirt on his body":

1. Absent a reference/citation to establish which frame(s) on the Z-film show him waving with his right hand, it is difficult to respond to the claim.

2. In the happening, the relevance of the claim is limited to the frame(s) immediately preceding the shot which struck President Kennedy. The problem is that the validity of the claim is destroyed by the inability of the Zapruder camera lens to capture on film the frame corresponding to the precise instant that shot struck. The reason for that inability was caused by a highway street sign—the famous Stemmons Freeway sign that was subsequently removed from *its* location in Dealey Plaza—that hid the limousine from the lens between frames 210 and 225 on the Zapruder film. Thus the reality is that there simply is no visual evidence that President Kennedy was waving at the time he was hit by the bullet in question.

3. The claim itself is dubious for this observer because I have never seen a photograph from that motorcade which shows President Kennedy waving with his hand positioned above the level of his head. Were there such a photo, the argument of "bunching/riding up/whatever" clothing might sustain the claim that the jacket rose during that wave. However, the only relevant photograph of which I am aware is Commission Exhibit No. 697, captioned "Photograph of Presidential limousine taken during motorcade." This shows the President waving with the elbow resting on the body of the open convertible in which he was riding. It appears on page 104 of the Warren *Report* in Chapter III, which was written by Arlen Specter. The citation for CE 697 is 17H 353.

4. Irrespective of rancorous debate concerning the correlation between shots and Z-film frames, the phenomenon of President Kennedy's waving style immediately preceding the shooting sequence may be clearly seen in a Zapruder frame which appeared in the October 2, 1964 issue of *Life* magazine. In that issue there is a six-page article written by then Congressman Gerald R. Ford, a member of the Warren Commission. Titled "Piecing Together the Evidence," the article includes

a color sequence of eight frames from the Zapruder Film. The first frame is identified as follows: "A moment before the first bullet was fired, the President and Mrs. Kennedy, Governor and Mrs. Connally, smiling and waving, were passing in front of the brick building where the assassin was taking aim. It is clear that the President's waving hand is not positioned above his head.

5. In 1993, Robert Groden published a book titled *The Killing of a President* in which he included on page 22 an enlargement of a Zapruder frame depicting the Presidential wave just prior to the limousine disappearing behind the Stemmons Freeway sign. The relationship of the elbow, hand waving, and head effectively compromises Arlen Specter's claim: "Waving with his right hand, as shown on the Zapruder film, would also tend to lift the president's jacket and shirt on his body."

COMMENT: VIII.

Regarding "Kennedy's back brace and muscular build would further hike up his garments": Depending upon unestablished variables, this claim may or may not be significant.

1. Absent measured dimensions of the back brace, there is no basis for Specter's term "would" as opposed to "could" in his claim. At the outset it is noted that Arlen Specter took the testimony of Parkland Hospital Doctors Charles Carrico and Malcolm Perry on two occasions. On March 25, he took their deposition in Dallas; on March 30 he took their testimony before the Commission in Washington. (It is also noted that he "prepared" each witness in Dallas prior to taking the testimony.) His deposition session with Dr. Carrico included these exchanges:

Mr. Specter. Would you continue to describe your observations of the President?

Dr. Carrico. . . . He was making no spontaneous movements, I mean, no voluntary movements at all. We opened his shirt and coat and tie and observed a small wound in the anterior lower third of the neck, listened very briefly, heard a few cardiac beats, *felt the President's back*, and detected no large or sucking chest wounds, and then proceeded to the examination of his head.

. . . .

S. You said you felt the President's back?

C. Yes.

S. Would you describe in more detail just what the feeling of the back involved at that time?

C. Without taking the time to roll him over and look or to wash off the blood and debris, and *while his coat and shirt were still on his arms, I just placed my hands at about his beltline or a little above and by slowly moving my hands upward detected that there was no large violation of the pleural cavity.*

. . . .

S. What did you observe as to the President's clothing with respect to the presence of a back brace, if any?

C. There was, on removing the President's shirt and coat, we noted he was wearing a standard back support.

S. Would you describe that back support, please?

C. As I recall, it was white cotton or some fibrous support, with staves, bones and if I remember buckled in the front.

S. *How wide was it?*

C. How wide?

S. Yes, sir.

C. *I don't know; I didn't examine below—you see—as I recall, it came to about his umbilicus—navel area.*

S. *Was there any Ace bandage applied to the President's hips that you observed?*

C. *No; I didn't remove his pants.*

S. Did you have any opportunity to observe that part of his body when his pants were removed?

C. I had the opportunity, but I didn't look. (6H 3-4)

In the March 30 testimony before the Commission, these exchanges took place:

Mr. Specter. Was President Kennedy wearing a back brace?

Dr. Carrico. Yes; he was.

S. Would you describe as precisely as you can that back brace?

C. As I recall, this was a white cotton or some sort of fiber standard brace with stays and corset, in a corset-type arrangement and buckles.

S. How far up on his body did it come?

C. Just below his umbilicus, as I recall.

S. How far down his body did it go?

C. I did not examine below his belt at that time.

S. Did you at any time examine below his belt?

C. I did not; no, sir.

S. Do you know if anyone else did?

C. Not in a formal manner.

S. What action did you take by way of treating President Kennedy on his arrival?

C. . . . We completed an emergency examination, which consisted of, as we have already said, his color, his pulse, we felt his back, determined there were no large wounds which would be an immediate threat to life there. . . .

S. Specifically, what did you do with respect to the back, Dr. Carrico?

C. This is a routine examination of critically ill patients where you haven't got time to examine him, fully. *I*

*just placed my hands just above the belt, but in this
case just above the brace, and ran my hands up his
back.*

S. To what point on his body?

C. All the way up to his neck very briefly.

S. What did you feel by that?

C. I felt nothing other than the blood and debris.

(3H 359-360) [Emphases added]

2. From his testimony, it is not obvious exactly how Dr.
    Carrico was able to provide his description of the back
    brace.

    a. When asked on deposition: (1) "How wide
        was it," his reply was "I don't know; it came
        to about his umbilicus—navel area"; (2) "Was
        there an Ace bandage applied to the President's
        hips that you observed?" his reply was "No, I
        didn't remove his pants"; (3) When asked "Did
        you have any opportunity to observe that part
        of his body when his pants were removed?"
        his reply was "I had the opportunity, but I
        didn't look."

3. When asked on formal testimony before the
    Commission: (1)"How far up on his body did it come?"
    his reply was "Just below his umbilicus, as I recall"; (2)
    "How far down his body did it go?" his reply was "I did
    not examine below his belt at that time"; (3) When asked
    "Did you at any time examine below his belt?" his reply
    was "I did not; no, sir"; (4) When asked "Do you know
    if anyone else did?" his reply was "Not in a formal
    manner"; (5) When asked "Specifically, what did you do
    with respect to the back, Dr. Carrico?" his reply was "I

just placed my hands just above the belt, but in this case just above the brace, and ran my hands up his back."

4. Assuming there is a close relationship between a normal belt position and the level of the umbilicus, and the doctor's testimony is that the back brace came "up on his body" to "just below the umbilicus" and that he "did not examine below his belt . . . at any time", it is difficult to believe that Dr. Carrico was the source of the datum that "Kennedy's back brace . . . would further hike up his garments."

5. Parkland Hospital Dr. Malcolm Perry was also questioned by Arlen Specter both on deposition and in testimony before the Commission. IN the deposition on March 25, the following exchanges are recorded:

Mr. Specter. Did you have any occasion to examine the President's clothing to ascertain direction of the missile?

Dr. Perry. No; I did not. The only aspect of clothing that I know about—I happen to recall pushing up the brace which he had on in an attempt to feel a femoral pulse when I arrived, and I could not, but the shirt had been removed by the personnel there in the emergency room, I assume.

S.   What did you observe as to the description of that brace?

P.   I couldn't give you a description. I just saw and felt the lower edge of one, and I reached to feel the left femoral pulse.

S.   Did you see whether the President was wearing any sort of an Ace bandage on the midsection of his body when his trousers were taken down?

P.   There was evidence of an Ace bandage—I saw it sticking out from the edge on the right side, as I recall. I don't believe it was on the midsection, although it may have been. I believe it was on his right leg—his right thigh.

S. Do you know whether it was on his left leg and thigh as well?

P: No, I don't; I just saw that briefly when I was reaching for that pulse and I didn't do any examination at all of the lower trunk or lower extremities.

S. Did you personally make any examination by feeling, or in any other way, of the President's back?

P. I did not. (6H 12)

In his Commission testimony on March 30, the following exchanges took place:

Mr. Specter: Will you continue then, Dr. Perry, as to what you observed of his condition?

. . . .

Dr. Perry. I pushed up the brace on the left side very briefly to feel for his femoral pulse, but did not obtain any.

. . . .

S. Now, you mentioned the President's brace. Could you describe it as specifically as possible?

P. No, sir; I did not examine it. I noted its presence only in an effort to reach the femoral pulse and I pushed it up just slightly so that I might palpitate for the femoral pulse, I did no more examination.

S. In the course of seeking the femoral pulse, did you observe or note an Ace bandage?

P. Yes, sir.

S. In the brace area?

P. Yes, sir. It was my impression, I saw a portion of an Ace bandage an elastic supporting bandage on the right thigh. I did not examine it at all but I just noted the bandage.

S. Did the Ace bandage cover any portion of the President's body that you were able to observe in addition to the right thigh?

P. No, sir; I did not go any further. I just noted its presence there at the junction of the hip. It could have been on the lower trunk or the upper thigh, I don't know. I didn't care any further. (3H 368-369)

6. Regarding the testimony of Dr. Perry as compared with that of Dr. Carrico, it is even more difficult to believe that Dr. Perry was the source of Specter's claim that "Kennedy's back brace . . . would further hike up his garments."

COMMENT IX.

.

It is also noteworthy that between March 20-24 in Dallas Arlen Specter took depositions from six Parkland Hospital nurses on duty in the Emergency Rooms area on November 22. Of them, two, Diane Bowron and Margaret Henchliffe, undressed and cleaned the body of President Kennedy in Trauma Room 2. Bowron's testimony appears at 6H 134-139; Henchliffe's testimony appears at 6H 140-143. Neither was asked questions, nor volunteered answers, concerning President Kennedy's back brace. Clearly it is difficult to believe that either of them was the source of Specter's claim that "Kennedy's back brace . . . would further hike up his garments,"

COMMENT X.

Regarding the claim that "Kennedy's . . . muscular build would further hike up his garments", this specification of the "bunching" argument might possibly apply to the suit jacket, but it is not clear how it could apply to a shirt restrained by a belt. And inasmuch as the May 13 expert witness testimony of FBI Agent Robert A. Frazier (5H 59-60) establishes that the holes in both jacket and shirt align perfectly with each other, the argument betrays a stretch of the imagination that is beyond understanding by persons of informed common sense. In any event, absent a reference/citation on behalf of the claim, it is enough to remember the old saw: "That which is gratuitously asserted may be gratuitously denied."

NOTE

[1] *Report of the President's Commission on the Assassination of President John F. Kennedy*, Washington: GPO, 1964, Commission Exhibit 1020.

CHAPTER IV

GOVERNOR CONNALLY

The five-page fourth chapter in Senator Specter's memoir, *Passion for Truth*, is something of a chronological oddity in that its focus is on a nationally prominent witness—John B. Connally—whose most important testimony had already been rejected by the Warren Commission. The chronological reality is simply this: By the time the Commission took the testimony of the Texas Governor on April 22, Arlen Specter had already put together the essential pieces in the construction of the Single-Bullet Theory, an account which could not accommodate Governor Connally's mental reconstruction of the shooting sequence. At the same time, however, the Commission was in the awkward stance of having to receive courteously and respectfully the testimony of a longtime personal friend and political ally of Lyndon B. Johnson, the President of the United States who had created the CommissIon. Whether by design or simply fortuitous occurrence, the awkward conundrum was resolved by way of a personnel substitution that effectively end-ran the problem.

Senator Specter's account of Governor Connally's testimony states concisely the reality of the situation:

> Even before Connally testified, it was clear he had his mind set about the events of November 22. As far as I know, no investigator from the commission or any other federal agency had interviewed John Connally before his

appearance in Washington. But I knew that the governor had discussed the shooting with others.

(The essential chronology to be kept in mind as the Connally testimony is recounted by Specter is simple but critical: The origin of the Single-Bullet Theory developed from the testimony of autopsy Doctor James J. Humes taken by Specter on March 16, corroborated by his autopsy associates, Doctors Boswell and Finck; Specter deposed Kennedy's surgeons, Parkand Doctors Carrico and Perry on March 25, when they endorsed Humes' testimony, and repeated it in Commission testimony on March 30; thus by the time Connally testified on April 21, a substantial outline of the theory was already in place.)

The circumstances of the selection of Arlen Specter for the interrogation of this high-profile witness, John Connally, make for fascinating reading in *Passion for Truth*:

> Several days before John Connally was scheduled to arrive in Washington, Rankin told me that the chief justice had ordered him to take the governor's testimony. Connally, riding in front of the president, fell into my area. But I understood. Warren had great confidence in Rankin, and it was appropriate that the general counsel handle the most important witnesses. And I knew that the chief justice found my detailed queries tedious.
>
> Lee Rankin asked me how he should approach the questioning of Governor Connally. In order to get all the information from the governor, I replied, it was necessary to correlate the medical findings, including the tests done at Edgewater [sic; Edgewood Arsenal in Maryland was the Army Weapons Research Center] and the X rays, with the velocity of the bullet and the path it followed. I pointed out to Rankin that the bullet had a muzzle velocity of approximately 2,000 feet per second; and that, on the basis of the tests at Edgewater with a

gelatin solution and compressed goat meat, the bullet would have an exit velocity of about 1,900 feet per second. The velocity decreased as the bullet entered slightly to the left of the govenror's right armpit, exited beneath his right nipple, leaving a large exit wound, and entered the dorsal aspect of his wrist and exited the volar aspect, finally lodging in his thigh. I presented a longer sequence to Rankin, taking in the path of the Lincoln limousine, the seating arrangements in the car, and other factors.

By the time I had finished, Rankin, knowing he had little time to immerse himself in such detail, shook his head in despair. 'You'll have to question Connally,' he said.

I hadn't intended to discourage Rankin and displace him as Connally's questioner. But I wouldn't say I regretted it either. (69-70)

Note! Senator Specter's memoir utilizes a writing style that is very readable and interesting-holding, but somewhat chronologically piecemeal from the perspective of organization of subject material. Thus, the above four paragraphs is quoted material from the seven pages of material in his previous chapter titled "Quick Reflexes," which was the topic of my Chapter III above.

From this point forward, Specter's account is taken from his five-page chapter titled **GOVERNOR CONNALLY**, on pages 71-75.

*   *   *

It is recalled from passing mention above that the record indicates erstwhile Senior Assistant Counsel Francis Adams was present at the April 21 testimony session of Governor Connally. Whether that record is factually accurate or not is irrelevant to the reality: Junior Assistant Counsel Arlen Specter was calling the shots as of April 21, 1964. Not only had he displaced Warren's choice of Rankin as the interrogator of Connally, but he also deliberately chose to end-run the presumed wishes of Warren concerning the style of the interrogation. The account in *Passion for Truth* is eye-opening:

> One subject that had intrigued the younger staff was the purpose of Kennedy's visit to Texas. The media had speculated that the trip was politically motivated, and several young commission lawyers thought Connally should be asked about that explicitly. We considered it important to put it on the record. I guessed that the chief justice might not like my exploring this background issue. To get the governor's candid response on a subject he had not expected—and to explore the area before the chief justice could preempt me—I led off with that question. (73)

(Remembering that Arlen Specter had most of his Single-Bullet Theory pieces in place prior to his April 21 interrogation of Governor Connally, it is amusing to recognize the style in which he "prepared his witness for the testimony:

> Connally's testimony would generally follow the outline we had discussed at our brief morning meeting. I thought the governor should know about some additional facts and testimony the commission had gathered, so he could weigh them along with his own experience. In the morning I had told Connally of factors that suggested he might have been struck by the same bullet that had first passed through Kennedy's neck. Connally summarily, emphatically rejected that possibility. 'It is not conceivable to me that I could have been hit by the first bullet,' he testified. Connally reasoned that he heard the first shot, did not hear the second shot, which he assumed struck him, and was in his wife's lap when he heard the third shot strike the president's head. (73-74)

Within that context, Connally's answer to the question of the purpose of the trip to Texas was irrelevant to the substance of his testimony as developed in Senator Specter's memoir. One thing seems certain: The 34-year-old Assistant District Attorney from Philadelphia, Arlen Specter, was not overwhelmed by the roster of luminaries and observers who attended the center-stage performance on April 21. It is an impressive roster:

- Six of the seven Commissioners—Warren/Russell/ Cooper/Boggs/ McCloy/Dulles—were there;
- General Counsel Rankin was there;
- Four Assistant Counsel colleagues—Adams/Ball/Belin/ Redlich—are recorded as present;
- Two observers—Charles Murray and Charles Rhyne— representing Walter E. Craig, president of the American Bar Association who had been chosen to represent Oswald's interests at the Commission hearings were there;
- Texas Attorney General Waggoner Carr was there;
- Two of Connally's surgeons—Drs. Charles Gregory and Robert Shaw—were there;
- Connally's wife, Nellie, was there.

*   *   *

Whether Arlen Specter's Single-Bullet Theory was or was not conceivable to Texas Governor John B. Connally is simply irrelevant to the Warren Commission's rejection of Connally's insistence that he could not have been hit by a bullet which first struck President Kennedy.

It is difficult to appreciate the brevity of Senator Specter's focus maintained in his memoir account of Governor Connally's testimony concerning "the assassination itself." He writes in *Passion for Truth*:

When we got to the assassination itself, Connally's testimony was among the most graphic and detailed we heard. 'What is the best estimate you have,' I asked the governor, 'as to the time span between the sound of the first shot and the feeeling of someone hitting you in the back which you just described.'

'A very, very brief span of time,' Connally answered. '. . . I knew I had been hit, and I immediately assumed, because of the amount of blood, and, in fact, that it had obviously passed through my chest, that I had probably been fatally hit. . . . And then, of course, the third shot sounded, and I heard the shot very clearly. I heard it hit him. I heard the shot hit something, and I assumed again—it never entered my mind that it hit anybody but the president. I heard it hit. It was a very loud noise, just that audible, very clear. Immediately I could see on my clothes, my clothing, I could see on the interior of the car—which, as I recall was a pale blue—brain tissue, which I immediately recognized, and I recall very well, on my trousers was one chunk of brain tissue as big as almost my thumb, and again, I did not see the president at any time either after the first, second, or third shots. . . .'

Following that dramatic testimony, Specter's memoir is content to close his account with a scene that, while emotionally touching, has an importance not immediately obvious, but is of incalculable importance to Arlen Specter:

> Toward the end of his testimony, I asked Connally, 'What was the nature of the exit wound on the front side of your chest, Governor?'
>
> 'If the committee would be interested,' Connally said, I would just as soon you look at it. Is there any objection to any of you looking at it?' There was no objection, and Connally took off his shirt to show a large, ugly four-inch-diameter scar under his right nipple, from the exit wound. While Connally's shirt was off, Lee Rankin's secretary, Julie Eide, came in. Seeing the governor bare-chested, she gasped and walked out. (74)

Left unresolved is the reality that the essence of Governor Connally's testimony—"It is not conceivable to me that I could have been hit by the first bullet"—remained a contradiction for the emerging Single-Bullet Theory sponsored by Assistant Counsel Arlen Specter.

Note! The "incalculable importance" alluded to above is an additional incident in Governor Connally's testimony that marks a critical development in Arlen Specter's Single-Bullet Theory. In the course of the scene where Connally exhibited his chest wound, there was a measurement taken by Drs. Robert Shaw and Charles Gregory, two of the three surgeons who had attended Connally in Parkland Hospital.

The schedule for that day, April 21, had planned a morning conference to explore several trajectory and ballistics factors involved in the "Magic Bullet" of Specter's theory. Connally's Parkland surgeons, Drs. Shaw and Gregory, were invited paticipants in that conference.

The Warren Commission schedule for April 21 called for an afternoon testimony session to begin at 1:30, in which four witnesses would be questioned by Mr. Specter in the following order: Dr. Shaw/ Dr. Gregory/Governor Connally/Mrs. Connally.

As indicated, during Connally's testimony he exhibited his back and chest wounds, at which time the doctors used a caliper to measure the downward angle of those entry/exit wounds. Dr. Shaw reported it as 25°.

It will be recalled that in March 16 testimony, autopsy surgeon Dr. James Humes—endorsed by colleagues, Drs. Boswell and Finck—had estimated that downward angle to be "approximately 45°". In turn, that 45° angle was used by Specter—on March 30—in a compound assumption question he posed for Dr. Charles Carrico and Malcolm Perry, who had attended President Kennedy at Parkland Hospital. Within the framework of that assumption, both Carrico and Perry conceded—in Commission testimony—Humes's autopsy report that the anterior throat wound was an exit wound. Thus, as of

March 30, Specter had in place the first leg of Bullet 399's remarkable journey: A posterior neck entry/throat exit.

The problem for the second leg of Bullet 399's journey was accommodating the Humes/Carrico/Perry estimated 45° downward angle through Kennedy on a straight line path of entry/exit through Connally's chest. Thus, the April 21 measurement by Drs. Shaw and Gregory—25°—was, presumably, a welcome gain of 20° toward the "correct" angle for Specter's emerging theory.

*   *   *

In the happening, the Warren Commission constructed a crafty ambiguity in an effort to accommodate both the Governor's testimony and Specter's theory. The result was this gem as its third of 12 conclusions presented in Chapter I of its *Report*:

> Although it is not necessary to any essential findings of the Commission to determine just which shot hit Governor Connally, there is very persuasive evidence from the experts to indicate that the same bullet which pierced the President's throat also caused Governor Connally 's wounds. However, Governor Connally's testimony and certain other factors have given rise to some differences of opinion as to this probability but there is no question in the mind of any member of the Commission that all the shots which caused the President's and Governor Connally's wounds were fired from the sixth floor window of the Texas School Book Depository. (19)

There is little, if any, in the succeeding 800+ pages of the *Report* that answers several obvious questions generated by this "conclusion":

1. Who are the "experts" who provided the "very persuasive evidence" that the same bullet which "pierced the

President's throat" also caused Governor Connally's wounds?

2. What is the "very persuasive evidence"?
3. What is meant by "pierced" the President's throat?
4. Another question follows from that language in the Commission's conclusion: Governor Connally's testimony aside, what are the "certain other factors that have given rise to some differences of opinion as to this probability" (the Single-Bullet Theory)?

CHAPTER V

BULLET 399

The ten-page fifth chapter in Part Two of Senator Specter's memoir, *Passion for Truth*, is titled "Bullet 399." It is a critically important chapter for understanding the evolution of the Single-Bullet Theory. So it is interesting to note an observation he makes on the first page: "It would have made more sense to investigate the activities at Parkland Hospital, where Kennedy and Connally were treated, before taking testimony from the autopsy surgeons, who had worked on Kennedy's body after it left Texas." (76) In the happening, the testimony of the autopsy surgeons was taken on Monday, March 16, and the testimony of the Parkland surgeons was taken on March 30. Though that chronology was not a Warren Commission decision for which Arlen Specter was responsible, the decision to follow that logical disorder in the organization of chapters in Part Two of his book certainly is his responsibility.

Such being so, Senator Specter focuses his chapter on data relevant to the role of the autopsy doctors in the development of his theory. From my perspective, the most eye-catching sentence in the chapter reads: "*The Bethesda doctors, while performing the autopsy, knew that the Parkland team had given Kennedy external heart massage.*" [Emphases added] (79) This sentence will function as the focal point of my critique of his chapter. And that critique will concentrate on two questions: (1) Who told the Bethesda doctors that the

Parkland team had given Kennedy external heart massage?;
and (2) When had the Bethesda doctors been provided that
information?

*   *   *

The first allusion to external heart massage appears in the
March 9 testimony of Secret Service Agent Roy H. Kellerman.
In the context of informal conversation between him and FBI
agents James W. Sibert and Francis X. O'Neill—present as
observers during the autopsy—Mr. Specter asked Kellerman
a very general question: "Did you have a discussion with either
of those two gentlemen about anything while you were at the
morgue?" Kellerman's answer is an unwelcome exercise in the
use of ambiguous pronouns: The relevant comment reads at
2H 93:

> The only thing I can recall discussionwise—I just
> forget which one it was, one of the two—this was **before
> we even knew that a shell had been found from the
> hole in the President's shoulder.** We couldn't determine
> what happened to it; they couldn't find any leeway as to
> what happened to it; when it hit the President's shoulder;
> where did it go. So **it was our contention that while he
> was lying on the stretcher in Dallas, and the
> neurosurgeon was working him over no doubt with
> pressure on the heart, this thing worked its way out.**
> (2H 93) [Emphasis added]

COMMENT

1. Two assumptions are inferentially warranted:

    •   Kellerman's "which one it was, one of the two" refers
        to FBI Agents Sibert and O'Neill.

- Kellerman is referring to himself and either Sibert or O'Neill (or both) when he says "we" as in "this was before *we* even knew that a shell had been found from the hole in the President's shoulder."

2. With those assumptions, it may be further inferred that "our contention" means *their* hypothesis—reached "before we even knew that a shell had been found"—that while he [Kennedy] was lying on the stretcher in Dallas, and the neurosurgeon was working him over no doubt with pressure on the heart, this thing [the bullet] worked it way out."

3. It may be objected that the assumptions and inferences are not warranted. And tortured logic might possibly sustain the objection. What would nevertheless remain is this: As of March 9, Kellerman's sworn testimony is that "*before we even knew that a shell had been found from the hole in the President's shoulder . . . it was our contention that while he was lying on the stretcher in Dallas, and the neurosurgeon was working him over no doubt with pressure on the heart, this thing worked its way out.*" (2H 93)

4. Arlen Specter carefully explored that sensitive testimony with his question: "When you say 'our contention' what do you mean by that"? To which Kellerman answered clearly: "One of the agents—I forget which one it was; it could have been Sibert or O'Neill, but I am not sure." Either way—Sibert or O'Neill—Kellerman's testimony concerning the "when"—means "before we even knew that a shell had been found."

5. Kellerman's March 9 testimony introduces another—this time two-dimensional—problem: When and how did he learn that during the emergency room treatment of President Kennedy in Parkland Hospital, "the neurosurgeon was working him over no doubt with pressure on the heart? Consideration of that problem awaits analysis below.

*   *   *

As of Monday, March 9, Assistant Counsel Arlen Specter had a very serious problem that needed quick resolution:

- Secret Service Assistant Agent in Charge Roy H. Kellerman, has testified that he and FBI Agents James Sibert and Francis O'Neill share a "contention" reached before they were aware that a bullet had been found on a stretcher at Parkland Hospital.
- The contention involves an awareness of external cardiac massage which accounts for the bullet found on the stretcher. Never asked by Specter, so never answered by Kellerman, was the basis for the awareness. If it was an oversight, one can but wonder whether Arlen Specter's "preparation" of his witness regretted that reality.
- The problem is resolution of "when"—before or following discovery of the bullet—did the autopsy doctors embrace the hypothesis that external cardiac massage at Parkland Hospital generated the bullet found on the stretcher. In turn, that "when" leads to the allied question: *How* did the autopsy doctors know about the external cardiac massage. The possibilities, which seem few, are deferred for further discussion below.
- The autopsy doctors are scheduled to give testimony on Monday, March 16.

This much seems certain: Arlen Specter's embryonic Single-Bullet Theory could not accommodate Kellerman's "contention", which stands in conflict with the theory's essential necessity that the frontal throat wound was an exit wound. Apparently he chose to deal first with the Secret Service/FBI alignment by way of an informal interview with the FBI agents.

*   *   *

Strangely, the only mention of the names Sibert and O'Neill in Specter's chapter "Bullet 399" appears in another chronological ambiguity found in two paragraphs on page 79 of *Passion for Truth*:

> At Bethesda, Ball and I tried to clear up some confusion over how far the bullet that struck Kennedy's neck had traveled through his body. The now-famous preliminary report of FBI agents O'Neill and Sibert, filed in December 1963, stated that one bullet entered Kennedy's body 'just below his shoulder to the right of the spinal column at an angle of 45 to 60 degrees downward, that there was no point of exit, and that the bullet was not in the body.' An FBI report said in January the bullet 'penetrated to a distance of less than a finger's length.'
>
> *The Bethesda doctors, while performing the autopsy, knew that the Parkland team had given Kennedy external heart massage.* [Emphasis added] They also knew that a whole bullet had been found on a Parkland stretcher. Initially they surmised that the bullet on the stretcher might have been pushed out the back of Kennedy's neck by the massage. When I later questioned FBI agents Sibert and O'Neill, they told me they had overheard the autopsy surgeon's hypotheses during the examination and used them as the basis of their report.

COMMENT

1. Regarding the Sibert-O'Neill Report, despite its significance for the angle of "45 to 60 degrees downward", which is incompatible with the 17°43'30" eventually calculated in the May 24 reenactment of the assassination, it is irrelevant to the topic at hand, Specter's interview of the agents.

2. Regarding "When I later questioned FBI agents Sibert and O'Neill, they told me that they had overheard the autopsy surgeon's hypotheses during the examination and used them as the basis of their report":

Inasmuch as they were never deposed, and never gave testimony to the Warren Commission, it must be assumed that "when I later questioned FBI agents Sibert and O'Neill" refers to the March 12 interview to be analyzed presently. It remains to be seen whether Specter's account of that interview reflects their telling him that "they had overheard the autopsy surgeons' hypotheses and used them as the basis of their report."

The documentary account of the interview reads as follows:

AS: mln

MEMORANDUM

March 12, 1964

TO: Mr. J. Lee Rankin

FROM: Arlen Specter

SUBJECT: Interview of FBI agents at Autopsy

On March 12, 1964, I interviewed Special Agents Francis X. O'Neill and James W. Sibert in my office from approximately 10:00 a.m. to 10:45 a.m.

SA O'Neill and SA Sibert advised that the autopsy surgeons made substantial efforts to determine if there was a missile in President Kennedy's body to explain what happened to the bullet which apparently entered the back of his body. They stated that the opinion was expressed by both Commander Humes and Lt. Col. Finck that the bullet might have been forced out of the back of the President's body upon application of external heart massage. They stated that this theory

was advanced after SA Sibert called the FBI
laboratory and talked to SA Killion who advised
that a bullet had been found on a stretcher at
Parkland Hospital. Sibert relayed that information
to the doctors.

SA O'Neill and Sibert advised that they did
not recall any discussion of the theory that the
bullet might have been forced out of the body by
external cardiac massage until *after* SA Sibert
reported the finding of the bullet on the stretcher;
however, neither agent could exclusively rule out
the possibility that such a hypothesis was advanced
prior to that time, but each expressed the opinion
that he thought that theory was expressed after
information was obtained about the bullet and
the stretcher. SA Sibert advised that he made no
notes during the autopsy. SA O'Neill stated that
he made only a few notes, which he destroyed
after his report was dictated. SA O'Neill advised
that he is sure his notes would not have shown
when the doctors expressed the thought that
the bullet might have been forced out by
external heart massage, in relation to the time
that they learned of the presence of the bullet
on the Parkland Hospital stretcher. [Emphases
added]

I also questioned SA Sibert and SA O'Neill
about their interviews of ASAIC Kellerman and
SA Greer on the portions of the FBI report which
Kellerman and Greer have repudiated.

SAs Sibert and O'Neill stated that they
interviewed SAs Kellerman and Greer formally on
November 27, 1963, and talked to them only
informally at the autopsy. SA O'Neill stated that
he is certain that he had a verbatim note on

Kellerman's statement that the President said 'Get
me to a hospital' and also that Mrs. Kennedy said,
'Oh, no.' SA O'Neill stated that he was sure those
were direct quotes from Kellerman because O'Neill
used quotation marks in his report which indicated
that he had written those precise words in his
notes, which notes have since been destroyed after
the report was dictated.

SA O'Neill noted that Mr. Kellerman did not
repeat that language in the interview of November
27, 1963, and that in the later interview O'Neill
took down what Kellerman said without leading
or directing him in any way.

I also asked the two Special Agents about the
language in their reports that Greer glanced around
and noticed that the President had evidently been
hit and thereafter got on the radio and
communicated with the other vehicles, stating
that they 'desired to get the President to the
hospital immediately.' SAs O'Neill and Sibert
advised that to the best of their recollection SA
Greer told them just that, but they probably
did not make any notes of those comments since
their conversation with Greer was an informal
one at the time of the autopsy and they did not
have an opportunity to make extensive notes in
accordance with their normal interviewing
procedures.

Dictated from 11:45 a.m. to 12:00 noon[1]

COMMENT

1. Regarding "They stated that the opinion was expressed by
    both Commander Humes and Lt. Col. Finck that the bullet
    might have been forced out of the back of the President's

body upon application of external heart massage. They stated that this theory was advanced after SA Sibert called the FBI laboratory and talked to SA Killion who advised that a bullet had been found on a stretcher at Parkland Hospital. Sibert relayed that information to the doctors.

Some of this March 12 account does not square very well with that given by Secret Service Agent Kellerman three days earlier. The context for the following comparison is the telephone call concerning the found bullet:

• *Kellerman testimony*

Mr. Specter. When did you first hear about it?
Mr. Kellerman. The phone call with Mr. Rowley that morning after we had got to the morgue.
S.   What time was this?
K.   I am only guessing; 9 o'clock in the evening.
S.   Nine o'clock in the evening. You had said morning; you didn't mean morning; you meant 9 o'clock in the evening when you had a telephone call. From whom was the call again?
K.   Mr. Rowley, Chief of Secret Service.
S.   You got a phone call from Mr. Rowley?
K.   Yes.
S.   Who had called him, if you know?
K.   This I don't know.
S.   But at that time Chief Rowley advised of the detection of the bullet on the stretcher and brought you up to date with what information as known at that time?
K. Yes, sir. (2H 99-100)

• *Specter Memorandum of FBI Agents*

"They stated that this theory was advanced after SA Sibert called the FBI laboratory and talked to SA Killion who advised that a bullet had been found on a stretcher at Parkland Hospital. Sibert relayed that information to the doctors."

So, there appear to be two telephone calls: one an incoming call from Secret Service Chief James Rowley reported in sworn testimony; the other an outgoing call from Sibert to the FBI lab as related in Specter's dictated memorandum. Which way is not a critical issue. What is important is the significance of Specter's inclusion of the minor different version in an interview whose effective function—as will be seen momentarily—is to discredit a crucial element in Kellerman's testimony relating to when during the autopsy a specific hypothesis was advanced.

2. I suggest for the consideration of the future historians that the genuine function of the memorandum is to establish a desired record relating to the "when" question under consideration. And if such be so, the key paragraph is the third, which is recalled from above and reads:

> SA O'Neill and SA Sibert advised that they did not recall any discussion of the theory that the bullet might have been forced out of the body by external cardiac massage until *after* SA Sibert reported the finding of the bullet on the stretcher; however, neither agent could exclusively rule out the possibility that such a hypothesis was advanced prior to that time, but each expressed the opinion that he thought that theory was expressed after information was obtained about the bullet and the stretcher. SA Sibert advised that he made no notes during the autopsy. SA O'Neill stated that he made only a few notes, which he destroyed after his report was dictated. SA O'Neill advised that he is sure his notes would not have shown when the doctors expressed the thought that the bullet might have been forced out by external heart massage, in relation to the time that they learned of the presence of the bullet on the Parkland Hospital stretcher.

COMMENT

1. Regarding "SA O'Neill and SA Sibert advised that they did not recall . . . .": Absent a record of the interview, Arlen Specter more properly should have reported that "It is my recollection that SA O'Neill and SA Sibert advised . . . ."

   It is recalled from Chapter II that Specter's account of his preparation for signature of an affidavit (which appears at 7H 439-440) from Senator Yarborough) suggests a phenomenal memory for a verbatim recall of an unrecorded interview. Indeed, the memoir account indicates that the typed record of the interview was so accurate that Yarborough mistakenly believed, at first, that he had been secretly recorded by Specter. However, inasmuch as Yarborough signed the affidavit prepared for him by Specter, the incident merely serves to emphasize the meticulously phenomenal accuracy of Specter's memory.

   In this instance, a record of an interview—held 3+ months before the Yarborough interview—with two FBI agents was dictated one hour following the interview. Nevertheless there is a significant difference between the two situations: Yarborough signed an affidavit—a sworn statement; the FBI agents did not sign the Memorandum. And inasmuch as the FBI agents were never on Commission record as commenting on the accuracy of the Memorandum, there simply is no way of either endorsing or rejecting its accuracy.

2. It is also recalled that Kellerman's sworn testimony on March 9 reads: "*before we even knew that a shell had been found from the hole in the President's shoulder . . . it was our contention that while he was lying on the stretcher in Dallas, and the neurosurgeon was working him over no doubt with pressure on the heart, this thing worked its way out.*" And it is remembered that "our contention" refers to Kellerman and either/or both Sibert and O'Neill.

Compare that with Specter's language in the unrecorded Memorandum of March 12: "*O'Neill and Sibert did not recall any discussion of the theory that the bullet might have been forced out of the body by external cardiac massage until after SA Sibert reported the finding of the bullet on the stretcher.*"

Again the problem: When is "when"?

Kellerman (sworn testimony) establishes a time line of approximately 9:00 p.m. during the autopsy; Specter's account has it that O'Neill and Sibert advised that they did not recall . . . until after Sibert reported the finding of the bullet. The "when" question becomes a "why" question: *Why* did Specter not ask the FBI agents the same pinpoint question he asked the Secret service agent: When was the call made?

3. Regarding Specter's account that ". . . neither agent could exclusively rule out the possibility that such a hypothesis was advanced prior to that time, but each expressed the opinion that he thought . . .": From my perspective, Arlen Specter is to be admired for the generous accommodation he accords the "possibility" and "opinion" of these FBI agents in his March 12 interview of them.

Historians who may, however, assume that generosity to be habitual, may wish to evaluate as a comparison/contrast the style of Assistant Counsel Arlen Specter in his March 10 interrogation of the eighteen-year-old Commission witness Arnold Rowland. Rowland's name does not appear in *Passion for Truth*, but Specter exhibits a somewhat different style in a not so gentle interrogation of him that may be read at 2H 165-190. A similar comment may be made concerning Specter's deposition of Darrell Tomlinson at 6H 128-134, a very important witness whose name does appear on pages 96-97 and 120 in *Passion for Truth*, comment about which is deferred for consideration below.

4. Regarding "SA O'Neill advised that he is sure his notes [which he had destroyed after his report was dictated] would not have shown when the doctors expressed the thought that the

bullet might have been forced out by external heart massage":
Assuming such to be so, it is simply an irrelevant advisement
because the interview issue is not whatever may have been
the timetable for the *doctors* expression of anything. The
only relevant issue for Specter's interview is whether the FBI
agents corroborate or deny the sworn testimony of the Secret
Service Agent Roy Kellerman.

Thus Specter's Memorandum of March 12 is
disappointing in its silence concerning the only genuinely
relevant question which may be inferred as the logical purpose
for his interview of Sibert and O'Neill: During the autopsy,
did you join Kellerman to become the 'our' in his 'our
contention'—'*before we even knew that a shell had been
found from the hole in the President's shoulder . . . that while
he was lying on the stretcher in Dallas, and the neurosurgeon
was working him over no doubt with pressure on the heart,
this thing worked its way out*'?

5. The last three paragraphs of the March 12 Memorandum
    serve no real function concerning the "when" timing issue of
    autopsy data:

    •   FBI agents interview of SS Agents Kellerman and
        Greer;
    •   Kellerman's statement concerning what the President
        and Mrs Kennedy said;
    •   Distinctions between formal and informal comments
        in FBI reports. These distinctions could be, in a
        different study, a fascinating exercise in investigative
        methodology used by the FBI.

*   *   *

The third major event in my study of that pivotal week
between March 9, when Kellerman testified, and March 16, when
the autopsy doctors testified, was Arlen Specter's interview of
the autopsy doctors as his "preparation" for their testimony.

Senator Specter introduces this subject on page 77 in *Passion for Truth*:

> I wanted to talk to the autopsy surgeons in advance to prepare an orderly presentation of their testimony. Redlich's ban on pre-testimony interviews was also still in effect, so I got authorization from Rankin. *An interview was set for Friday, March 13.* [Emphases added] Frank Adams was not in Washington that day, so I asked Joe Ball to come with me to Bethesda Naval Hospital, just north of Washington, where Humes and Boswell were based. Ball was the most experienced trial lawyer on the commission. *And that Friday afternoon,* Ball was the only other lawyer around.

Note! In addition to the twice-mentioned "Friday", in this paragraph, There are two other allusions in *Passion for Truth* to the Friday, March 13 date for the interview:

- "Our Friday interview with Humes and Boswell produced a revelation: The bullet that passed through Kennedy's neck proceeded in a straight line, struck nothing solid, and exited with great velocity." (80)
- "When Joe Ball and I talked to Humes and Boswell on the Friday before they testified, we told them that they would be testifying without the aid of photographs and X-rays." (89)

Further comment on this "Friday, March 13" interview is deferred for consideration below.

COMMENT: I.

1. There is no indication when the Friday, March 13 interview of the autopsy surgeons was arranged. In the event, one of them, Dr. Pierre Finck was on military duty in Panama on

that date. Inasmuch as his testimony was scheduled for Monday, March 16, it must be assumed that Specter deemed it unnecessary to "prepare" *all* of the autopsy surgeons. That convenient absence from the interview is a matter of wry irony when it is remembered that the first allusion to "external cardiac massage" had surfaced in the testimony of Secret Service Agent Roy A. Kellerman on Monday, March 9, when he recounted a question he had posed for Dr. Finck at the autopsy. Further mention of that sequence is deferred for consideration below. It is at best unfortunate that he was not available for the "preparation" interview on Friday, March 13.

2.   Regarding "Ball was the most experienced trial lawyer on the commission. And that Friday afternoon, Ball was the only other lawyer around": It is a matter of wonderment whether the nature of the preparation of Drs. Humes and Boswell mandated the interview presence of "the most experienced trial lawyer on the commission." Inasmuch as Arlen Specter had not thought it necessary to have a colleague present for the March 12 interview of the FBI agents, it seems odd that he wished a witness for the interview with the autopsy surgeons.

3.   It is noted here in the context of "Redlich's ban on pretestimony interviews," there had developed among the Assistant Counsel a debate over the propriety of preparing witnesses for testimony. The lineup was Rankin's assistant, Norman Redlich, v. Arlen Specter/David Belin/ Joseph Ball. Apparently Redlich won the battle, but lost the war by way of Specter endrunning him via Rankin.

As for the Bethesda meeting, Specter continues:

We began the interview by reviewing the autopsy reports and the general procedures the doctors had used. We couldn't go over the surgeons' notes because Humes had burned them in his fireplace. Some have suggested that Humes was trying to hide his mistakes, or worse. Humes had responded to an extraordinary situation, with FBI agents in the middle of his autopsy room and the president's wife and brother sitting outside waiting for him to finish. I concluded that he was inexperienced and naive, not realizing how many people would be looking over his shoulder, but not at all malicious. (77-78)

COMMENT: II.

Regarding "We couldn't go over the surgeons' notes because Humes had burned them in his fireplace", obvious questions are unfortunately ignored in Senator Specter's memoir:

1. From the perspective of his "historical lens", why did Specter never determine for the record *why* the notes were destroyed?
2. From the perspective of his "legal lens", why did Specter never determine for the record whether Dr. Humes regarded those notes as his personal property?
3. If Dr. Humes regarded the burned notes as his personal property, then presumably he must have regarded notes of his autopsy colleagues as *their* personal property. And if the burned notes included those of his colleagues, by what authority did he destroy them?

    (It is of course possible that neither of Dr. Humes's assistants, Dr. Boswell or Dr. Finck, took notes during the autopsy. If so, it seems an extraordinary lapse of protocol that the senior authority takes notes while the juniors are able to avoid that normally tedious task.)

COMMENT: III.

Regarding "Humes had responded to an extraordinary situation, with FBI agents in the middle of his autopsy room and the president's wife and brother sitting outside waiting for him to finish":

1. It is not clear why the presence of two FBI agents constituted an "extraordinary situation," whereas there is no mention of either of the three Secret Service Agents, two of whom remained throughout the autopsy proceedings. (And it will be remembered that one of them—Kellerman—was the source of the "when" problem as of his testimony on March 9.) There is an interesting subtle distinction made apparent by this negative tone identifying the FBI agents as an "extraordinary situation" in the middle of "*his* [Humes's] autopsy room". The contrast in tone differs sharply from that conveyed by Specter elsewhere in his memoir account. Indeed, as seen above, he clearly welcomed the assistance of those same FBI agents in his interview of them on March 12 as an exercise in damage control of Kellerman's "our [Kellerman and FBI agents] contention" central to the "when" question that required solution prior to the scheduled testimony of the autopsy doctors on March 16.

    Moreover, it is somewhat surprising to read Specter speak of "Humes's autopsy room". As a Commander in the U.S. Navy at the time of the autopsy, it has never been explained why at least two Navy Admirals, and an Army General, were present as observers in "Humes's" autopsy room. The failure to explain *their* presence does nothing to allay residual suspicions among some critics that this was an autopsy in which military, as opposed to medical, protocol governed the proceedings.

2. It is amusing to realize the versatility of FBI agents Sibert and O'Neill, who play a dual role in Specter's account of things in his *Passion for Truth*:

    •   They are viewed *negatively* as an "extraordinary situation" to excuse "skipped steps" of Dr. Humes in the autopsy of November 22.

- They are viewed *positively* to compromise the testimony of Secret Service Agent Kellerman's testimony concerning the autopsy of November 22.

*   *   *

Returning to a familiar theme, I am sometimes uneasy concerning my understanding of Senator Specter's chronology in his memoir account of important events related in *Passion for Truth*. An example is the sequence of five paragraphs on pages 79-80.

- The first paragraph begins : "At Bethesda, Ball and I tried to clear up some confusion over how far the bullet that struck Kennedy's neck had traveled through his body." I presume that "At Bethesda" refers to the Bethesda interview on Friday, March 13.
- The second paragraph begins: "The Bethesda doctors, while performing the autopsy, knew that the Parkland team had given Kennedy external heart massage."
- The third paragraph begins: "As the autopsy progressed, the surgeons realized that the bullet had passed farther through the president's neck."
- The fourth paragraph begins: "The morning after the autopsy, Humes had called Dr. Malcolm Perry, one of the Parkland team, to ask about Kennedy's neck."
- The last paragraph begins: "Our Friday interview with Humes and Boswell produced a revelation."

Clearly, the sequence of begins and ends with data developed during the course of Specter's Friday, March 13 interview of the doctors. The uncertainty is whether the data in paragraphs 2-4 were generated in that same interview. Of particular interest is the plural noun—*doctors*—used in paragraph 2's sentence: The question for the present inquiry is that familiar "when": *Who* knew what and *when* was it known *during* the autopsy?

Sequential logic suggests to me that all five paragraphs relate to information generated during the Friday, March 13 interview of Drs. Humes and Boswell at Bethesda Hospital. Absent qualifying evidence to the contrary, I presume the validity of the logic.

*   *   *

Absent declaration or disclaimer, it is difficult to understand exactly what was Arlen Specter's objective in his "preparation" of the autopsy doctors for their impending testimony scheduled for three days following the interview. His language is recalled:

> At Bethesda, Ball and I tried to clear up some confusion over how far the bullet that struck Kennedy's neck had traveled through his body. The now-famous preliminary report of FBI agents O'Neill and Sibert, filed in December 1963, stated that one bullet entered Kennedy's body 'just below his shoulder to the right of the spinal column at an angle of 45 to 60 degrees downward, that there was no point of exit, and that the bullet was not in the body.' An FBI report said in January the bullet 'penetrated to a distance of less than a finger's length.' (79)

COMMENT

Regarding "At Bethesda, Ball and I tried to clear up some confusion over how far the bullet that struck Kennedy's neck had traveled through his body":

1. As of the March 13 interview, there is an unwarranted conclusive claim that it had been established as settled that the bullet struck Kennedy's *neck*. It is a matter for wonder whether confusion can ever be resolved by way of an unsupported declaration. Specter's very next sentence indicates

that as of the December report of the FBI agents the bullet had entered "just below his [Kennedy's] shoulder". The only confusion lies in unanswered questions generated by the unexplained substitution of *neck* for *shoulder!* The questions are both simple and unanswered: (1) Who changed the bullet's entry location? (2) When was that change made? (3) What was the evidence supporting the change? and (4) On whose authority was the change made?

It may of course be argued on behalf of Senator Specter's obvious space limitations in his *Passion for Truth* that he cannot be expected to answer in a general memoir all possible questions that may be raised by his claims. What seems reasonable to suggest, however, is that he should be expected to provide reference/citation for those of his claims which remain in reasonable dispute forty years after the event.

2. As for trying to clear up some confusion, it is difficult to determine exactly what confusion surrounds the key issue under present analysis: "*The Bethesda doctors, while performing the autopsy, knew that the Parkland team had given Kennedy external heart massage.*" It is recalled that followup for an earlier observation deferred discussion of SS Agent Kellerman as the source of the information about heart massage at Parkland Hospital. His testimony on March 9 included his statement: "our contention [meaning Kellerman and either/both Sibert and O'Neill] that while he was on the stretcher in Dallas, and the neurosurgeon was working over him no doubt with pressure on the heart, this thing worked itself out." In that context, the following exchange ensued:

Mr. Specter. You had a discussion and when you say 'our contention' by that do you mean that was the conclusion you came to?
Mr. Kellerman. Conclusion—that is right, sir—as to where this bullet went into the shoulder and where did it go.

S.   While you are on that subject, was there any conversation at the time of the autopsy on that matter itself?

K.   Very much so.

S.   Would you relate to the Commission the nature of that conversation and the parties to it?

K.   There were three gentlemen who were performing this autopsy. A Colonel Finck—during the examination of the President, from the hole that was in his shoulder, and with a probe, and we were standing right alongside of him, he is probing inside the shoulder with his instrument and I said, 'Colonel, where did it go?' He said, 'There are no lanes for an outlet of this entry in this man's shoulder.'

S.   Did you say anything in response to that?

K.   I said, 'Colonel, would it have been possible that while he was on the stretcher in Dallas that it works itself out?' And he said, "Yes."

S.   Was there any additional conversation of any sort between you and Colonel Finck at that time?

K.   Not on that point; no, sir; not on that point. (2H 93)

The exchange then shifted to discussion of the head wound suffered by President Kennedy. Eventually, Mr. Specter returned to the earlier inquiry:

S.   Did you have any conversation with either Special Agent O'Neill or Special Agent Sibert of the FBI on November 22, 1963, other than your conversations about the wounds on President Kennedy?

K.   No.

S.   Mr. Kellerman, while we are discussing this in relationship to your conversations with Special Agents O'Neill and Sibert, were there any other comments made by anybody else at the autopsy about the path of that bullet into Mr. Kennedy's back,

relating to whether there was any point of exit or
anything of that sort?

K. Colonel Finck did all the talking, sir. He was the
    only one.

S. Now, have you told us everything Colonel Finck said
    about that subject?

K. Very much so; yes, sir.

S. So that there is nothing that was said on that subject
    other than what you have already told us about?

K. No; that is right. (2H 94)

3. The only obvious confusion seems to be the difficulty
    Mr. Specter may have had in accepting Mr. Kellerman's
    testimony, and his decision not to call FBI agents Sibert and
    O'Neill as witnesses for either corroboration or rejection of
    Kellerman's testimony—none of which had to do with "how
    far the bullet that struck Kennedy's neck had traveled through
    his body."

COMMENT: I

It but remains to establish a critical reality in remembering
those two key points in Kellerman's testimony. The two key
have already been stated, and restated above:

1. The "our contention" testimony: "**before we even knew
    that a shell had been found from the hole in the
    President's shoulder . . . it was our contention that
    while he was lying on the stretcher in Dallas, and the
    neurosurgeon was working him over no doubt with
    pressure on the heart, this thing worked its way out.**"
    (2H 93)

2. The Kellerman/Specter exchange:

Kellerman. A Colonel Finck—during the examination
    of the President, from the hole that was in his

shoulder, and with a probe, and we were standing right alongside of him, he is probing inside the shoulder with his instrument and I said, 'Colonel, where did it go?' He said, 'There are no lanes for an outlet of this entry in this man's shoulder.'

Specter. Did you say anything in response to that?

Kellerman. I said, 'Colonel, would it have been possible that while he was on the stretcher in Dallas that it works itself out?' And he said 'Yes.' (2H 93)

. . . .

Specter. Mr. Kellerman . . . were there any other comments made by anybody else present at the autopsy about the path of the bullet into Mr. Kennedy's back, relating to whether there was any point of exit or anything of that sort?

Kellerman. Colonel Finck did all the talking, sir. He was the only one. (2H 94)

And the critical reality to be remembered is this: Points 1. and 2. occurred in exactly that chronological order.

COMMENT: II

Returning again to Senator Specter's memoir account in *Passion for Truth*, where he indicates on page 79 that *The Bethesda doctors, while performing the autopsy, knew that the Parkland team had given Kennedy external heart massage*, this much seems clear: Either they must have known it from Kellerman's testimony on March 9, or on some other basis that remains undisclosed to this day. I suggest to the future historians that if there was indeed a known source of this knowledge other than Kellerman's testimony, then the failure of both the Warren Commission's *Report*, and Senator Specter's memoir to disclose it is simply incomprehensible. I presently incline to believe there *was* another source for that information, discussion of which is deferred for consideration below.[F]

COMMENT: III

It is noted that Kellerman's reference is to **Dr. Finck** as the autopsy surgeon who probed the shoulder/back wound during the autopsy, and to whom Kellerman asked the question: **"Colonel, would it have been possible that while he was on the stretcher in Dallas that it works itself out?"** And he said **"Yes."** From the record Dr. Pierre Finck was a U.S. Army Lt. Col. summoned to the autopsy, after it had begun, by U.S. Navy Commander James Humes, the chief autopsy surgeon. He was summoned by Dr. Humes through the Wound Ballistics Pathology Branch of the Armed Forces Institute of Pathology at the Army's Walter Reed Hospital in the Washington, D.C. area. And he was the only one of the three autopsy surgeons who had previous autopsy experience with gunshot wound deaths.

Accordingly, it seems significant to note Arlen Specter's sentence construction in the presumed context of the Friday, March 13 "preparation" interview of the doctors: "When I later questioned FBI agents Sibert and O'Neill, they told me that they had overheard the **autopsy surgeon's hypotheses** during the examination and used them as the basis for their report." Note that "surgeon's" is a singular possessive, and "hypotheses" is a plural noun. Recalling the Kellerman testimony, Finck was the only doctor involved in his exchange involving the "hypothesis" that external massage at Parkland Hospital could have resulted in the bullet "working itself out". Neither Humes nor Dr. Boswell, the third autopsy surgeon, was a party to the formation of that hypothesis.

And if there was more than one hypothesis (as suggested by Specter's "hypotheses")—from the autopsy surgeon, Dr. Finck— "which the FBI agents Sibert and O'Neill used as the basis for their report," the other Finck hypotheses went unreported in Specter's memoir.

Either way—Dr. Finck's hypothesis generated with Kellerman—or the mysteriously plural Finck's "hypotheses" created by Specter—entail the absurd incongruity that Dr. Finck was not present for the "preparation" interview of the autopsy surgeons on Friday, March 13.

COMMENT: IV.

It is also recalled that Senator Specter's memoir account of the March 13 Bethesda meeting generated an unexpected phenomenon:

> Our Friday interview with Humes and Boswell produced a revelation: The bullet that passed through Kennedy's *neck* [emphases added] proceeded in a straight line, struck nothing solid, and exited with great velocity. The doctors had not mentioned this in their autopsy report." (80)

This became the beginning point for an extraordinary line of questioning subsequently undertaken by Specter on March 16 during the testimony of Dr. Humes, the details of which are deferred for examination below. For the moment, it is enough to observe that Dr. Humes, though lacking experience in gunshot wound autopsies, was an obviously welcome witness for Arlen Specter's emerging Single-Bullet Theory, which requires a bullet passing through Kennedy's *neck* [not "shoulder"] as found in the Kellerman-Sibert/O'Neill-Finck hypothesis during the course of the autopsy. In the happening, that hypothesis gave way to an entirely new evaluation developed according to Dr. Humes's account of a telephone conversation between himself and Dr. Malcolm Perry, who had rendered emergency treatment for President Kennedy of Parkland Hospital in Dallas.

And *that* observation recalls the earlier mention of another facet of Specter's account of his Friday, March 13 "preparation" interview of autopsy doctors Humes and Boswell at Bethesda Hospital. It reads:

> The morning after the autopsy, Humes had called Dr. Malcolm Perry, one of the Parkland team, to ask about Kennedy's *neck* [emphases added]. They talked for about half an hour. Perry told Humes that he'd had to perform a tracheotomy on Kennedy to insert a breathing tube. There was no bullet hole in Kennedy's throat because Perry had performed the 'trache' there, obliterating any evidence of that wound. When all the facts came in it became clear that the *neck* [emphases added] shot had exited Kennedy's throat. (79-80)

With Humes's account of that telephone call to Perry, everything was in place for the rejection of the Kellerman-Sibert/O'Neill-Finck hypothesis reached during the autopsy. In turn, the rejection of that hypothesis was followed by the development of the Single-Bullet Theory.

*   *   *

It is difficult to evaluate the quality of Senator Specter's *Passion for Truth* account of his *Friday, March 13 interview* of autopsy doctors Humes and Boswell. The reason for the difficulty is that there is no credibly authentic evidence it took place on that date. Informative though the data may be, the ten-page chapter—"Bullet 399"—offers only one reference/citation relevant to the account of the interview. And that reads: "Joseph Ball, interview with the author. Tape recording. Washington. 7 June 1996." The direct quote from Ball's interview—for which there is no transcript—is irrelevant to the substance of the account.

There is, however, on file in the National Archives a fascinating document for a *March 11 interview*. It reads:

AS: mln

MEMORANDUM

March 12, 1964

TO: Mr. J. Lee Rankin
FROM: Arlen Specter
SUBJECT: Interview of Autopsy Surgeons

On the afternoon of March 11, 1964, Joseph
A. Ball, Esq., and I went to Bethesda Naval
Hospital and interviewed Admiral C. B. Holloway
[sic; Galloway], Commander James J. Humes and
Commander "J" Thornton Boswell. The interview
took place in the office of Admiral Holloway, who
is the commanding officer of the National Naval
Medical Center, and lasted from approximately
3:30 p.m. to 5:30 p.m.

Commander Humes and Commander Boswell,
along with Lt. Col. Pierre A. Finck, who is currently
in Panama, conducted the autopsy and Admiral
Holloway was present at all times. They described
their activities and findings in accordance with
the autopsy report which had been previously
submitted as Commission Report #77.

All three described the bullet wound on
President Kennedy's back as being a point of
entrance. Admiral Holloway then illustrated the
angle of the shot by placing one finger on my back
and the second finger on the front part of my chest
which indicated that the bullet traveled in a
consistent downward path, on the assumption that
it emerged in the opening on the President's throat
which had been enlarged by the performance of
the tracheotomy in Dallas.

Commander Humes explained that they had spent considerable time at the autopsy trying to determine what happened to the bullet because they found no missile in the President's body. According to Commander Humes, the autopsy surgeons hypothesized that the bullet might have been forced out of the President on the application of external heart massage after they were advised that a bullet had been found on a stretcher at Parkland Hospital.

Dr. Humes and Dr. Boswell were shown the Parkland report which describes the wound of the trachea as being "ragged", which they said was characteristic of an exit rather than an entrance wound. Dr. Humes and Dr. Boswell further said that it was their current opinion that the bullet passed in between two major muscle strands in the President's back and continued on a downward flight and exited through his throat. They noted, at the time of the autopsy, some bruising of the internal parts of the President's body but tended to attribute that to the tracheotomy at that time. Dr. Humes and Dr. Boswell stated that after the bullet passed between the two strands of muscle, those muscle strands would resist any probing effort and would not disclose the path of the bullet to probing fingers, as the effort was made to probe at the time of the autopsy.

We requested that Dr. Humes and Dr. Boswell prepare or have prepared drawings of the consequences of the shots on the President's body and head, and they also elaborated upon the facts set forth in their autopsy report.

Dictated from 11:30 to 11:45 a.m.[2]

COMMENT: I.

Clearly, the chronological problem is whether the Specter/ Ball preparation interview of Drs. Humes and Boswell occurred on Wednesday, March 11 or Friday, March 13.

1. The March 12 Memorandum from Specter to Rankin says it occurred on March 11 from 3:30 to 5:30 p.m.
2. The account in Senator Specter's *Passion for Truth*, indicates on page 77: "An interview was set for Friday, March 13. Frank Adams was not in Washington that day, so I asked Joe Ball to come with me to Bethesda Naval Hospital, ... And that Friday afternoon, Ball was the only other lawyer around." And it is recalled that two other entries in that account reinforce the claim for Friday, March 13:

   • Page 80: "Our Friday interview with Humes and Boswell produced a revelation: The bullet that passed through Kennedy's neck proceeded in a straight line, struck nothing solid, and exited with great velocity."
   • Page 89: "When Joe Ball and I talked to Humes and Boswell on the Friday before they testified [Monday, March 16], we told them that they would be testifying without the aid of photographs and X-rays."

3. In an effort to resolve the chronological disorder, I wrote Senator Specter a letter, dated March 21, 2004, requesting verification or rejection of the authenticity of an unreferenced/ uncited copy of the March 12 memorandum of the interview of the autopsy doctors. That letter remains unanswered.
4. On April 14, 2004 I wrote the National Archives concerning the authenticity of that document. In a letter dated April 22, I received an answer which included the following: "The citation for the documents you refer to are RG 272, Reading File of Outgoing Letters and Internal Memorandums 1963-1964, Entry 26, Box 1."

Clearly, the Specter Memorandum of the March 12 interview of the autopsy doctors is an authentic document. Just as clearly, the citation does not address any question concerning its credibility.

5. Thus, comments 1 and 4 offer documentary support for the claim that Specter's interview with the autopsy doctors occurred on Wednesday, March 11.

Conversely, however, that claim poses a disturbing challenge for Senator Specter's memoir account on behalf of its Friday, March 13 date for that interview. Moreover, there is an additional inferential support for the interview being on Friday, March 13, by way of a passing remark in Dr. Humes's testimony on Monday, March 16. Specification of that point is deferred for presentation in its proper context below.

COMMENT: II.

Deferring further consideration of the chronology issue, an examination of differing emphases in the two accounts of the interview discloses different agenda items:

The *Memorandum* account includes:

1. "On the afternoon of March 11, Joseph A. Ball, Esq., and I went to Bethesda Naval Hospital and interviewed Admiral C. B. Holloway, Commander James J. Humes and Commander 'J' Thornton Boswell."

Other than that possibility suggested above, concerning military orders, Specter never explains the reason for the presence of a Navy Admiral for the "preparation" interview of the "Autopsy Surgeons". Moreover, it is a careless oversight that the Admiral's name—Calvin B. Galloway—is misspelled. (Coincidentally, the same spelling error appears in the Sibert-O'Neill Report alluded to by Specter on page 79 in his account.) In the happening, Admiral Galloway performed a surprisingly dramatic gesture, albeit one for whose enlightenment it is not at all clear in Senator Specter's account:

> All three described the bullet wound on President Kennedy's back as being a point of entrance. Admiral Holloway then illustrated the angle of the shot by placing one finger on my back and the second finger on the front part of my chest which indicated that the bullet traveled in a consistent downward path, on the assumption that it emerged in the opening on the President's throat which had been enlarged by the performance of the tracheotomy in Dallas.

Certainly the absence of measurable finger placements on Specter—"my back and front of my chest"—does not provided meaningful locations for medical laymen readers.

More importantly, what is the significance of *the Admiral's* demonstration of the angle unless intended as an authoritarian instructive clue for either or both sets of witnesses: lawyers and autopsy surgeons? Such may or may not be so, but if so what remains unknown is the answer to the question: What was the instruction being conveyed by this high-ranking U.S. Navy observer of the autopsy proceedings? Absent *any* explanation by Specter of the meaning of the admiral's gesture, it is difficult to understand why Specter included the incident in his Memorandum to Rankin.

Independently of anything else, this much seems reasonably clear: Admiral Galloway's demonstration, as recorded in Specter's Memorandum of March 12, functions as the U.S. Navy's commitment to a decision "which indicated the bullet traveled in a consistent downward path, on the assumption that it emerged in the President's throat which had been enlarged by the performance of the tracheotomy in Dallas." If such be so, there is no need for articulating the obvious inference to be drawn: The demonstration effectively eliminates any need for expert testimony regarding the trajectory of the bullet.

2. Regarding "According to Commander Humes, the autopsy surgeons hypothesized that the bullet might have been forced out of the President on the application of external heart massage *after* they were advised that a bullet had been found on a stretcher at Parkland Hospital": Inasmuch as Arlen Specter was aware from Kellerman's sworn testimony two days prior to this Memorandum account, the hypothesis was developed in "our contention" of Kellerman/Sibert/O'Neill/Finck *prior* to their awareness of the found bullet. Whatever may have been the function of this particular "preparation" interview recounted in the Memorandum, it is odd that Specter would not have raised this point in the interview of Humes and Boswell— particularly odd in the absence of Finck from the interview.

3. Regarding "Dr. Humes and Dr. Boswell were shown the Parkland report which describes the wound of the trachea as being 'ragged', which they said was characteristic of an exit rather than an entrance wound": This use of the term "ragged", and Specter's account of the Humes/Boswell evaluation of it, is an exercise in distortion that is tedious to follow and understand. I think, however, that an understanding of the exercise is worth the tedium. The point of the following survey of autopsy procedure is to establish the sequence of specific steps taken in the postmortem examination.

   a. The term, "ragged", in reference to the trachea, appears in the context of the "Parkland report" which is not identified in the preparation interview of the doctors, but which appears in the March 16 testimony of Dr. Humes, by way of the following at 2H 362-363:

   Mr. Specter. And have you had occasion . . . to examine the report of Parkland Hospital which I made available to you?

Commander Humes. Yes, sir; I have.

S.   May it please the Commission, I would like to note this as Commission Exhibit No. 392, and subject to later technical proof, to have it admitted into evidence at this time for the purpose of having the doctor comment about it.

. . . .

S.   What did your examination of Parkland Hospital records disclose with respect to this wound on the front side of the President's body?

H.   The examination of this record from Parkland Hospital revealed that Doctor Perry [The doctor who performed the tracheotomy on President Kennedy at Parkland] had observed this wound as had other physicians in attendance upon the President, and actually before a tracheotomy was performed surgically, an endotracheal tube was placed through the President's mouth and down his larynx into his trachea which is the first step in giving satisfactory airway to a person injured in such fashion and unconscious.

. . . .

The person who performed that procedure, that is installed the endotrachea [sic] tube noted that *there was a wound of the trachea below the larynx, which corresponded in essence with the wound of the skin which they had observed from the exterior.*

S.   How is that wound described, while you are mentioning the wound?

H.   Yes, sir.

. . . .

This report was written by a doctor—or of the activities of Dr. James Carrico, Doctor Carrico in inserting the endotracheal tube noted a *ragged* wound of trachea immediately below the larynx. [Emphases added]

The report, as I recall it, and I have not studied it in minute detail, would indicate to me that Dr. Perry realizing from Dr. Carrico's observation that there was a wound of trachea would quite logically use the wound which he had observed as a point to enter the trachea since the trachea was also damaged, that would be a logical place in which to put his incision.

In speaking of that wound in the neck, Dr. Perry told me that before he enlarged it to make the tracheotomy wound it was a "few millimeters in diameter."

Of course by the time we saw it, as my associates and as you have heard, it was considerably larger and no longer at all obvious as a missile wound.

. . . .

To complete the examination of the area of the neck and chest, I will do that together, we made the customary incision that we use in a routine postmortem examination which is a Y-shaped incision from the shoulders over the lower portion of the breastbone and over to the opposite shoulder and reflected the skin and tissues from the anterior portion of the chest.

We examined in the region of this excised surgical wound which was the tracheotomy wound and we saw that there was some bruising of the muscles of the neck in the depths of this wound as well as laceration or defect in the trachea.

At this point, of course, I am unable to say how much of the defect in the trachea was made by the knife of the surgeon, and how much of the defect was made by the missile wound. That would have to be ascertained from the surgeon who actually did the tracheotomy.

. . . .

In attempting to relate findings in the President's body to this wound which we had observed low in his neck, we then opened his chest cavity, and we very carefully removed the lining of his chest cavity and both of his lungs. We found that there was, in fact, no defect in the pleural lining of the President's chest.

    b. The first question is what is the significance of a reported "ragged wound of trachea" in terms of determining the path of the bullet as either back to front or front to back? Inasmuch as the trachea is an internal structure of the respiratory system, it is difficult to understand how any "wound of the trachea" can be identified as either an entrance or an exit wound. Obviously skin must be penetrated prior to any bullet damaging the internal trachea.

4. Regarding "Dr. Humes and Dr. Boswell further stated that it was their current opinion that the bullet passed in between two major muscle strands in the President's back and continued on 'a downward flight and exited through the throat': If "their current opinion" was reached following Admiral Galloway's demonstration—"which indicated that the bullet traveled in a consistent downward path, on the assumption that it emerged in the opening on the President's throat"—it would be an unlikely probability that their "current opinion" would be other than what they indicated it to be.

5. Particular attention is called to *this* point in Arlen Specter's Memorandum of March 12 concerning the "preparation" interview of the autopsy doctors: "*We requested* [emphasis added] that Dr. Humes and Dr. Boswell prepare or have prepared drawings of the consequences of the shots on the President's body and head, ..."

There have been, and continue to be, sharp differences in claims regarding the precise location of the wound caused by the entry of the so-called "magic bullet" made prominent in Arlen

Specter's Single-Bullet Theory. But there has never been dispute of the fact that photographs were taken during the course of the autopsy. Presuming that one or more of the photographs clearly showed that location, the refusal to allow the autopsy doctors access to those photographs prior to, and during, their testimony has never been satisfactorily explained by defenders of the Warren Commission. So, in the happening, Drs. Humes and Boswell were forced to rely on their memories of events 3+ months earlier to advise an illustrator who constructed the drawings requested by Specter. Apparently this procedure was a desired exception to lawyers' normal preference for "best evidence."

It is recalled that support for the date of the interview of the autopsy doctors being Friday, March 13, included a page 89 entry in *Passion for Truth*: "When Joe Ball and I talked to Humes and Boswell, in Bethesda on the Friday before they testified, we told them that they would be testifying without the aid of photographs and X rays." The next two sentences in the account read: "Humes asked if it would be helpful to have some sketches made of the president's body. Most helpful, I said."

So, there is an unexplained difference between the Memorandum account of a Wednesday, March 11 interview, which has Specter *requesting* drawings, and the memoir account of a Friday, March 13 interview, which has Humes *asking* whether it would be helpful to have some sketches made of the president's body—an offer Specter thought "most helpful". As a matter of harmless humor, it is noted that the memoir version of this request/ offer appears in a chapter—the followup to "Bullet 399"—titled "The Biggest Mistake"! (However amusing this coincidence may be, it will become clear below, in the analysis of "The Biggest Mistake" that Specter is *there* referring to the Commission decision—Chief Justice Earl Warren decision?—to withhold the photographs and X rays from the legal counsel as well as from the autopsy doctors.)

* * *

The last segment of this version of a fascinatingly extraordinary week—which began with the Monday, March 9 testimony of Secret Service Assistant Special Agent in Charge Roy A. Kellerman—concerns the Monday, March 16 testimony of Dr. James J. Humes, the chief autopsy surgeon. The other two autopsy surgeons, Drs. "J" Thornton Boswell and Pierre A. Finck, also testified that day, but the record shows clearly that their function was to endorse the testimony of Humes, although Finck was questioned more thoroughly because of his use of a technical "teaching scheme" he had devised for use in tracing bullet paths through bone. Be that as it may, the numbers convey the relative quantitative contributions of each to the proceedings: Humes's testimony is found at 2H 347-376; Boswell's at 2H 376-77; Finck's at 2H 377-384. The relevant questions/answers convey the essential significance of the testimony of Humes's assistants:

- Mr. Specter. Have you been present here today during the entire course of Doctor Humes' testimony?

Commander Boswell. I have, sir, yes.
S. Do you have anything you would like to add by way of elaboration or modification to that which Doctor Humes has testified?
B. None, I believe. Doctor Humes has stated essentially what is the culmination of our examination and our subsequent conference, and everything is exactly as we had determined our conclusions. (2H 377)

- Mr. Specter. You heard the whole of Doctor Humes' testimony, did you not?

Colonel Finck. Yes, I did. (2H 379)

. . . .

S. And do you share the opinions which he expressed
   in their entirety during the course of his testimony
   here today?

F. I do.

That testimony relating to events in a military-controlled hospital is not really surprising when it is remembered that in 1964—Remember the Gulf of Tonkin Resolution and the Vietnam War?—a subordinate military career officer did not tend to contradict publicly the account of a military officer to whom he was subordinate.

Presuming that Arlen Specter and Joseph Ball did not undertake two "preparation" interviews of autopsy doctors James Humes and J. Thornton Boswell, the question is obvious: Why are there different dates—March 13 and March 11—given in the two accounts of the interview?

For the jury of future historians, I will argue on behalf of the memoir account of a preparation of witnesses interview on Friday, March 13. The argument is based on the following data:

• Specific mention of a Friday interview occurs four times in the memoir account.
• The name of Specter's colleague, Assistant Counsel Joseph Ball appears five times in Specter's memoir as being present at the interview of the autopsy doctors.

Inasmuch as the year 2000 publication of Senator Specter's *Passion for Truth* included on page 77 a reference/citation of his tape recording interview of Mr. Ball in Los Angeles on May 27, 1996, it seems a reasonable assumption that Mr. Ball—and/or his family—was aware of his role in Specter's upcoming memoir account. And it is simply beyond my present belief that Arlen Specter, a prominent U.S. Senator at the time of his interview of then 94-year-old Joseph Ball would fabricate either the memoir account of the March 13, 1964 interview of the autopsy doctors, or Joseph Ball's role in that interview.

From that reasonable assumption, I will argue that Assistant Counsel Arlen Specter simply pre-dated from March 13 to March 11 an account of the interview, and then dictated a memorandum of its record on March 12. The plausibility of the argument depends of course on its reasonableness factor. And obviously, the first question is why would he undertake a venture as risky as predating to create such an important document for the National Archives?

SPECULATION

When there are two authentic—but differing—accounts of the same interview, and there is no documented reconciliation of them, and their author declines explanation of the phenomenon, any determined critic of the author's methodology must necessarily indulge in reasonable conjecture. In undertaking the present exercise, it will be remembered that neither account constitutes sworn testimony.

The first question for resolution is this: Is there anything in the memoir's account of the March 13 interview that conflicts with anything in the record of the March 12 interview of the FBI agents? If the answer is yes, methodological prudence suggests that the formal record of the March 13 interview be predated to eliminate that conflict.

I submit that there is such a conflict: The March 13 interview account declares:

> The Bethesda *doctors*, while performing the autopsy, knew that the Parkland team had given Kennedy external heart massage. They also knew that a whole bullet had been found on a Parkland stretcher. Initially, they surmised that the bullet on the stretcher might have been pushed out of the back of Kennedy's neck by the message. When

I later questioned FBI agents Sibert and O'Neill, they told me that they had overheard the autopsy surgeons *hypotheses* during the examination and used them as the basis of their report. [Emphases added] (79)

Certainly there are at least two subtle differences in details of this account from the March 9 sworn testimony of Secret Service Agent Roy Kellerman: (1) In the March 13 account, the Bethesda *doctors* and *hypotheses*—plural nouns—stand in opposition to the Kellerman-Sibert/O'Neill-*Finck* "our contention" *hypothesis* developed during the autopsy; and (2) "When I *later* questioned FBI agents Sibert and O'Neill" conveys the impression that Specter's interview of those agents followed that of the autopsy doctors, as opposed to *preceding* it by one day.

As regards (1), It is recalled that Dr. Finck—the *only* autopsy doctor who was party to a hypothesis *during* the autopsy—is not a party to the "preparation interview" of March 13.

As regards (2), "*Later* questioned" can only be explained as an oversight uncorrected in the printed account of the pre-dating exercise that shifted from March 13 to March 11 the interview of the autopsy doctors.

When it is remembered that the interview was a "preparation" interview for the scheduled March 16 testimony of the doctors, it should be expected that the testimony will be consistent with the March 13 account published 34 years following the testimony.

• The heart of the March 13 memoir account declares:

The Bethesda doctors, while performing the autopsy, knew that the Parkland team had given Kennedy external heart massage. They also knew that a whole bullet had been found on a Parkland stretcher. Initially they surmised that the bullet on the stretcher might have been pushed out the back of Kennedy's neck by the massage. (79)

What is missing from this non-documented account is that elusive "when" did the doctors know about the external heart massage in relation to "when" they knew about the whole bullet found on a Parkland stretcher.

- The relevant testimony of Dr. Humes on March 16 mentions only in passing the subjects of external heart massage and the found bullet.

Mr. Specter. And at or about that time when you were trying to ascertain, as you previously testified, whether there was any missile in the body of the President, did someone from the Secret Service call your attention to the fact that a bullet had been found on a stretcher at Parkland Hospital?
Commander Humes Yes, sir; they did. (2H 367)

[The Warren *Report* indicates on pages 59-60 that the autopsy began at about 8 p.m. and concluded at approximately 11 p.m. It is recalled that Kellerman's testimony on March 9 indicated— with correction from Specter—that this call from the Secret Service came into the autopsy morgue around 9 p.m.]

S. And in that posture of your examination, **having just learned of the presence of a bullet on a stretcher,** did that call to your mind any **tentative explanatory theory of the point of entry or exit of the bullet** which you have described as entering at Point "C" on Exhibit 385?
H. Yes, sir. We were able to ascertain with absolute certainty that the bullet had passed by the apical portion of the right lung producing the injury which we mentioned.

   I did not at that point have the information from Doctor Perry about the wound in the anterior neck, and while that was a possible explanation for the point of exit, we also had to consider the possibility that the missile in some rather inexplicable fashion had been stopped in its path through the President's body and, in fact, then had fallen from the body onto the stretcher.

S: And what theory did you think possible, at that juncture, to explain the passing of the bullet back out the point of entry; **or had you been provided with the fact that external heart massage had been performed on the President?**

H: Yes, sir; we had, and we considered the possibility that some of the physical maneuvering performed by the doctors might have in some way caused this event to take place.

S: Now, have you since discounted that possibility, Doctor Humes?

H: Yes; in essence we have. When examining the wounds in the base of the President's neck anteriorly, the region of the tracheotomy performed at Parkland Hospital, we noted, and we noted in our record, some contusion and bruising of the muscles of the neck of the President. We noted that at the time of the postmortem examination.

COMMENT

1. It is reasonable to presume that "having just learned" of the bullet, means following the telephone call about the bullet. Such being so, the **tentative explanatory theory of the point of entry or exit of the bullet** occurred *after* the doctors were aware of the bullet via the telephone call. If either this presumption or this timing of the doctors' tentative explanatory theory is in error, then the question as asked by Specter is an ambiguity that effectively precludes a single answer.

2. Regarding **"theory of the point of entry or exit of the bullet"**: This is a poor option inasmuch as the followup—

"the bullet which you have described as entering at Point "C" on Exhibit 385?"—is one of the three drawings which the doctors had the naval illustrator prepare for their testimony. That drawing is clearly marked showing the bullet entry to be from the posterior neck to and through the throat. Stated differently, **the testimony of Dr. Humes on March 16 never stated, implied or even considered, the possibility that the path of the bullet was from anterior to posterior.**

*   *   *

Senator Specter, writing in his *Passion for Truth* memoir published in 2000 indicates the evolution of the Single-Bullet Theory in these terms:

> I have been credited, or condemned, as the author of the Single-Bullet Conclusion ever since [Edward Jay] Epstein published *Inquest*, the earliest of the conspiracy books. Gerald Ford, for one, sends his Single-Bullet Theory queries my way. 'Anytime I've had an opportunity, or if I'm asked about the Single-Bullet Theory,' Ford told me recently, 'I respectfully say, "You ought to talk to the author of it. He knows more about it than I."'
>
> While I later put the pieces together, Humes laid them out, even if he did not think the bullet went through Connally's wrist. I have always been willing to take on the mantle of authorship that Epstein first thrust upon me, mostly because I have always had a sense that the Single-Bullet Conclusion is correct. I have also had the sense that if the conclusion turned out to be incorrect, that would be okay, too, because it was an honest, good-faith, soundly reasoned judgment. Let the chips fall where they may. . . . (82)

I incline to believe that when the future historians rearrange the puzzle pieces—from today's plausible conjecture to tomorrow's verifiable accuracy—to present an account that corrects the errors in the Warren *Report*, the chips will fall in a pattern very much different from the "honest, good-faith, soundly reasoned" argument of the Single-Bullet Theory masterminded by Arlen Specter.

NOTES

[1] Harold Weisberg, *Post Mortem* c1975, 537-538.

[2] Harold WEisberg, Post Mortem, c1975, 539-540.

CHAPTER VI

THE BIGGEST MISTAKE

The five-page sixth chapter in Part Two of Senator Specter's memoir, *Passion for Truth*, is titled "The Biggest Mistake." Therein he gives positive proof of the basic humanity of his and his colleagues' capacity for the phenomenon of self-serving rationalization. They are willing to utilize an indefensible methodology that manipulates data to serve their own hypotheses, while simultaneously reserving the right to indulge in selective, belated criticism of their superiors for decisions similar to those they themselves practice when it suits their purpose. The following are offered as demonstration of relevant examples of the phenomenon. In Specter's view, the "Biggest Mistake" of the Warren Commission was the decision to withhold from the Assistant Counsel the use of photographs and X-rays taken during the autopsy of the body of John F. Kennedy. Speaking of his former colleague Counsel, David Belin, Senator Specter's memoir account says in 2000:

> When Belin and I had dinner together shortly after the commission nixed the photos and X rays, he suggested resigning from the probe. 'It was discussed,' he told me in April 1996. 'I don't think that either one of us thought about doing it.' In the end I submitted a memo to the commission on April 30, 1964, saying the photos and X rays were indispensable to our investigation. (87-88)

(Recalling a passing comment I made in the previous chapter, it seems that the human condition is also obvious when Senator Specter exercises selective prudence concerning ownership of an April 30, 1964 Memorandum while practicing silence in 2004 in response to an inquiry about his ownership of a March 12, 1964 Memorandum.)

I can only wonder whether Senator Specter is serious when he indicates that "the photos and X rays were indispensable to our investigation." They didn't use them, but he nevertheless was able to sell the Warren Commission his Single-Bullet Theory without them, and they in turn based their *Report*'s conclusions on his theory-turned conclusion—all of which suggests they were in fact dispensable. Left unsaid is what Arlen Specter could and would have done differently if he had had access to them.

Be all that as it may, in the present instance the lawyers' criticism was directed toward the decision-maker(s) responsible for denying the staff lawyers access to the autopsy photographs and X-rays. What Specter does not explain very well is the reason for the dualism in the criticism. Rather he simply says: "We did not doubt the autopsy surgeons' testimony about the wounds. But we thought all the evidence should be presented." (86) And his reasoning reads:

> Any investigator likes to have all the facts before drawing conclusions. That applies to corroborative evidence, such as photographs and X rays, as well as to general testimony. A picture is usually worth a thousand words. The photographs and X rays could have gone a long way toward resolving the controversy over the direction and location of the shots. (87)

A brief moment's reflection produces an awareness of at least three flaws in that reasoning:

(1) While it is undoubtedly prudent for an investigator to have all the facts before drawing conclusions, in the normal

course of Arlen Specter's "legal lens" focus as a prosecutor, the investigator was normally a police officer who was seldom the decision-maker in determination of which of the known facts were to be used in drawing the conclusions. When, as in the case of the Warren Commission, the "investigator"—the staff lawyer—was also the interrogator of the witness, it is the record of the testimony elicited by the investigator-interrogator which determines the conclusions that will be drawn by the Commission;

(2) Whether the ratio is 1,000 words to 1 picture—is not important alongside the reality that *the picture cannot speak for itself.* Accordingly, whether it is 1,000 words or some other number, witness testimony—expert or otherwise—is the only genuine source of the authenticity of the physical evidence and the credibility of the human witness. Thus, ultimately it is witness testimony that generates the facts upon which the investigator necessarily relies in drawing conclusions;

(3) Given the continuing rancorous debate among "expert medical witnesses" concerning both the photographs and X-rays ever since they have been made available to *selected* observers, it is difficult to realize how they *would*—as opposed to Specter's *could*—"have gone a long way toward resolving the controversy over the direction and location of the shots."

Surprisingly, Senator Specter indicates that the Assistant General Counsel, Norman Redlich—author of the "ban" on "preparation" interviews—opposed the ban on the use of the photographs and X rays. (86) Not surprisingly, Senator Specter indicates his close colleagues—David Belin and Joseph Ball—joined him in criticism of the refusal to utilize the pictorial evidence from the autopsy. He quotes Belin, who, in his 1973 book, *November 23, 1963: You Are the Jury*, wrote on page 345:

It was a disastrous decision. It was a decision with which Joe Ball and I, as well as Arlen Specter, disagreed. It was a decision that gave rise to wild speculation and rumor. It was a decision which violated basic elementary rules of evidence familiar to every law student in America that when a person testifies he should have the "best evidence" available.

Even as I am not inclined to dispute the value of the art of forensics in legal education, any reader of Belin's wisdom concerning "best evidence" will be well-advised to read his account of the function of the March 20 photographs he used in questioning his March 23 Commission witness, Howard L. Brennan. This is the witness subsequently identified by both Belin and former Warren Commissioner Gerald R. Ford, as "the most important witness who appeared before the Commission."[F] Conflicting photographic evidence in Brennan's testimony, however, seriously compromised the quality of his testimony and, hence, any claim to superlative ranking as a witness. (See Warren *Report* at 144-145.)

In that same vein, it is noteworthy to recall a photography sequence that I related in a previous publication. On May 24, 1964, Arlen Specter participated in an FBI-Secret Service reenactment of the assassination in Dealey Plaza. Following the reenactment in Dealey Plaza, there was a photography session in what was identified as a nearby Railway Express Agency garage. Senator Specter's memoir is silent concerning the session's purpose as well as its significance. Nevertheless, it is a memorable learning experience to recount what apparently happened. At the very least, three photos seem indisputably authentic.

• In the Doubleday Publisher's edition of the Warren *Report*, between pages 428-429, there is an unnumbered 32-page insert of photographs. There is no such insert in the U.S. Government Printing of the *Report*, although some of the photos also appear in scattered pages of the official 888-page report. One of the photos—number 12 in the Doubleday edition—indicates a copyright held by Station KRLD, of Dallas, Texas. That picture shows two FBI agents seated in a limousine as stand-ins for President Kennedy and Governor Connally. It carries the caption: "Two FBI agents re-enacting the assassination. One, left, has a chalk patch on the back of his jacket, where the first bullet hit President Kennedy. The man with circle drawn around dot on his jacket is seated in the position of Governor Connally of Texas."

In that photo, the path of the bullet, indicated by a broken line with arrow, does not corroborate the path to which the autopsy doctors testified. I am unaware of any documentation that discloses whether the Commission did or did not see that picture. Nor I am I aware of any attempt to reconcile its bullet path with Dr. Humes's testimony of March 16.

• There is, however, a reference/citation for a photograph that appears at page 96 in Volume XVIII of the Commission/ Hearings/ Exhibits/Depositions/Affidavits/Statements/Whatever. Identified as Commission Exhibit 903, its caption reads: "Photograph taken at garage, following reenactment of assassination on May 24, 1964, depicting probable angle of declination of bullet which passed through President Kennedy and Governor Connally." This photo shows Arlen Specter holding a pointer at an angle demonstrating clearly the bullet path used in the reenactment.

(It is neither explained nor obvious why that exhibit appears sandwiched between Commission Exhibits 902—depicting frame 313 (the head shot from the Zapruder film)—and 904—a copy of the original Zapruder film, which carries the extraordinary footnote "1". That note reads: "These exhibits were not reproduced because of their length. Selected frames from these films, however, are depicted in Commission Exhibit No. 885." But, in turn, the caption for CE 885 will leave a diligent researcher questioning it thoroughly: "Album of black and white photographs of frames from the Zapruder, Nix and Muchnore films.")

• Nowhere in either the Warren *Report* or in its accompanying 26 volumes of ostensibly supporting data is found a second picture, clearly taken in the same garage, depicting Arlen Specter and his pointer in a photo taken from the opposite side of the limousine. Unlike CE 903, however, this photo shows the backs of both stand-ins in a pointer-determined bullet path that does not come close to lining up with the chalk mark on the jacket of the Kennedy standin seated in the limousine. This photo includes a caption which reads:

> Arlen Specter holds the tip of the probe against the location of Governor Connally's back wound. In order for the bullet's trajectory to have passed through the President and entered Connally, the President's wound needed to be six inches higher than its actual location, which is shown by the white spot on the jacket, below Specter's hand.

This photo appears—without claimed credit or copyright—on page 125 in Robert J. Groden's 1993 book, *The Killing of a President*. Absent such claim, I incline to believe that it, like CE 903, lies in the public domain as a government agency photograph.

Left unmentioned by either Specter or Belin is why General Counsel Rankin, and/or Commission Chairman, Chief Justice Warren, were so unyielding in their refusal to allow the autopsy's pictorial evidence. That refusal stands considerably apart from the tone and substance of the Chief Justice's welcoming remarks in his lecture given the lawyers at the outset of their employment in January, 1964: "Truth Is the Client." Indeed, when Specter relates that "as hard as we pressed for the materials, Rankin consistently refused. We were told that the Kennedy family opposed having the photographs and X rays made available," that adamant stance of the decision makers assumes an awkward posture as it relates to who really controlled the direction of the Commission's work. More appropriate, but unasked by the outraged lawyer, is the underlying question ignored by Senator Specter: By what right did the Kennedy family assume ownership of these government documents? Perhaps David Belin put it best when he wrote in his *November 23, 1963*:

> The reverberations from the decision to withhold publication of the autopsy photographs and X rays will be felt for many decades as part of the overall diminution of the confidence that the American people have in the integrity of their elected officials. (348)

And he could have added, "and the account of the Warren Commission as found in its *Report* of September 1964." Indeed, many critics of that report have found it difficult to reconcile its "conclusions" with the evidence upon which they are supposedly based. Certainly a reading of second chapter—"Truth Is the Client"—in Senator Specter's memoir account contributes little toward such a reconciliation.

Indeed, a careful examination of Senator Specter's memoir, *Passion for Truth*, generates a fascinating awareness. With the exception of this ban on autopsy photographs and X-rays, the thirty-four-year-old Arlen Specter was commendably willing, at times, to challenge decisions of his superiors on the Warren Commission:

• As mentioned above, when Redlich banned unsworn "preparation" interviews of witnesses prior to testimony, Specter simply bypassed him with a successful appeal to their mutual superior, Rankin.

• When the lawyers learned that the Commission had voted not to publish testimony from the public sessions and depositions, Specter writes: "The staff contacted the members of Congress serving as commissioners who had not been present at the vote on publication. Those commissioners took action to see that the record was published." (59)

• When Warren ordered Rankin to take Governor Connally's testimony, Specter's warning lecture to Rankin on the complexity of the assignment ended with Rankin subdelegating the questioning of Connally to Specter. (69-70)

• Perhaps the most brazen example is also connected with the testimony of Governor Connally. In Specter's words:

> One subject that had intrigued the younger staff was the purpose of Kennedy's visit to Texas. The media had speculated that the trip was politically motivated, and several young commission lawyers thought that Connally should be asked about that explicitly. We considered it important to put this on the record. I guessed that the chief justice might not like my exploring this background issue. To get the governor's candid response on a subject he had not expected—and to explore the area before the chief justice could preempt me—I led off with that question.
> . . . .
> As I was questioning Connally, I noticed Chief Justice Warren's impatience. When I finished, Warren left no doubt, on the record. Before swearing in Mrs. Connally, he said, 'Mrs. Connally, would you mind telling the story of this affair as you heard it, and we will be brief and will start right off with the shooting itself, and Mr. Specter will also examine you . . . .' Without the inflection, those words do not jump out. But Warren's tone left no room for doubt. 'We *will* be brief,' he stressed. His statement that 'we will start right with the shooting itself' made clear that he did not want me to explore any of the background. Having covered the background and a reasonable amount of detail with the governor, I tried to comply with the chief justice's interdiction.

Pursuing the question of whether the autopsy photographs and X-rays were really necessary for the Warren Commission, for Dr. Humes's testimony, and for Arlen Specter himself, the exchanges that occurred in the March 16 testimony session are genuinely educative. The following account, though not an exactingly precise order of questions, is an accurate extract of essentials in a fascinating sequence.

I asked Humes a number of questions when he testified before the commission to suggest the benefits of making the actual photographs and X rays available to the commission. 'Would it be helpful to the artist, in redefining the drawings if that should become necessary, to have available to him the photographs or X rays of the president?' I asked at one point.

'If it were necessary to have them absolutely true to scale,' Humes said, 'I think it would be virtually impossible for him to do this without the photographs.'

'And what is the reason for the necessity for having the photographs?' I asked.

'I think it is most difficult to transmit into physical measurements the—by word—the exact situation as it was seen to the naked eye.' Humes replied. 'I cannot transmit completely to the illustrator where they were situated.' Responding to another of my questions, Humes said. 'The pictures would show more accurately and in more detail the character of the wounds . . . . They would also perhaps give the commissioners a better—better is not the best term, but a more graphic picture of the massive defect.'

Following that answer, Warren closed the matter with Humes. 'Before we get off that,' the chief justice said, 'may I ask you this, Commander: If we had the pictures here and you could look them over again and restate your opinion, would it cause you to change any of the testimony you have given here?'

'To the best of my recollection, Mr. Chief Justice,' Humes said, 'it would not.' Humes gave that answer only moments after saying that the 'photographs are far superior to my humble verbal description . . . ' (89-90)

COMMENT

1. Any analysis of these six paragraphs must be undertaken with the awareness that Dr. Humes's testimony occupies 29 pages in Volume II of the Commission Hearings.
2. The Warren *Report* indicates that "The hospital received the President's body for autopsy at approximately 7:35 p.m.[277] X-rays and photographs were taken preliminarily and the pathological examination began at about 8 p.m.[278] (The reference/citation for [277] and [278] is Dr. Humes testimony at 2H 349.
3. Regarding Humes's answer, "I think it is most difficult to transmit into physical measurements the—by word—the exact situation as it was seen to the naked eye. I cannot transmit completely to the illustrator where they are situated" to Specter's question, "And what is the necessity for having the photographs?", a reader of *Passion for Truth* should be aware of this reality: There is a large sentence segment missing between the two sentences in Humes's answer.

    Humes's full answer reads at 2H 350:

> I think it is most difficult to transmit into physical measurements the—by word—the exact situation as it was seen to the naked eye. *The photographs were—there is no problem of scale there because the wound, if they are changed in size and proportion to the structures of the body and so forth, when we attempt to give a description of these findings, it is the bony prominences, I cannot, which we used as points of references,* [Emphases added] I cannot transmit completely to the illustrator where they are situated.

    If I understand Dr. Humes's syntax, I translate his answer to mean that there is no scale problem with the wounds, but there is with bony prominences. And if my translation is accurate, it is understandable why Specter chose to edit the sentence. Had that missing sentence fragment been retained in Humes's answer, Specter would have imprudently risked his memoir readers' attention to a never-defended criticism of an essential datum in the autopsy methodology utilized by Dr. Humes. Among other reasons, that methodology was faulty because it chose not to use a wound location determined by a fixed distance from the top of the head, as opposed to the variable distances inherent in measurements of 14 centimeters from the "tip of the right acromion process" and 14 centimeters below the "tip of the right mastoid process." Simply stated, variances between the length of the human neck and the breadth of the human shoulders preclude reliable measurements based upon those "bony prominences" as points of reference.

And the reality is this: Arlen Specter's Single-Bullet Theory is dependent upon a bullet trajectory that presents impossible variances between witness testimony and trajectory angle calculations established by the Commission-FBI-Secret Service Reenactment of May 24, 1964. This reality awaits further analysis below.

4. Regarding Chief Justice Warren's hypothetical question to Dr. Humes: "If we had the pictures here and you could look them over again and restate your opinion, would it cause you to change any of the testimony you have given here?" Inasmuch as Humes had not previously seen them, it is strange to see the word "again" as in "look them over again". That point aside, Arlen Specter's reaction to Humes's answer does not convey a flattering tone:

Humes's reply: "To the best of my recollection, Mr. Chief Justice . . . it would not."

Specter's reaction: "Humes gave that answer only moments after saying that the "photographs are far superior to my humble verbal description . . . ."

The tone of Specter's comment is even less warranted when paired with the context for Humes's answer. Humes's answer to Warren was given on page 2H 372 of his testimony. Humes's comment to which Specter reacted—"photographs are far superior to my humble verbal description"—may be found in context on page 369 of his testimony:

> Senator Cooper: May I ask a question?
>
> Dr. Humes. Yes, sir, Senator.
>
> C. [Referring to CE 385, the Naval illustrator's drawing of the neck-throat wound] Assuming that we draw a straight line from Point "C" which you have described as a possible point of entry of the missile, to Point "D" which you saw as an incision of the tracheotomy—
>
> H. Yes, sir.
>
> C. What would be the relation of the bruise at the apex of the pleural sac to such a line?
>
> H. It would be exactly in line with such a line, sir, exactly.
>
> C. What was the character of the bruise that you saw there?
>
> H. The bruise here, *photographs are far superior to my humble verbal description* [Emphases added], but if I let my hand in cup-shaped fashion represent the apical parietal pleura, it was an area approximately 5 cm, in greatest diameter of purplish blue discoloration of the parietal pleura. Corresponding exactly with it, with the lung sitting below it, was a roughly pyramid-shaped bruise with its base toward the surface of the upper portion of the lung, and the apex down into the lung tissue, and the whole thing measured about 5 cm., which is a little—2 inches in extent, sir.

CE 385—the illustrator's drawing—visualizes internal structures of the neck that would not be seen on photographs taken, it is recalled from comment 2. above, "preliminarily [to the] pathological examination [which] began at about 8 p.m." Thus, the "character of the bruise" and Humes's representation of "the apical parietal pleura" pointed out by Humes in answer to Commissioner Cooper's question were depicted on the drawing, and not on any photograph.

So, when Humes answered Chairman Warren's question whether photographs "would cause you to change any of the testimony you have given here," and Humes answered "To the best of my recollection, Mr. Chief Justice, it would not", it is the only possible answer in the circumstance of Humes not having seen the photographs. I find it difficult to believe that Arlen Specter did not understand the difference between Humes's *incompetence* to answer Warren's hypothetical "if", concerning photographs, with his *competence* to answer Cooper's question concerning a drawing, the data for which Humes himself had dictated to the illustrator. Stated differently, Humes testified about drawings, not photographs. So if he were to be shown photographs, could it change his testimony about drawings that depicted internal data that could not possibly have been shown in the photographs? Obviously not. If Specter's reaction was one of perplexity, it should have been properly directed against the Chairman's question, not Humes's answer.

*   *   *

Senator Specter memoir relates that he "finally saw the original autopsy photographs and X rays, along with computer-enhanced images, at a branch of the National Archives in April, 1999." His first comment is appropriately terse: "The photos are gruesome." It is not surprising that he also includes this judgment:

I was also struck by the president's clearly robust physical condition, which somehow made the photographs even more ghastly. Kennedy, at forty-seven

[sic], had well-defined, muscular shoulders and arms, a flat stomach, and a full head of brown hair. (88)

COMMENT

1. It is noteworthy to realize that both Dr. Humes and Mr. Specter—the main collaborators in development of data incorporated into the Single-Bullet Theory—were impressed with the muscular physique of John F. Kennedy. Whether the subject was explored in the interview of March 13 when Specter prepared Humes for his March 16 testimony is not a matter of record. What is on record is the fact that the subject was raised in the sworn testimony.

2. It is remembered that CE 385 is the Naval illustrator's drawing of the back/neck bullet entry and throat exit path of what eventually became prominent in the Single-Bullet Theory. The record reads at 2H 365-366:

> Mr. Specter. Would it be accurate to state that the hole [in CE 393, Kennedy's suit jacket] which you have identified as being the point of entry is approximately 6 inches below the top of the collar, and 2 inches to the right of the middle seam of the coat?
>
> Commander Humes. That is approximately correct, sir. . . .
>
> . . . .
>
> S. Now, how, if at all, do the holes in the shirt and coat conform to the wound of entrance which you described as point "C" on Commission Exhibit 385?
>
> H. We believe that they conform quite well. When viewing—first of all, the wounds or the defects in 393 and 394 coincide virtually exactly with one another. [CE 393 is Kennedy's suit jacket; CE 394 is his shirt] They give the appearance when viewed separately and not as part of the clothing of a clothed person as being perhaps, somewhat lower on the

Exhibits 393 and 394 than we have depicted them in Exhibit 385. We believe there are two reasons for this. 385 is a schematic representation, and the photographs would be more accurate as to the precise location, but more particularly the way in which these [clothing] defects would conform with such a [wound] defect on the torso *would depend on the girth of the shoulders and configuration of the base of the neck of the individual, and the relative position of the shirt and coat to the tissues of the body at the time of the impact of the missile.* [Emphases added]

S. As to the muscular status of the President, what was it?

H. The President was extremely well-developed, an extremely well-developed muscular young man with a very well-developed set of muscles in his thoraco and shoulder girdle.

S. What effect would that have on the positioning of the shirt and coat with respect to the position of the neck in and about the seam?

H. *I believe this would have a tendency to push the portions of the coat which show the defects somewhat higher on the back of the President than on a man of less muscular development.* [Emphases added]

COMMENT

1. The first problem for the Single-Bullet Theory is seemingly impossible: a. The bullet holes in the suit jacket and shirt—measured as approximately six inches below the top of the jacket collar—must match the bullet entry hole in the body; but b. The bullet entry hole in the body must be higher than the bullet exit hole in the throat.

2. The solution for that first problem is twofold: a. Humes: "The way in which these [clothing] defects would conform with such a [wound] defect on the torso would depend on the girth of the

shoulders and configuration of the base of the neck of the individual, and the relative position of the shirt and coat to the tissues of the body at the time of the impact of the missile. b. Humes: "The President was extremely well-developed, an extremely well-developed muscular young man with a very well-developed set of muscles in his thoraco and shoulder girdle. . . . I believe this would have a tendency to push the portions of the coat which show the defects somewhat higher on the back of the President than on a man of less muscular development.

3. There is nothing in the record which indicates whether Arlen Specter enthusiastically embraced Dr. Humes's solution as of the testimony session on March 16. The record merely indicates that Specter's next question was not a follow-up to the Humes solution. Rather, the next exchange reads:

    S. Now, does the one [defect] which you have described as the entry of the bullet go all the way through?
    H. Yes, sir; it goes through both layers.

4. As indicated above, by 1999, when Senator Specter visited the National Archives and inspected the autopsy photographs, he was a believer:

    I was also struck by the president's clearly robust physical condition, which somehow made the photographs even more ghastly. Kennedy, at forty-seven [sic], had well-defined, muscular shoulders and arms, a flat stomach, and a full head of brown hair. (88)

5. There are other problems with the Single-Bullet Theory. However, they must await analysis below.

*   *   *

It is surprising to learn that Senator Specter's 1999 examination of the autopsy photographs was not assisted by

Dr. Humes, his chief autopsy surgeon witness. Rather, he writes:

> Dr. Boswell, who lived near the archives center, came over to help me interpret the materials during my two-hour inspection. The bullet wounds, as shown on the photographs, were consistent with the Single-Bullet Conclusion. The entrance wound on the neck was about an inch below the shoulder line in the president's back. The exit wound, at the site of the tracheotomy in his throat, was lower. The massive head wound was also consistent with a shot from above and behind.
>
> When the autopsy surgeons testified before the commission in 1964, they didn't know whether the photographs and X rays would ever be made available as a check against their testimony. They put their hands on the Bible and swore to tell the truth, subject to stiff penalties for perjury. My contacts with Humes, Boswell, and Finck convinced me that they were telling the truth. (88-89)

COMMENT

1. Left unmentioned is whether Dr. Boswell's interpretation of the materials included corroboration for their authenticity.
2. Senator Specter's assurance of consistency between the photographs and the Single-Bullet Conclusion is not surprising. Indeed, inasmuch as examination of these materials is presently available for qualified experts who apply for permission see them, if would be extraordinary if, after 35 years, Specter had found inconsistencies by way of pictorial evidence challenging his Single-Bullet Theory-turned-Conclusion-turned Fact.
3. Above mention is recalled of the 1998 anecdotal explanation by Dr. Humes for his burning draft notes of the autopsy proceedings. It is unfortunate that Senator Specter did not ask for Dr. Boswell's explanation in 1999 for his astonishing

placement of the mark for the Single-Bullet Theory's bullet hole on the autopsy face sheet, which includes the notation, "Verified GG Burkley." That placement was, and remains, embarrassingly uncomfortable for defenders of that Theory/Conclusion/Fact, despite Boswell's disavowal of it as a harmless human error. And perhaps it was. But be that as it may, Boswell's mark on the face sheet absolutely contradicts data in the official death certificate—"a second wound occurred in the posterior back at about the level of the third thoracic vertebra"—signed on November 23, 1963 by the White House Presidential physician, Admiral (Dr.) George Gregory Burkley.

And mention of that name brings to mind a troubling question: Why was Admiral Dr. George Burkley neither summoned nor deposed as a witness, or even interviewed as a knowledgeable observer, by the Warren Commission in its investigation of the assassination of President John F. Kennedy. Taken in sum, his credentials for that investigation are unique: He was a member of the traveling party aboard Air Force One to and from Dallas; He was in the Presidential motorcade; He was in the emergency room at Parkland Hospital; He was in the autopsy room at Bethesda Hospital. It seems beyond rational comprehension that his genuine credentials as a witness were prioritized by the Warren Commission as below that of each of the 552 witnesses heard in the course of its 1964 investigation.

CHAPTER VII

THE MAGIC BULLET

Senator Arlen Specter used the title *The Magic Bullet* for the seventh chapter in Part Two of his memoir, *Passion for Truth*. I am not certain whether he intended the term "magic bullet" to be understood as it is defined in *Webster's New World College Dictionary*, Fourth Edition, 1999, 863: "any invention, discovery, solution, etc. that solves a particular problem." Or whether he is using the term as an adjective—"magic"—modifying the noun—"bullet" in the context of his Single-Bullet Theory/Conclusion/Fact. Whatever his intention, I incline to believe that any debate over Specter's usage would be a misplaced priority inasmuch as less than half of his chapter is concerned with the bullet featured in his theory. In an eight-page chapter, only 12 of the 30 paragraphs therein are devoted to the bullet about which the chapter is ostensibly concerned.

The first of those fourteen paragraphs reads:

> When I'd introduced the whole bullet at the commission hearing, I had promised, 'We shall produce later, subject to sequential proof, evidence that the stretcher on which this bullet was found was the stretcher of Governor Connally.' The Parkland depositions would put that evidence on the record. (95)

COMMENT I.

1. In this instance, "when" is a conjunctive, connected with the

verb, "introduced". Thus, as used here, "when" means "at the time I'd introduced".

2. The commission hearing to which Specter refers is the March 16 testimony of Dr. Humes, which may be read at 2H 347-376. The following excerpt is from page 367:

> Mr. Specter. Now, Doctor Humes, at one point in your examination of the President, did you make an effort to probe the point of entry with your finger?
> Commander Humes. Yes, sir. I did.
> S. And at or about that time when you were trying to ascertain, as you previously testified, whether there was any missile in the body of the President, did someone from the Secret Service call your attention to the fact that a bullet had been found on a stretcher at Parkland Hospital?
> H. Yes, sir; they did.

In the course of ensuing Specter-Humes exchanges concerning the found bullet, Commissioner Dulles sought clarification whether that bullet had come from President Kennedy's stretcher.

> Mr. Dulles: Could I ask a question about the missile, I am a little bit—the bullet, I am a little bit—confused. It was found on the stretcher. Did the President's body remain on the stretcher while it was in the hospital?
> Commander Humes. Of that point I have no knowledge. The only—
> D. Why would it—would this operating [the tracheotomy on Kennedy] have anything to do with the bullet being on the stretcher unless the President's body remained on the stretcher after he was taken into the hospital: is that possible?
> H. It is quite possible, sir.

D. Otherwise, it seems to me the bullet would have to have been ejected from the body before he was taken or put on the bed in the hospital.

H. Right, sir. I, of course, was not there. I don't know how he was handled in the hospital, in what conveyance. I do know he was on his back during the period of his stay in the hospital; Doctor Perry told me that.

D. Yes; and wasn't turned over.

H. That is right.

D. So that he might have been on the stretcher the whole time, is that your view?

The Chairman [Warren]. He said he had no view. He wasn't there, he doesn't know anything about it. (368)

(Though there is no indication that Specter welcomed Warren's interruption of Dulles' "might have" question, this is an extraordinary,if not singular, instance in which Warren effected summary closure of a fellow Commissioner's questioning a witness. Be that as it may, Dulles used a different approach with his next question: "Yes, I wonder of there is other evidence of this.")

Thus, it was only *at that point* that Specter made his grand "promise" that "the evidence will show that it was from Governor Connally's stretcher that the bullet was found."

Mr. Specter: There has been other evidence, Mr. Dulles. If I may say at this point, *we shall produce later, subject to sequential proof, evidence that the stretcher on which this bullet was found was the stretcher of Governor Connally.* We have a sequence of events on the transmission of that stretcher which ties that down reasonably closely, so that on the night of the autopsy itself, as the information I have been developing indicates, the thought preliminarily was that was [sic; that "it"— the bullet—was] from President Kennedy's stretcher, and that is what led to the hypothesis which we have been exploring about, but which has since been rejected. But at any rate the evidence will show that it was from Governor Connally's stretcher that the bullet was found. [Emphases added] (368)

3.   Note carefully that Senator Specter's memoir account refers to a "whole" bullet. One of the extraordinary characteristics of the "magic bullet" is that it had to be going fast enough to cause seven wounds

   — in-out Kennedy's neck/in-out Connally's chest (fracturing a rib)/in-out Connally's wrist (fracturing the radius bone)/ in Connally's thigh
   — but simultaneously going slow enough to remain in a nearly undamaged condition when found on Connally's stretcher. Among the marvels in Specter's theory is the utilization of what he termed "sequential proof" in his memoir account.

4.   Thus, Senator Specter misleads his readers in writing, "When [at the time] I'd introduced the whole bullet at the commission hearing, . . .". He introduced *a discussion* of the bullet, but he certainly did not—at that time—enter that bullet into the record as a Commission Exhibit. Nor, at the time he initiated the discussion, did he promise to produce evidence that the bullet was found on Connally's stretcher. That promise came only in response to Dulles' unwelcome questions. And it remains to be seen whether he made good on the promise.

COMMENT: II.

Regarding "The Parkland depositions would put that evidence on the record.": Prior to a discussion of Arlen Specter interviews of personnel at Parkland Hospital, there is another thread that must be inserted into this dissection of his memoir account. It involves a dimension of the methodology utilized within the Warren Commission. This is taken from Chapter VI of *Passion for Truth*, at page 90:

> Ball, Belin, and I had asked Rankin to authorize the lawyers to take sworn depositions, just as lawyers do in pretrial discovery proceedings in civil cases. Belin and I urged Joe Ball to take up the matter with his close friend, the chief justice. When the lawyers submitted their preliminary reports, due February 18, the commission brass saw the number of witnesses we needed to interview. It would have stretched the investigation to bring all these witnesses to the VFW Building [in Washington]. Ball reported back that Warren had agreed to let us take sworn testimony in the field. The chief justice, Ball said, wanted 'to get things cleaned up.'

This is an example of a unique procedure devised by a commission appointed "to ascertain, evaluate and report upon the facts relating to the assassination of the late President John F. Kennedy and the subsequent violent death of the man charged with the assassination."

By definition, assassination is a crime of murder. As of 1963, however, it was not a Federal crime to murder the President of the United States. The result was a bizarre methodology, authorized by the Chief Justice of the United States, in which a civil law discovery process—deposition by attorneys—was utilized to investigate a murder that was not a federal crime.

And regarding "the subsequent violent death of the man charged with the assassination", I suggest that the brutality of the shocking televised murder of an undefended, handcuffed designated assassin is silently rendered insignificant by not identifying the nature of his "violent death". At first glance, that insignificance was diminished by the Warren Commission *Report*'s generous nod in the direction of fairplay:

In fairness to the alleged assassin and his family, the Commission on February 25, 1964, requested Walter E. Craig, president of the American Bar Association, to participate in the investigation and to advise the Commission whether in his opinion the proceedings conformed to the basic principles of American justice. Mr. Craig accepted this assignment and participated fully and without limitation. He attended Commission hearings in person or through his appointed assistants. All working papers, reports, and other data in Commission files were made available, and Mr. Craig and his associates were given the opportunity to cross-examine witnesses, to recall any witness heard prior to his appointment, and to suggest witnesses whose testimony they would like to have the Commission hear. This procedure was agreeable to counsel for Oswald's widow. (WR xiv-xv)

On second glance, I am unaware of specific examples—in either the Warren *Report* or its 26 Volumes of Hearings/Depositions/Affidavits/ Exhibits—of details specifying how either Mr. Craig, or his assistants, undertook "to participate in the investigation and to advise the Commission whether in his/their opinion the proceedings conformed to the basic principles of American justice."

*   *   *

As introduction to the "Parkland depositions" Arlen Specter took in Dallas beginning Friday, March 20, he wrote in *Passion for Truth* on Page 95:

Shortly after Kennedy was pronounced dead at 1:00 p.m., Commission Exhibit 399—the so-called magic bullet—had rolled off a stretcher on the ground floor at Parkland. . . . Working backward, we had to determine

from whose stretcher Bullet 399 had fallen. To find out,
I intended to take the sworn testimony of every doctor,
nurse, orderly, and bystander who had been interviewed.

COMMENT

1. There is no factual basis for any claim that the bullet in
   question—CE 399—"rolled off a stretcher". Indeed, the
   testimony of Darrell C. Tomlinson, who found the bullet, is
   quoted by Specter on page 96 as saying: "I bumped the wall
   [with a stretcher] and a spent cartridge or bullet rolled out
   that apparently had been lodged under the edge of the mat
   [on the stretcher]."

2. Regarding ". . . we had to determine from whose stretcher
   Bullet 399 had fallen. I intended to take the sworn testimony
   of every doctor, nurse, orderly, and bystander who had been
   interviewed":

   • Independently of how many doctors, nurses,
     orderlies, or bystanders were deposed by Specter, his
     key witness was Tomlinson, who does not seem to
     fit in any of the categories of Specter's deponents.
   • ". . . who had been interviewed" By whom? When?
     Under oath? With opportunity to correct error(s)?

3. It is noted that Specter's account of the depositions limits
   itself to an either/or possibility: Connally's stretcher, or
   Kennedy's stretcher. In the happening, there was another
   emergency patient—a child named Ronald Fuller—in no way
   connected with the events of the assassination, who received
   emergency treatment during the general time frame that
   services were provided Kennedy and Connally. That account
   is beyond the scope of my present analysis. In 1967, Josiah
   Thompson published a book titled *Six Seconds in Dallas*.
   Anyone interested in the account of treatment given the Fuller
   child will find it on pages 161-165 of Thompson's book.

*   *   *

Much energy, paper and ink have been expended over the past forty years in an unyielding debate concerning problems with the bullet in Arlen Specter's Single-Bullet Theory, which is absolutely committed to three shots. In this present study, I concentrate on three of those problems: Timing; Trajectory; Ballistics. In undertaking the following commentary on those problems, I cannot emphasize too emphatically the complex phenomenon of their interrelationships. For identification and order they can be presented separately, but *data for one necessarily impacts with consequences for each of the others.*

Thus the relationships are reciprocal: Each affects and is affected by each.

Timing

Though an important question, this is an uncomplicated issue involving simple math calculations. Beginning with an uncontested Zapruder Frame 313 depiction of the third shot—the fatal head shot—and working backward to the first shot, the first question involves the time required for one assassin to get off three shots with the designated rifle.

- The FBI firing tests used with the designated rifle established that a minimum of 2.3 seconds was required for each of the second and third shots. (WR 115)
- Examination of the Zapruder camera by the FBI established that "18.3 pictures or frames were taken each second, and therefore, the timing of certain events could be calculated by allowing 1/18.3 seconds for the action depicted from one frame to the next." (WR 97)
- 2 shots @ 2.3 seconds each = 4.6 seconds firing time.
- 4.6 seconds x 18.3 frames = 84.18 frames.
- Frame 313-84.18 frames = *Frame 228/229 for the first shot.*

The problem is this: Frame 228/229 for the first shot does not quite match an inference of Frame 217.5 drawn from FBI calculations generated by its photography expert Lyndal L. Shaneyfelt. Those calculations were used by the Warren Commission in its *Report* account, based on Shaneyfelt's testimony on April 23.

That report reads:

As the President rode along Elm Street for a distance of about 140 feet, he was waving to the crowd.[281] Shaneyfelt testified that the waving is seen on the Zapruder movie until around frame 205, when a road sign blocked out most of the President's body from Zapruder's view through the lens of his camera. However, the assassin continued to have a clear view of the President as he proceeded down Elm.[282] When President Kennedy again came fully into view in the Zapruder film at frame 225, he seemed to be reacting to his neck wound by raising his hands to his throat.[283] (See Commission Exhibit No. 895, p. 103.) According to Shaneyfelt the reaction was 'clearly apparent in 226 and barely apparent in 225.'[284] It is probable that the President was not shot before frame 210, since it is unlikely that the assassin would deliberately have shot at him with a view obstructed by the oak tree when he was about to have a clear opportunity. It is also doubtful that even the most proficient marksman would have hit him through the oak tree. In addition, the President's reaction is 'barely apparent' in frame 225, which is 15 frames or approximately eight-tenths of a second after frame 210, and a shot much before 210 would assume a longer reaction time than was recalled by eyewitnesses at the scene. Thus, the evidence indicated that the President was not shot until at least frame 210 and that he was probably hit by frame 225. The possibility of variations in reaction time in addition to the obstruction of Zapruder's view by the sign precluded a more specific determination than that the President was probably shot through the neck between frames 210 and 225, which marked his position between 138.9 and 153.8 feet west of station C.[285] (WR 98, 105) [Pages 99-104 = The narrative is interrupted by inclusion of Commission Exhibits 887, 889, 891, 893, 895, 697.]

(Two points in clarification of data:

1. ". . . [T]he agents concluded that at frame 166 of the Zapruder film the President passed beneath the foliage of the large oak tree and the point of impact on the President's back disappeared from the gunman's view as seen through the telescopic lens.[277] (See Commission Exhibit No. 889, p. 100.) For a fleeting instant, the President came back into view in the telescopic lens at frame 186 as he appeared in an opening among the leaves.[278] (See Commission Exhibit 891, p. 101.) The test revealed that the next point at which the rifleman had a clear view through the telescopic sight where the bullet entered the President's back was when the car emerged from behind the tree at frame 210.[279]" (WR 98)

2. "Station C" was an FBI-designated point which represents the intersection of Houston and Elm Streets. It was used by the FBI to calculate distances the limousine had traveled on Elm Street by the times of the three shots.[276])

Note! The citations for Endnotes [276] through [285] are 5H 145-157 (Shaneyfelt).

Inasmuch as the road sign blocked Zapruder's lens between frames 210-225, the FBI tests split the difference and used the average for those frames—217.5—to calculate the incredibly precise number *17°43'30"* as the downward angle of fire for the first shot! It may of course be reasonably argued that my simple math calculations for the timing problem establish a precise Frame—228/229—for the first shot. And that argument is sound. My defense is this: My math calculations use as good or better a methodology than the Warren *Report's* expert witness uses in reaching the *probable* (but very precise!) downward angle of fire as being 17°43'30" (Stated differently, the precision demanded for a bullet to pass through Kennedy's neck and throat without touching bone—which would deflect a straight line trajectory—is arguably greater than that needed to resolve the simple timing issue.)

Trajectory

By definition, this problem involves more than the simple math calculations in the timing issue. *Webster's New World Dictionary* reads on page 1518:

> **trajectory** the curved path of something hurtling through space, esp. that of a projectile from the time that it leaves the muzzle of a gun.

It will be recalled from passing mention above that the trajectory for the Single-Bullet Theory requires a straight line bullet path from the muzzle of the rifle into Kennedy's neck and out his throat, into Connally's back and out his chest, in and out of Connally's wrist, and into Connally's thigh. And while there can be no way of knowing whether Arlen Specter discussed trajectory matters with Drs. Humes and Boswell when he interviewed of them on Friday, March 13, it is clear from his examination of Dr. Humes on Monday, March 16 that he was interested in Humes's views on the path of the bullet through Kennedy's neck. (And it is remembered that inasmuch as the autopsy never did not include dissection of the neck, Humes's opinions in this area of Specter's inquiry about a bullet path were necessarily inferences developed following the autopsy.)

Senator Specter provides his readers with an unexpected insight into his methodology when he includes the following on page 81 in his *Passion for Truth*:

> There was a real question whether Humes should be asked at all about matters beyond his immediate personal knowledge, such as his view on the trajectory of the bullets or the metallic flakes in Governor Connally's wrist. Under the technical rules that apply in court, such testimony might be barred. But the commission made the common sense decision to ask Humes and other witnesses for their views, impressions, and opinions on a variety of issues. Questions about outside subjects might produce more answers about inside subjects. For example, by asking Humes—who had never examined Connally—about damage Connally might have suffered, we were probing at the same time about resistance the bullet met in passing through Kennedy's neck, an area within Humes's sphere. From this freewheeling questioning, the Single-Bullet Conclusion developed naturally.

COMMENT:

1. Aside from the unmentioned reasons why such a practice "might be barred" in a court, witness views about "outside subjects" is a strange way of requiring them to perform their obligation to tell "the truth, the whole truth, and nothing but the truth" in matters beyond their competence. Unmentioned by Specter is the inherent possibility of abuse of witnesses in a legal environment in which they do not have the protection of the adversarial system.

2. Specter's "for example" is ludicrous: Asking about damage Connally *might* have suffered has no utility for resolution of the trajectory problem of a bullet in Kennedy's neck for the simple reason that Humes had no first-hand knowledge of

what happened in Kennedy's neck. Certainly Specter is correct when he says that Kennedy's neck was "an area within Humes's sphere." What Specter ignores is the fact that Humes never explored that sphere. Clearly when an autopsy surgeon fails—as is the case with Humes—to dissect the neck, he cannot be credited with a competence to give credible testimony on the trajectory of a bullet through that neck. So the reality is impossible: Competence cannot be based on nonperformance.

3. In the happening, Humes's testimony was of considerable value to Specter for three reasons:

    •   The first reason was the inference generated by/from Humes's telephone conversation with Parkland Hospital's Dr. Malcolm Perry. Humes claimed as of November 23, 1963, and maintained until his death in 2003, that he knew nothing about Kennedy's anterior throat wound until informed of it by Dr. Perry in a telephone conversation on the morning following the autopsy of November 22. From that information, he inferred that the back/neck wound was an entry wound and that anterior throat wound was the exit for that bullet. Thus, Specter was indebted to Humes for the first leg—Kennedy entrance and exit—of the journey of that remarkable bullet.

    •   The second reason was Humes's expression on March 16 of a valuable opinion regarding the bullet entry of the back/neck wound as being an "approximately 45°" angle of entry of that bullet in Kennedy's back/neck. In turn, the value of that "45°" angle entry became important as an assumed fact in Specter's subsequent questioning of the two Parkland doctors—Charles Carrico and Malcolm Perry—who had seen the anterior throat wound on President Kennedy. The March 16 Humes testimony was developed in the following account from 2H 370. The context is discussion of two of the three drawings Humes had had made by the Naval illustrator. CE 385 is the neck/throat wound; CE 388 is the Head Wound.

Mr. Specter. Dr. Humes, can you compare the angles of declination of 385, point "C" to "D", with 388 "A" to "B"?

Commander Humes. You will not, and again I must apologize for the schematic nature of these diagrams drawn to a certain extent from memory and to a certain extent from the written record. It would appear that the angle of declination is somewhat sharper on the head wound, 388, than it is in 385.

The reason for this, we feel, by the pattern of the entrance wound at 388 "A" causes us to feel that the President's head was bent forward, and we feel this accounts for the difference in the angle, plus undoubtedly the wounds were not received absolutely simultaneously, so that the vehicle in which the President was traveling moved during this period of time, which would account for a difference in the line of flight, sir.

S. Aside from the slight differences which are notable by observing those two exhibits, are they roughly comparable to the angle of decline?

H. I believe them to be roughly comparable, sir.

S. Can you state for the record an approximation of the angle of decline?

H. Mathematics is not my forte. *Approximately 45 degrees from the horizontal.* [Emphases added]

• Humes's opinion was also important for Specter's second leg of the magic bullet journey—from Kennedy's throat into Connally's back.

In *Passion for Truth*'s account this reads on page 81: "When I showed him photographs of the positions that Kennedy and Connally had occupied in the Lincoln, Humes suggested that the same bullet might have exited into Kennedy's neck and then passed through Connally's chest." The testimony exchange reads on page 2H 375:

Mr. Specter. What wounds did Governor Connally sustain in the chest area, based upon the records of Parkland Hospital [CE392], which you have examined, Doctor Humes?

Commander Humes. Governor Connally received in his chest a wound of entrance just—this is again from 392—'just internal to the right scapula close to the axilla which had passed through the latissimus dorsi muscle, shattered approximately ten centimeters of a lateral and anterior portion of the right fifth rib, and emerged just below the right nipple anterially.'
These were the wounds of the chest of Governor Connally.

S.   Now assuming that there were only three missiles fired, and bearing in mind the positions of President Kennedy and Governor Connally from the photograph marked Commission Exhibit 398, do you have an opinion as to the source of the missiles which inflicted the wound on President Kennedy marked 385-C to D [the Naval illustrator's drawing], and the wound in Governor Connally's chest which you have just referred to?

H.   Yes. I would preface this statement by the following: As I testified earlier in the afternoon, as much as we could ascertain from our X-rays and physical examinations, this missile struck no bony structures in traversing the body of the late President. Therefore, I believe it was moving at its exit from the President's body at only very slightly less than that velocity, so it was still traveling at great speed.

I believe in looking at Exhibit 398, which purports to be at approximately the time the President was struck, *I see that Governor Connally is sitting directly in front of the late President, and suggest the possibility that this missile, having traversed the low neck of the late President, in fact traversed the chest of Governor Connally.* [Emphases added]

(Note that Dr. Humes goes *beyond* opinion regarding trajectory—the path of the projectile—when he observes of the bullet that "I believe it was moving at its exit from the President's body at only very slightly less than that velocity [with which it entered the President's body], so it was still traveling at great speed." As will be seen presently, Specter was not as enthusiastic about other Humes opinions, those in the field of ballistics.)

Ballistics

By definition, this problem involves more than the simple math calculations in the timing issue. *Webster's New World Dictionary* reads on page 110:

ballistics 1. The science dealing with the motion and impact of projectiles, such as bullets, rockets, bombs, etc.
2. the study of the effects of firing on a firearm or bullet, cartridge, etc.

The problem may be identified as the question: How can there be seven wounds caused by a bullet that fractured two bones and remained virtually undamaged? Attempted answers have often taken on the characteristics of an exercise in semantics utilizing hair-splitting distinctions in matters of word usage and context. At one end of the exercise spectrum are critics of the Single-Bullet Theory who insist on referring to the Commission Exhibit 399—the "magic bullet"—as being in pristine condition. That argument is countered with scorn from those who will argue that a bullet is pristine only at the moment it leaves the weapon from which it fired. At the other extreme is a logical argument that utilizes a reverse "slice the salami" exercise in which incremental additions of premises to intermediate conclusions eventually produce a desired conclusion reached by way of deductive syllogistical argument. And somewhere in between the extremes most of the debaters joust with varying degrees of success measured by the cheers of partisan judges.

I incline to believe that the ballistics problem was the most troublesome for Arlen Specter's creation of his Single Bullet Theory.

Brilliant as a prosecutor, quick and resourceful as a debater, he was nevertheless a medical layman forced to rely on conflicting medical opinions for crucial conclusions. Having successfully negotiated the first steps—(1) one bullet entered the neck and exited the throat of Kennedy, and (2) Humes's opinion that the same bullet could have passed through Connally's chest—Specter's next step was obviously that taken in his exchange with Humes, as related in *Passion for Truth* on pages 81-82:

> I asked Humes whether he thought that Bullet 399 could have caused Connally's other wounds, to the right wrist and left thigh. Humes could only rely on the Parkland Hospital records to answer. 'I think that extremely unlikely,' he replied. 'The reports, again Exhibit 392 from Parkland, tell of an entrance wound in the lower midthigh of the governor, and X rays taken there are described as showing metallic fragments in the bone, which apparently by this report were not removed and are still in Governor Connally's thigh. I can't conceive of there they came from this missile.'

COMMENT

Presuming that Specter would have *welcomed* an affirmative answer to his question, it is harmlessly amusing to wonder whether

Specter would have been uneasy with that welcome answer despite the fact that "Humes could only rely on the Parkland records" for his answer. Regardless of that speculation, Humes did not support the final leg of the magic bullet's journey in Specter's theory.

Specter then tried for the intermediate step—the bullet's journey through Connally's wrist—which also produced a Humes negative. He writes on page 81-82:

> Humes also did not think Bullet 399 had caused the wounds to Connally's wrist, because of metallic fragments found in that wound. 'The reason I believe it most unlikely that this missile could have inflicted either of these wounds is that this missile is basically intact; its jacket appears to me to be intact, and I do not understand how it could possibly have left fragments in either of these locations.' At this point, then, there was no Single-Bullet Theory. Humes had given us vital information indicating that the bullet had exited from Kennedy's throat at high speed. The theory that the bullet then went through Connally's chest and wrist and then lodged in the governor's thigh would have to be checked out against his X rays, a suggestion Humes made. *The key lay in the size and weight of the metal fragments.* [Emphases added]
>
> We would later prove that Bullet 399 could indeed have passed through the president and then inflicted all of the governor's wounds. We would make the case partly by weighing Bullet 399 and the metal fragments taken from Connally's body. Together, the nearly whole bullet and the fragments weighed no more than an ordinary bullet.

COMMENT

1. As of the conclusion of Dr. Humes's testimony on March 16, there are two problems requiring resolution for the

emerging Single-Bullet Theory: (1) Photographic evidence and ballistics tests of the striking power of bullets; and (2) Composition and weight of bullet fragments. As of 2004, these problems remain unresolved because of conflicting opinions among equally credentialed experts.

2. Strangely, however, Arlen Specter does not believe the problems remain unresolved. Indeed, his memoir account conveys a decisive tone on page 82:

> Affirmation came initially during my questioning of Dr. Charles Gregory, the orthopedist who had treated Connally's wrist. I asked Gregory about the size and weight of the metal fragments. 'They would represent in lay terms flakes, flakes of metal,' he said. I asked the orthopedist to estimate the fragments' weight. 'It is something less than the weight of a postage stamp,' he said. Gregory, in answer to my questions, said it was indeed possible that Bullet 399 had passed through the governor's wrist and lodged in his thigh. Humes had never consulted Gregory about the fragments' minuscule weight.

This paragraph concludes Specter's account of the development of his Single-Bullet Theory in this chapter of his memoir. He devotes several paragraphs to anecdotal discussion of Kennedy's clothing, but nothing further about his formulation of the theory.

3. That closure in turn raises a question regarding the extraordinary language: "Affirmation came initially during my questioning of Dr. Charles Gregory, the orthopedist who had treated Connally's wrist":

Presumably, in this usage "affirmation" means simply a positive declaration by Dr. Gregory. And there is nothing improper about that. But when tied with "initially" there is the suggestion that Dr. Gregory was not alone in his affirmation. An interested observer may find it educative to pursue the following relevant sequence:

- On March 23, Arlen Specter deposed Dr. Gregory in Dallas. The testimony may be found at 6H 96-104. It reads in part:

Mr. Specter. Did you observe any foreign objects identifiable as bits of fragments or portions of a bullet missile?

Dr. Gregory. A preliminary X-ray had indicated that there were metallic fragments or at least metallic fragments which cast metallic shadows in the soft tissues around the wounded forearm. Two or three of these were identified and were recovered and observed to be metallic in consistency. These were turned over to appropriate authorities for further disposition.

S. Approximately how large were those fragments, Dr. Gregory?

G. I would judge that they were first—flat, rather thin, and that their greatest dimension would probably not exceed one-eighth of an inch. They were very small.

S. Would you have sufficient experience with gunshot wounds to comment as to whether a 6.5 mm. bullet could have passed through the Governor's wrist in the way you have described, leaving the fragments which you have described and still have virtually all the bullet missile intact, or *having 158 grains of a bullet at that time?* [Emphases added]

G. Well, I am not an expert on ballistics, but one cannot escape certain ballistic implications in this business.

. . . .

S. Would you have any idea at all as to what the fragments which you observed in the Governor's wrist might weigh, Doctor?

G. No, not really, but it would have been very small—very small. (98-99)

- On March 31, FBI Agent Robert A. Frazier testified as a firearms expert with training that included ballistics. He was examined by Assistant Counsel Melvin Eisenberg and gave testimony recorded at 3 H 390-441. It includes the following:

Mr. Eisenberg. Mr. Frazier, did you determine the weight of the exhibit—that is, 399?

Mr. Frazier. Yes, sir. Exhibit 399 weighs 158.6 grains.

E. How much weight loss does that show from the original weight?

F. We measured several bullets, and their weights varied, which is a normal situation, a portion of a grain, or two grains, from 161 grains—that is, they were all in the vicinity of 161 grains. One weighed—160.85, 161.5, 161.1.

E. In your opinion, was there any weight loss?

F. There did not necessarily have to be any weight loss to the bullet. There may be a slight amount of lead missing from the base of the bullet, since it is exposed at the base, and the bullet is slightly flattened; there could be a slight weight loss from the end of the bullet, but it would not amount to more than 4 grains, because 158.6 is only a grain and half less than the normal weight, and at least a 2 grain variation would be allowed. So it would be approximately 3 or 4 grains. (430)

As a firearms layman I lack expertise in ballistics, and defer to the future historians their evaluation of Frazier's data in the context in which he testified. But there is a chronology puzzlement that has nothing to do with ballistics expertise:

March 23: In the deposition of Dr. Gregory, Mr. Specter asks a question which alludes to the "magic bullet" weighing *158 grains* after passing through Governor Connally's wrist. (6H 98)

March 31: In his testimony given before the Commission, FBI agent Robert A. Frazier, the ballistics expert, stated that *158.6* grains is the weight of Exhibit 399, the "magic bullet" in Mr. Specter's Single-Bullet Theory. (3H 430)

Puzzlement: Where did Mr. Specter get the "*158*" number used in the Dr. Gregory deposition eight days prior to securing the *158.6* number from the FBI ballistics expert?

- On April 21, Dr. Gregory gave testimony before the Warren Commission. At that time he was examined by Assistant Counsel Arlen Specter, and gave testimony which may be found at 4H 117-129. It reads in part:

Mr. Specter. Will you continue to show what that X-ray shows with respect to metallic fragments, if any?

Dr. Gregory. Three shadows are identified as representing metallic fragments. There are other light shadows in this film which are identified or interpreted as being artifacts.

S. What is the basis of distinction between that which is artifact and that which is a real shadow of the metallic substance?

G. A real shadow of metallic substance persists and can be seen in other views, other X-ray copies, whereas artifacts which are produced by irregularities either in the film or film carrier will vary from one X-ray to another.

S. Is it your view that these other X-ray films led you to believe those are, in fact, metallic substances?

G. As a matter of fact, it is the mate to this very film, the lateral view marked "B" which shows the same three fragments in essentially the same relationship to the various levels of the forearm that leads me to believe that these do, in fact, represent metallic fragments.

S. Will you describe as specifically as you can what those metallic fragments are by way of size and shape, sir?

G. I would identify these fragments as varying from five-tenths of a millimeter in diameter to approximately 2 millimeters in diameter, and each fragment is no more than a half millimeter in thickness. They would represent in lay terms flakes, flakes of metal.

S. What would your estimate be as to weight in total?

G. I would estimate that they would be weighed in micrograms which is very small amount of weight. I don't know how to reduce it to ordinary equivalents for you. It is the kind of weighing that requires a microadjustable scale, which means that it is something less than the weight of a postage stamp. (120)

Dr. Gregory, by his declaration at the outset of his testimony, was not a ballistics expert. So, whether he was accurate in his dismissive remark concerning the weight of the bullet fragments ("something less than a postage stamp") must remain an unknown dependent upon his credibility as a witness in matters of weights and measures of postage stamps. I suggest for the historians that a meaningful comparative analysis of the weights of bullet fragments and postage stamps may ultimately depend on whether there is a standard size and weight of a postage stamp.

Be that as it may, it is difficult to leave Specter's account of the importance of Dr. Gregory's contribution to the Single-Bullet Theory without at least passing mention that other witnesses expressed varying degrees of agreement—and disagreement—with the opinions of Dr. Gregory. Indeed, there were two remarkable conferences held in Washington, the first on April 14, the second on April 21 (the same day that "affirmation" of Arlen Specter's Single-Bullet Theory emerged during the course of his taking Dr. Gregory's Commission testimony. That notion of "affirmation" takes on a somewhat extraordinary meaning in the context of the April 21 conference.

*   *   *

At this point I again express my indebtedness to Harold Weisberg, for inclusion, in his 1975 publication, *Post Mortem*, of documents relevant to my own writing. This time I am interested in two Memorandums For The Record written by Assistant Counsel Melvin Eisenberg on April 22. They may be seen in *Post Mortem*, 501-504.

(They may be seen in their entirety, but not fully read because of a serious problem of uneven legibility.)

- The subject of both addresses a critical problem of timing: "To determine which frames in the Zapruder movies show the impact of the first and second bullets". Present at the April 14 conference were:

Commander James J. Humes, Director of Laboratories of the Naval Medical School, Bethesda, Maryland;

Commander J. Thornton Boswell, Chief Pathologist, Naval Medical School, Bethesda, Maryland;

Lt. Col. Pierre A. Finck, Chief of Wound Ballistics Branch, Armed Forces Institute of Pathology;

Dr. F. W. Light, Jr., Deputy Chief of the Biophysics Division at Edgewood Arsenal, Maryland, and Chief of the Wound Assessment Division at Edgewood Arsenal; Messrs. Malley, Gauthier, Shaneyfelt, and two other unidentified agents of the FBI; Messrs. Kelley and Howlett of the Secret Service; and Messrs. Redlich, Specter, and Eisenberg of the Commission staff.

There is a roster of 11 paragraphs, lettered (a) through (k) constituting the "consensus of the meeting." My present interest is in (i) because of its asterisk footnote entry. The thrust of the paragraph is that Governor Connally could not have been hit in the back after Zapruder frame 236 because he was turned to his right and would have taken a bullet in the side rather than the back. The asterisk note reads: "Mr. Specter disagrees with this and feels the Governor was in a position to receive the chest wound up to 242."

• Present at the April 21 Conference were: Drs. Light, Olivier, Dolce;

Dr. Charles F. Gregory and Dr. Robert Shaw of Parkland Hospital, Dallas, Texas;

Messrs Gauthier, Shaneyfelt, and one other unidentified agent of the FBI; and

Messrs. Redlich, Specter, Belin and Eisenberg.

Later in the proceedings, Governor and Mrs. Connally, Mr. Rankin and Mr. McCloy joined the conference.

There is a roster of five paragraphs, (a) through (e) constituting the "consensus of the meeting." My present interest is in paragraph (b) because of its footnote entry. The paragraph reads:

After Governor Connally straightened up at frames 224-26 he started a turn to the right. As a result of this turn, at no time after frame 236 was Governor Connally in a position such that a bullet fired from the presumed site of the assassin would have caused the wound in the chest cavity which Governor Connally sustained—that is, after frame 236 the Governor presented a side view to the assassin rather than a back view. 1/ Mr. Specter disagrees.

I was surprised to read the final paragraph of Eisenberg's Memorandum of Record for the April 21 Conference:

In a discussion after the conference Drs. Light and Dolce expressed themselves as being very strongly of the opinion that Connally had been hit by two different bullets, principally on the ground that the bullet recovered from Connally's stretcher could not have broken his radius without having suffered more distortion. Dr. Olivier withheld a conclusion until he had the opportunity to make tests on animal tissue and bone with the actual rifle.

I am not aware of any writing—by any defender of the work of the Warren Commission and/or its *Report*—that may be regarded as a favorable review of Harold Weisberg's book, *Post Mortem*, which he published in 1975. But it seems difficult to believe that his critics could object to his reasonable observation regarding that paragraph:

> Of course it was nothing new that wound ballistics experts could not accept as fact that 399 had struck a wrist; it is common knowledge and experience that even jacketed bullets do not cause such substantial bone damage and suffer no distortion. All the expert testimony before the Commission was to this effect. (504)

Further, it seems even more difficult to believe that he had no basis for his provocative judgment suggestion, "But consider what this conference says of the Commission's investigation":

> —Dr. Dolce, who 'was very strongly of the opinion' that 399 'could not have' caused the wrist wound, was never called before the Commission;
> —Dr. Light, who agreed with Dr. Dolce, did testify before the Commission but was never asked why he felt 399 could not have wounded the wrist. In response to Specter's hypothetical question, Dr. Light indicated that the passage of a single bullet through the two victims was a possibility based on the circumstances outlined by Specter (e.g., that 399 was found on Connally's stretcher!) Specter even had the audacity to ask Light, 'And what

about that whole bullet [399] leads you to believe that the one bullet caused the President's neck wound and all of the wounds on Governor Connally?' Light's reply was polite but firm: 'Nothing about the bullet. Mainly the position in which they were seated in the automobile.' (5H 95) Thus, Dr. Light's expert opinion was kept carefully out of the record;

—Dr. Olivier's tests, in anticipation of which he withheld an opinion at this conference, produced nothing but mangled, distorted bullets (CEs 853, 856, 857). Specter never asked Olivier if 399 could have done what the official theory demands and emerged in such perfect condition;

—Nothing was done to investigate the suggestion of the wound ballistics experts that Connally might have been hit by 2 separate bullets, a possibility incompatible with the lone assassin finding. Particularly helpful in this area might have been the spectographic and NAA tests so carefully kept out of the record.

This memo takes criticism of Specter's Commission work out of the realm of 'Monday morning quarterbacking.' Specter *knew* the fatal flaws in his theory at the very time he was trying to build a record in support of that theory; he *knew* what scientific tests had to be done, which experts had to be called. He ignored the flaws, ignored the tests and ignored the experts and devised a solution to the crime he had to know was impossible. [Emphasis in original]

And can it be regarded as anything less than culpable that, with a record like this, especially a suppressed memo of a secret conference like this, the authors of the Report could write: 'All the evidence indicated that the bullet found on the Governor's stretcher could have caused all his wounds.'? (R95)

It may of course be argued that Weisberg had no basis for claiming *he* knew what Specter *knew*—and that point would be well taken. But it is difficult to fault Weisberg's suggestion for things to be considered. Indeed, there is an allied comment he made elsewhere in *Post Mortem*, that should have been repeated with emphasis in the context of the April 21 Conference. On page 84, in the context of bullet fragments from the magic bullet, he wrote: "There was the fragment Dr. Shires saw in the postoperative chest X-ray (which I think accounts for his never being asked to testify before the members of the Commission although he was the physician in charge of the Governor's case)."

The chronological sequence is fascinating:

- Dr. George T. Shires was the Chairman of the Department of Surgery at Parkland Hospital. At the time of the assassination he was attending a conference in Galveston, Texas. Flown to Dallas to supervise the treatment given Governor Connally, he performed the surgery on Connally's thigh wound.

On March 23, at *1635* hours, Arlen Specter took deposition testimony from Dr. Shires at Parkland Hospital. The deposition record may be found in 6H 104-113. The following exchange reads on page 111:

Mr. Specter. Do you have any knowledge as to what fragments there were in the chest, bullet fragments, if any?

Dr. Shires. No, again except for post-operative X-rays, there is a small fragment remaining, but the initial fragments I think Dr. Shaw saw before I arrived.

- Dr. Robert R. Shaw was Chief of Thoracic Surgery at Parkland Hospital. He performed the chest surgery on Governor Connally.

On March 23, at *1800* hours, Arlen Specter took deposition testimony from Dr. Shaw, at Parkland Hospital. The deposition record may be found at 6H 83-95. The following exchange reads on page 95:

> Mr. Specter. Did you find any fragments of bullets in his chest?
>
> Dr. Shaw. No; only fragments of shattered rib.

QUESTIONS

1. Why did Mr. Specter not ask Dr. Shaw the same question he had asked Dr. Shires? In the happening, nothing is resolved by way of Dr. Shaw being permitted to avoid X-ray evidence by way of Specter's equivocal question that may be understood to mean Shaw looked for something he didn't find.
2. When there is a conflict of testimony between equally credentialed witnesses, should one should be accorded more credibility than the other?
3. If the answer to that question is yes, on what basis should the credibility issue be resolved?
4. If, as is this case, there is a conflict between Dr. Shires's interpretation of post-operative X-rays and Dr. Shaw's declarative "No", which category of testimony should take precedence? And why?
5. I will argue that it is a fair inference to conclude that Arlen Specter's answer to the questions may be assumed by reason of:

    (a) His failure, in Doctor Shaw's deposition, to raise the issue generated by Dr. Shires's deposition—two hour earlier—allusion to post-operative X-rays;
    (b) His failure to call Dr. Shires as a witness before the Commission; and
    (c) His failure to acknowledge the conflicting testimony at the time of Dr. Shaw's Commission hearing, the practical effect of which was to deny the attendant Commissioners—Warren/Russell/Cooper/Boggs/

McCloy/Dulles—the opportunity to realize the existence of the credibility issue, and ask their own questions if they chose to resolve it?

I submit for the judgment of the future historians that such an inference is fair.

*   *   *

It is recalled that in the course of Dr. Humes's testimony, Commissioner Dulles expressed confusion concerning which stretcher—Kennedy's or Connally's—was the source of the bullet that has figured so prominently in the development of the Single-Bullet Theory. As Senator Specter indicated in his memoir account, at that time he promised: "We shall produce later, subject to sequential proof, evidence that the stretcher on which this bullet was found was the stretcher of Governor Connally." (80) Sixteen pages later, in his "Magic Bullet" chapter, he undertook to make good on the promise.

The first thing that caught my eye in reading the promise, was the expression, "sequential proof," which I immediately presumed to be an essential part of the promise. My first problem was that I didn't understand the meaning of *sequential* proof. Indeed, I had never seen or heard that term used before seeing Arlen Specter's use of it. Presuming it was a technical legal term, I checked *Black's Law Dictionary* for its meaning, only to learn that it was not in that reference, which identified 11 specific kinds of proof. Nor did I find it in three of the prominent conventional dictionaries: *Webster's New World Collegiate Dictionary*, the *Oxford English Dictionary*, *Webster's New Twentieth Century Unabridged*. I have asked lawyers, judges, and law enforcement persons if they can tell me what is "sequential proof"? None were able to do so. Inasmuch as I have neither seen nor heard it since reading Arlen Specter's use of it, I incline to believe it is a created "Specterism". Whatever the adjective, "sequential", may mean in Arlen Specter's usage, is beside the

more important question: What does he mean by proof? The
definition I find most appropriate in this context is taken from
Webster's New World Collegiate Dictionary, Fourth Edition, 1999,
1149: "Applies to facts, documents, etc. *that are so certain or
convincing as to demonstrate the validity of a conclusion beyond
reasonable doubt.*" [Emphases added] If that is Specter's meaning, it
but remains to see whether "the facts, documents, etc. are so certain
or convincing as to demonstrate the validity of his conclusion" that
Bullet 399 came from Governor Connally's stretcher.

*　　*　　*

Arlen Specter's March 16 promise to Commissioner Dulles—
he will produce "sequential proof" that Bullet 399 came from
Governor Connally's stretcher—entails his account of the deposition
of Darrell C. Tomlinson, whom Specter identifies as the "senior
engineer in charge of heating and air conditioning at Parkland." In
the happening, Tomlinson's important role on November 22 was to
provide manual operation of the emergency area elevator following
the arrival of the assassination victims at the hospital.

Following an informal "preparation" interview, Tomlinson's
March 20 testimony was taken on deposition by Arlen Specter.
Of the deposition, Specter states: "I went out of my way not to
lead Tomlinson or put words into his mouth, questioning the
engineer as carefully as possible. History was looking over my
shoulder." I urge the historians to take a long, attentive look
before rendering their judgments on his style of questioning the
engineer-turned-elevator operator on November 22.

There are four paragraphs devoted by Specter to Tomlinson.
The first reads in part:

> . . . Tomlinson got to the elevator at around 1:00
> p.m. and saw a stretcher in the elevator. He wheeled the
> stretcher off the elevator and put it up against the south
> wall of the ground floor. Another stretcher was resting
> about two feet from the wall. (96)

COMMENT

1. I am not certain what Specter means when he says "put it up against the south wall." Regardless of that, at the request of Specter, Tomlinson drew a diagram of what he called the "elevator lobby" in the emergency treatment area of the hospital. This diagram appears at 2H 673 of the Warren Commission records. It is noted that Assistant Counsel Specter made no criticism of the diagram at the time of the deposition. The diagram focused on the area of (1) the elevator entry on the north wall, (2) the hallway, and (3) the south wall opposite the elevator entry.

   Note! Tomlinson's deposition does not indicate that Specter had any objections to either the scheme or the information in the diagram.

2. The "another stretcher" resting "about two feet from the wall" was parallel with the south wall. The diagram marked that stretcher as "B". It was blocking a south wall entry to a Men's Restroom.

3. The stretcher removed from the elevator was marked "A". It was positioned parallel with the south wall next to Stretcher "B".

4. There are no scale measurements on the diagram. But if Stretcher B was, as Specter says, "about two feet from the wall," then Stretcher A was also about two feet from the wall. In turn, that raises again the question of what Specter meant when he said the stretcher taken from the elevator (A) was "put up against the south wall".

The second paragraph is the action paragraph:

'An intern or a doctor, I didn't know which, came to use the men's room there in the elevator lobby.' Tomlinson said. 'He pushed the stretcher [B] out from the wall to get in, and then when he came out, he just walked off and didn't push the stretcher back up against the wall, so

I pushed it out of the way where we would have clear area in front of the elevator.'

'Where did you push it to,' I asked.

'I pushed it back up against the wall,' Tomlinson said.

'What if anything happened then?' I asked.

'I bumped the wall,' Tomlinson said, 'and a spent cartridge or bullet rolled out that apparently had been lodged under the edge of the mat.'

The third paragraph introduces Specter's problem:

I was surprised. I had talked to Tomlinson briefly [the 'preparation'] before going on the record, as I did with all the witnesses, to organize the testimony for a more orderly presentation. Not only had Tomlinson told me a short time earlier that the bullet had come from the stretcher that he had wheeled off the elevator, but he'd said the same thing to the Secret Service. Now he was saying he wasn't certain whether the bullet came from Connally's stretcher or from the stretcher next to it.

This paragraph also introduces three interrelated problems for the historians' future judgments:

1. When Specter says "Not only had Tomlinson told me a short time earlier that the bullet had come from the stretcher that he wheeled off the elevator . . ." he is silently switching the locations of the two stretchers from their positions on the diagram constructed by Tomlinson— to which Specter had not made any objection.

2. When Specter says "but he'd said the same thing to the Secret Service," there is no foundation to establish that Specter's "preparation" of his witness had included any mention of a Secret Service interview that Specter is introducing into the deposition.

3. There is no time orientation for Specter's "now" in the "Now he was saying he wasn't certain whether the bullet came from Connally's stretcher or from the stretcher next to it."

Note! The further Specter goes with his account of the Tomlinson deposition, the more apparent it becomes that "sequential proof" has many unexpected turns in an increasingly convoluted sequence of self-serving questions.

The fourth paragraph is the "history" paragraph introduced in an earlier context:

> I went out of my way not to lead Tomlinson or to put words in his mouth, questioning the engineer as carefully as possible. History was looking over my shoulder. Tomlinson had marked on a diagram the locations of the two stretchers, labeled A and B, and their distances from the elevator. I gently asked, 'Now, Mr. Tomlinson, are you sure that it was stretcher A that you took off the elevator and not stretcher B?" After a lengthy exchange, Tomlinson said, 'Well, we talked about taking a stretcher off the elevator, but when it comes down on an oath, I wouldn't say for sure. I really don't remember.' (96-97)

And that is the end of Senator Specter's year 2000 account of his deposition of witness Darrell Tomlinson on March 20, 1964.

COMMENT

1. I repeat here my urging that historians take a "long, attentive look before rendering their judgments on his style of questioning the engineer-turned-elevator operator."
2. When Senator Specter wrote his memoir account of service on the Warren Commission, he should have been more

concerned with the *historians* as opposed to *history* looking over his shoulder. For the likelihood is high that the future historians will examine carefully his deposition of Tomlinson. And when it is remembered that Tomlinson was not accompanied by legal counsel in the proceeding, it is difficult to believe historians will be impressed by this mismatch in which an unsuspecting, increasingly confused witness was manipulated by an accomplished prosecutor's calculatedly clever questioning. I submit for their consideration that Arlen Specter gave new meaning to the adverb, "gently", when he said: "I gently asked, 'Mr. Tomlinson, are you sure that it was stretcher A that you took out of the elevator and not stretcher B?"

3. It is noted, and should be remembered, that the answer to Mr. Specter's question followed a presumably contextual orientation link—"After a lengthy exchange"—between the question and the forthcoming answer from Tomlinson. In the happening, such was not exactly so.

4. Indeed, when the future historians do evaluate Senator Specter's unreferenced/uncited account of the Tomlinson deposition they will probably be surprised by what they will learn when it is compared with the deposition recorded in 6H 128-134:

    -   On *page 131*, Assistant Counsel Mr. Specter asks the now-familiar question: "Mr. Tomlinson, are you sure that it was stretcher A that you took off the elevator and not stretcher B?" *The record answer reads:* "Well, really, I can't be positive, just to be perfectly honest about it, I can't be positive because I really didn't pay that much attention to it. The stretcher was on the elevator and I pushed it off there and I believe we made one or two calls before I straightened out the stretcher against the wall."
    -   Senator Specter, writing 36 years later in his memoir, *Passion for Truth*, follows that now-familiar-question

with: "After a lengthy exchange, Tomlinson said, 'Well, we talked about taking a stretcher off the elevator, but when it comes right down on an oath, I wouldn't say for sure. I really don't remember.'"

Whatever he may have meant by "After a lengthy exchange," Senator Specter's account is very misleading if he intends to convey as fact that Tomlinson's answer was given in direct answer to the *page 131* question.

• In the happening, following the *page 131* question, the record shows a total of 23 Q&A exchanges before Tomlinson gave the answer on record *page 132* as it appears in the memoir account linked to the page 131 question. But by the time of the answer on *page 132*, the 23 Q&A exchanges have introduced an entirely new contextual orientation neither mentioned nor hinted at prior to the *page 131* question.

The 8th through 12th of the Q&A exchanges read on pages *131-132*:

Mr. Specter. Now, just before we started this deposition, before I placed you under oath and before the court reporter started to take down my questions and your answers, you and I had a brief talk, did we not.

Mr. Tomlinson. Yes, sir.

S. And we discussed in a general way the information which you have testified about, did we not?

T. Yes, sir.

S. And at the time we started our discussion, it was your recollection at that point that *the bullet came off of stretcher A*, was it not? [Emphases added]

T. *B*. [Emphases added]

S. Pardon me, stretcher B, but it was stretcher A that you took off the elevator.

T. I believe that's right.

S. But there is no question but that at the time we started our discussion a few minutes before the court reported started to take it down, that your best recollection was that it was stretcher A which came off the elevator?

T. I believe that it was—yes.

COMMENT

1. It is remembered that just four days prior to this deposition of Tomlinson on March 20, Specter had promised Commissioner Dulles "evidence that the stretcher on which this bullet was found was the stretcher of Governor Connally."

2. Evidently, Specter's first step in that direction was taken in the "preparation" interview with Tomlinson, who quickly corrected him:

    S. And at the time we started our discussion, it was your recollection at that point that *the bullet came off of stretcher A*, was it not? [Emphases added]

    T. *B*. [Emphases added]

    S. Pardon me, stretcher B, but it was stretcher A that you took off the elevator.

    T. I believe that's right.

3. The next step in developing "sequential proof" was another inquiry between the *page 131* inquiry and its answer on *page 132*.

    It began with a question whether Tomlinson had ever been interviewed by "any other Federal representative, to which he answered that he had been interviewed by the FBI in late November, and the Secret Service in early December. Then followed this specific inquiry in the 22nd Q&A exchange:

    S. What did the Secret Service man ask you about?

T. Approximately the same thing [about the stretchers], only, we've gone into more detail here.

S. What did you tell the Secret Service man about which stretcher you took off of the elevator.

T. I told him that I was not sure, and I am not—I'm not sure of it, but as I said, I would be going against the oath which I took a while ago, because I am definitely not sure.

[Note! Tomlinson's "I told him that I was not sure" obviously refers to what Tomlinson told the Secret Service man, whereas "but as I said, I would be going against the oath I took a while ago" must be understood as being what Tomlinson said to Specter. "Must be" for the simple reason that Secret Service interviews were not depositions under oath, as was the case with the sworn testimony in the Specter-Tomlinson deposition.]

The next Q&A exchange [on *page 133*]—the 23rd since Specter asked the original question: "Now, Mr. Tomlinson, are you sure that it was stretcher 'A' that you took out of the elevator and not stretcher 'B'?" is what generated the answer to that question on page *131*:

S. Do you remember if you told the Secret service man which stretcher you thought you took off the elevator?

T. *Well, we talked about taking a stretcher off of the elevator, but when it comes down on an oath, I wouldn't say for sure, I really don't remember.*

NOTE

1. Again, Tomlinson's "we talked" obviously refers to Tomlinson and the Secret Service man, whereas "but when it comes down on an oath, I wouldn't say for sure" must be understood as being what Tomlinson is saying to Specter.

2. I submit this for the consideration of the future historians:
   The only way the answer makes sense to me is by dividing
   the answer into two parts to mean: (1) "we, the Secret service
   interviewer and I, Tomlinson, talked, while I was not under
   oath, about taking a stretcher off the elevator" and (2) "but,
   when it comes down to talking with you, Mr. Specter, under
   oath, I wouldn't say for sure, because I really don't remember
   it well enough to declare it positively on oath."

3. Whether that hypothetical interpretation of the question and
   answer exchange is reasonable is a matter for the future
   historians to decide. What seems indisputable is that Assistant
   Counsel Arlen Specter took advantage of a deposition style
   that would be unrealistic in the discovery process of civil law
   procedure. The Warren Commission depositions took place
   without legal counsel available for the deponent. In this
   Specter/Tomlinson deposition, the result was predictable
   confusion generated by repetition. The following example is
   instructive:

> S: And at the time we started our discussion, it was
>   your recollection at that point that the bullet came
>   off stretcher A, was it not?
> T: B.
> S. Pardon me, stretcher B, but it was stretcher A that
>   you took off the elevator.
> T. I believe that's right. (6H 131)
> . . . .
> S. Now, before I started to ask you questions under
>   oath, which have been taken down here, I told you,
>   did I not, that the Secret Service man wrote a report
>   where he said that the bullet was found on the
>   stretcher which you took off the elevator—I called
>   that to your attention, didn't I?
> T. Yes; you told me that.
> S. Now, after I tell you that, does that have any effect

on refreshing your recollection of what you told the Secret service man?

T.   No; it really doesn't; it really doesn't.

S.   So, would it a fair summary to say that when I first started to talk to you about it, your first view was that the stretcher you took off the elevator was stretcher A, and when I told you that the Secret Service man said it was—that you had said the stretcher you took off the elevator was the one that you found the bullet off, and when we talked about the whole matter and talked over the entire situation, you really can't be completely sure about which stretcher you took off the elevator, because you didn't push the stretcher that you took off the elevator right against the wall at first?

T.   That's right.

S.   And there was a lot of confusion that day, which is what you told me before?

T.   Absolutely. And, now, honestly, I don't remember telling him definitely—I know we talked about it, and I told him that it could have been. Now, he might have drawed his own conclusion on that. (6H 133)

. . . .

S.   You got the stretcher from where the bullet came from, whether it was brought down from the second floor?

T.   It could have been—I'm not sure that it was A I took off.

S.   But did you tell the Secret Service man which one you took off the elevator?

T.   I'm not clear on that—whether I absolutely made a positive statement to that effect.

S.   You told him it could have been B that you took off the elevator?

T. That's right.

S. But you don't remember whether you told him that it was A you took off of the elevator?

T. I think it was A—I'm not really sure.

S. Which did you tell the Secret Service agent—that you thought it was A that you took off of the elevator?

T. Really, I couldn't be real truthful in saying I told him this or that.

S. You just don't remember for sure whether you told him you thought it was A or not?

T. No, sir; I really don't remember. I'm not accustomed to being questioned by the Secret Service and the FBI and by you and they are writing down everything I mean.

S. That's all right. I understand exactly what you are staying and I appreciate it and I really just want to get your best recollection. We understand it isn't easy to remember all that went on, on a day like November 22, and that a man's recollection is not perfect like every other part of a man, but I want you to tell me just what you remember, and that's the best you can do today, and I appreciate that, and so does the President's Commission, and that's all we can ask of a man.

T. Yes, I'm going to tell you all I can, and I'm not going to tell you something I can't lay down and sleep at night with either. (133-134)

COMMENT

1. Whether defenders of the Warren Commission and its *Report* will be inclined to support my contention that Arlen Specter's inquisitorial style must bear heavy responsibility for contributing to Darrell Tomlinson's confusion, is irrelevant to one unchanging reality. Tomlinson Exhibit No. 2, Tomlinson's diagram of the elevator area, with its locations

of Stretchers A and B, and the men's room in location to the stretchers, was accepted without challenge by Specter, and appears as part of the Commission record in Volume XXI of its Hearings. If the future historians accept the authenticity of that Exhibit, it is difficult to imagine on what basis they can endorse the Warren *Report*'s finding: "Although Tomlinson was not certain whether the bullet came from the Connally stretcher or the adjacent one, the Commission has concluded that the bullet came from the Governor's stretcher." (WR 81)

2. Indeed, one can only wonder whether Commissioner Dulles—or any other member of the Warren Commission would have regarded this deposition testimony as the "sequential proof" promised four days earlier by Assistant Counsel Arlen Specter.

One can also but wonder whether this account would have put to rest Dulles' original confusion over whether the bullet had come from President Kennedy's stretcher. Specter's account provides two relevant sentences for what he may have meant as "sequential proof": "After Kennedy was in his casket, the sheets from his stretcher were gathered and placed in a linen hamper. *The stretcher was then wheeled over to Trauma Room 2. Kennedy's stretcher was never near the area where Tomlinson found the bullet.*" [Emphasis added] (97)

COMMENT

If that emphasized sentence *was* intended as part of a "sequential proof", it is a vulnerable proffer. In the November 1964 Parkland Hospital floor plan, Trauma Room 1, in which Kennedy was treated is directly across the hallway from Trauma Room 2 into which the Kennedy stretcher was wheeled following the removal of the sheets. And that hallway was the same hallway that had the elevator lobby where Tomlinson's diagram locates the stretchers. And since there is no way of knowing whether either/both stretcher(s) were eventually relocated for cleaning purposes, there is no way of knowing whether Kennedy's stretcher was subsequently taken to the area of the same elevator that had been used for Connally's stretcher.

This observation is not intended as support for any argument on behalf of the possibility that Bullet 399 came from Kennedy's stretcher. It merely points out the absurdity of rejecting such an argument on the basis of the claim that "Kennedy's stretcher was never near the area where Tomlinson found the bullet." However close—or distant—a measurement may have established the proximity of the stretchers, it is better left to the future historians to determine whether Specter's "never near" claim supports his contention that "We proved that the bullet could not have come from Kennedy's stretcher".

CHAPTER VIII

BEDLAM

The eighth chapter in Senator Specter's memoir, *Passion for Truth*, is titled "Bedlam." As his account indicates, that was the word aptly selected by Dr. Malcolm Perry to describe the scene in which he participated in a press conference held at Parkland Hospital within hours following the death of President Kennedy on November 22, 1963. In its most innocuous sense, *Webster's New World Collegiate Dictionary*, Fourth Edition, 1999, 129, defines its third meaning of "bedlam" as "any place or condition of noise and confusion." But a clear distinction must be made and maintained between "Parkland Hospital" and "the press conference held at Parkland Hospital." For, while Specter is properly critical of the lack of control by the organizers of the conference, he is generously supportive of the professional performance of the personnel in attendance during the emergency treatment rendered Kennedy and Governor Connally that tragic day. His second paragraph (in a total of 27) reads:

> Parkland's medical and professional staff were not immune to the drama that swept the hospital. 'Certainly, everyone was emotionally affected,' said Dr. Charles Carrico, a resident in general surgery who was the first to treat the wounded president. From all indications, Parkland's medical effort was superb. 'I think, if anything, the emotional aspect made us think faster, work faster and better,' Carrico said. (99)

Similarly, the first two sentences of the fourth paragraph do not convey a condition of confusion:

> Although the president's condition was clearly hopeless, the Parkland doctors made every conceivable, desperate effort to save him. They followed the ABCs of treatment: Airway. Breathing, Circulation. (99)

Inaptly, however, it is somewhat disappointing to read a tone of needless negativism in Specter's writing that appears at the bottom of the chapter's second page:

> But the Parkland examination was so cursory that the doctors did not even turn Kennedy over. They never saw the bullet entrance wounds in the back of his head and the back of his neck. The Parkland doctors saw only the exit wounds: the small hole on the front of Kennedy's neck and the large wound on the right side of the head. (100)

COMMENT

1. Regarding "They never saw the bullet entrance [wound . . . in] the back of his neck": As I so tediously demonstrated in Chapter VII above, the conclusion that President Kennedy's back/neck wound was an entrance wound has never been more than a speculative *inference* generated by the autopsy doctors sometime following the completion of the autopsy. And it will be recalled that what the paperwork identified as a "full autopsy" never included dissection of the neck in an effort to establish the path of the bullet.
2. Similarly, regarding "The Parkland doctors saw only the exit [wound]: the small hole on the front of Kennedy's neck . . .": The conclusion that the throat wound was an exit wound was merely the reciprocal *inference* generated by the autopsy doctors following the completion of the autopsy. A tit for

tat would merely observe that the autopsy doctors never saw what they identify as an exit wound.

3. If Senator Specter intended to write a memoir account devoid of references/citations for premises in his Single-Bullet Theory, he was perfectly free to do so. But when he chooses to declare as proven conclusions, what are merely self-serving inferences of his choice, he should be expected to support the argument by way of references/ citations.

* * *

Senator Specter's year 2000 memoir account recognizes clearly the indebtedness of 1964 Assistant Counsel Arlen Specter to autopsy surgeon, Dr. James J. Humes for the first leg of the "Magic Bullet" journey. Indeed, without Humes's inference that the throat wound was an exit wound, there can be no such thing as a Single-Bullet Theory. With that awareness, it is not surprising that the Senator's "historical lens" in "Bedlam" is generally distorted, even as that lens is not generally focused on Dr. Humes. Two paragraphs on page 101 in *Passion for Truth* demonstrate the point. The first reads:

> The Parkland doctors saw the clean, round quarter-inch hole in the front of the president's neck but didn't know about the wound in the back. It was a natural first thought, for some of them, that the hole in the president's throat might be an entry wound, since they knew of no other way the bullet might have entered his body. Dr. Ronald Jones's report, filed on the day of the assassination, stated that the hole in the front of the president's neck was 'thought to be a bullet entrance wound.'

COMMENT

1. Regarding "The Parkland doctors saw the clean, round quarter-inch hole in the font of the president's neck, but didn't

know about the wound in the back": This is a non sequitur remark. Whether they knew or did not know there was a hole in the back is irrelevant to their first impression—based on routine experience with gunshot wounds. That impression—gained from observation of the characteristics of the wound—suggested to them it was an entrance wound.

Curiously, there is no identification of the doctors who *saw* "the clean, round quarter-inch hole in the front of the president's neck," nor is there any indication *when* they reportedly saw it.

2. Regarding "It was a natural first thought, for some of them, that the hole in the president's throat might be an entry wound, since they knew of no other way the bullet might have entered his body": One can but wonder what is the basis for Senator Specter's observation about a "natural first thought, for some of them"?

In the Warren *Report*'s Appendix VIII, titled "Medical Reports From Doctors at Parkland Memorial Hospital, Dallas, Tex.", there are individual statements—each signed and dated November 22, 1963—of Drs. Charles J. Carrico, Malcolm O. Perry, Charles H. Baxter, Kemp Clark, Robert McClelland, F. Bashour, and M. T. Jenkins, included as Commission Exhibit 392, which appear on pages 519-528.

Those doctors' statements appear in the order of their listing herein. Dr. Carrico's relevant entry reads: "Two external wounds were noted. One small penetrating wound of ant. neck in lower 1/3." Dr. Perry's relevant entry reads: "A small wound was noted in the midline of the neck, in the lower third anteriorly." Dr. Baxter's comment reads: "The president had a wound in the mid-line of the neck." Dr. Clark's statement makes no reference to a throat wound. Dr. McClelland's account mentions "a fragment wound of the trachea." Dr. Jenkins makes a passing remark that "there was also obvious tracheal and chest damage." It is difficult to understand how Senator Specter translated these statements into his unreferenced/uncited judgment that "It was a natural first thought, for some of them, that the hole in the president's throat might be an entry wound, since they knew of no other way the bullet might have entered his body".

Note! Beyond Dr. Kemp Clark's statement, which includes the date "22 Nov 1963", there is also a time reference, which reads "1415 hrs." And Dr. Perry's statement includes "1630 hrs 22 Nov 1963." So, it is quite possible that Specter's allusion to "natural first thought" may refer to remarks attributed to them in a press conference held earlier that afternoon. Further comment on that press conference is deferred for presentation below.

3. Regarding "Dr. Ronald Jones's report, filed on the day of the assassination, stated that the hole in the front of the president's neck was 'thought to be a bullet entrance wound.'": Because there is something very special about this report, it is surprising that Senator Specter would include even passing mention of in his memoir. It is very special for these reasons:

    • It is not included with the statements of the others that appear as CE 392 in the 28 pages of Appendix VIII the Warren *Report*.
    • Rather, there *is* a written statement signed by Dr. Jones that may be found in Volume XX of the Commission Hearings, on page 333. This statement, stamped **TOP SECRET**, is dated 11-23-63, and has an identification mark "37a". There is no indication whether the date refers to the signed statement, or to the classification. Nor is there the time it was written. This document, is titled "Jones (Dr. Ronald C.) Exhibit No. 1". There is nothing to indicate if and when this statement was ever declassified.
    • The full sentence from which Specter quoted, reads: "Previously described severe skull and [illegible word; subsequently, in his March 24 deposition of Dr. Jones, Specter's reading identified this word as "brain"] was

noted as well as a small hole in anterior midline of neck thought to be a bullet entrance wound."

4. Absent explanation from Specter himself, it is not clear why this document was given a Top Secret security classification. Dr. Jones was not called as a witness before the Commission. However, a careful reading of his deposition testimony taken by Mr. Specter on March 24 may help us understand why he (Specter) might not have wanted a repeat performance before the Commission. This testimony may be read in its entirety in 6H 51-57. Beginning with the statement under consideration, it reads in part:

Mr. Specter. Did you observe any wounds?
Dr. Jones. As we saw him the first time, we noticed that he had a small wound in the midline of the neck, just above the suprasternal notch, and this was probably no greater than a quarter of an inch in its greatest diameter, and that he had a large wound in the right posterior side of the head.
S. When you say "we noticed," whom do you mean by that?
J. Well, Dr. Perry and I were the two that were there at this time observing.
S. Did Dr. Perry make any comment about the nature of the wound at that time? Either wound?
J. Not that I recall. (53)
. . . .
S. Will you describe as precisely as you can the wound in the throat?
J. The wound in the throat was probably no larger than a quarter of an inch in diameter. There appeared to be no powder burn present, although this could have been masked by the amount of blood that was on the head and neck, although there was no obvious amount of powder present. There appeared to be a

very minimal amount of disruption of interruption of the surrounding skin. There appeared to be relatively smooth edges around the wound, and if this occurred as a result of a missile, you would probably have thought it was a missile of very low velocity and probably could have been compatible with a bone fragment of either—probably exiting from the neck, but it was a very small, smooth wound.

S. Did you notice any lump in the throat area?

J. No, I didn't.

S. Was there any blood on the throat area in the vicinity of the wound which you have described of the throat?

J. Not a great deal of blood, as if in relation to the amount that was around the head—not too much. (54)

Eventually, Specter got around to asking his critical question concerning the anterior neck wound:

S. What led you to the thought that it was a bullet entrance wound, sir?

J. *The hole was very small and relatively clean cut, as you would see in a bullet that was entering rather than exiting from a patient. If this were an exit wound, you would think that it exited at a very low velocity to produce no more damage than this had done, and if this were a missile of high velocity, you would expect more of an explosive type of exit wound, with more tissue destruction than this appeared to have on superficial examination.* [Emphases added]

S. Would it be consistent, then, with an exit wound, but of low velocity, as you put it?

J. Yes; of very low velocity to the point that you might think that this bullet barely made it through the soft tissues and just enough to drop out of the skin on the opposite side. (55)

With that response, Mr. Specter shifted his attention to Dr. Jones's credentials:

S. What is your experience, Doctor, if any, in the treatment of bullet wounds?

J. During our residency here we have approximately 1 complete year out of the 4 years on the trauma service here, and this is in addition to the 2 months that we spend every other day and every other night in the emergency room during our first year, so that we see a tremendous number of bullet wounds here in that length of time, sometimes as many as four or five a night.

S: Have you ever had any formal training in bullet wounds?

J. No.

S. Have you ever had occasion to observe a bullet wound which was inflicted by a missile at approximate size of a 6.5 mm. bullet which passed [56] through the body of a person and exited from a neck without striking anything but soft tissue from the back through the neck, the missile came from a weapon of a muzzle velocity of 2,000 feet per second, and the victim was in the vicinity of 160 to 250 feet from the weapon?

J. No; I have not seen a missile of this velocity exit in the anterior portion of the neck. I have seen it in other places of the body, but not in the neck.

S. What other places in the body have you seen it, Dr. Jones?

J. I have seen it in the extremity and here it produces a massive amount of soft tissue destruction.

S. Is that in a situation of struck bone or not struck bone or what?

J.   Probably where it has struck bone.

S.   In a situation where it strikes bone, however, the bone
     becomes so to speak a secondary missile, does it not,
     in accentuating the soft tissue damage?

J.   Yes.

The next question area is surprising because Mr. Specter invites
a Parkland doctor to undertake speculation, something which, as
will be seen below, is not a routine methodology he used with a
Parkland doctor.

S.   Dr. Jones, did you have any speculative thought as
     to accounting for the point of wounds which you
     observed on the President, as you thought about it
     when you were treating the President that day, or
     shortly thereafter?

J.   With no history as to the number of times that the
     President had been shot or knowing the direction
     from which he had been shot, and seeing the wound
     in the midline of the neck, and what appeared to be
     an exit wound in the posterior portion of the skull,
     the only speculation that I could have as far as how
     this could occur with a single wound would be that it
     would enter the anterior neck and possibly strike a
     vertebral body and then change its course and exit in the
     region of the posterior portion of the head. However,
     this was—there was some doubt that a missile that
     appeared to be of this high velocity would suddenly
     change its course by striking, but at the present—at that
     time, if I accounted for it on the basis of one shot, that
     would have been the way I accounted for it.

S.   And would that account take into consideration the
     extensive damage done to the top of the President's
     head?

J.   If this were the course of the missile, probably—
     possibly could have accounted for it, although I would

possibly expect it to do a tremendous amount of damage to the vertebral column that it hit and if this were a high velocity missile would also think that the entrance wound would probably be larger than the one that was present at the time we saw it.

S. Did you observe whether or not there was any damage to the vertebral column?

J. No, we could not see this.

S. Did you discuss this theory with any other doctor or doctors?

J. Yes; this as discussed after the assassination.

S. With whom?

J. With Dr. Perry—is the only one that I recall specifically, and that was merely as to how many times the President was shot, because even immediately after death, within a matter of 30 minutes, the possibility of a second gunshot wound was entertained and that possibly he had been shot more than once.

COMMENT: I

1. Regarding the sequence of Specter's questions—

Q. When you say "we noticed" whom do you mean by that?

A. Well, Dr. Perry and I were the two that were there at this time observing.

Q. Did Dr. Perry make any comment about the nature of the wound at that time" Either wound?

A. Not that I recall—

It will be remembered that Mr. Specter took this deposition of Dr. Jones on March 24 at 10:20 a.m. (6H 51) The sequence of scheduled depositions prepared for Specter by the Parkland Hospital Administrator called for the depositions of the two

Parkland surgeons, Drs. Carrico and Perry, starting at 9:30 a.m., on March 25. One can only wonder whether he had any apprehensions for an impending sworn testimony interview with Dr. Perry along lines of conversation Perry may have had with Dr. Jones on November 22.

2. Regarding Specter's question "What led you to the thought that it was a bullet entrance wound?": Dr. Jones's first comment was the typical medical evaluation: "The hole was very small and relatively clean cut, as you would see in a bullet that was entering rather than exiting from a patient." But his second comment could not have been for Arlen Specter on March 24 a welcome lecture on ballistics:

> If this were an exit wound, you would think that it exited at a very low velocity to produce no more damage than this had done, and if this were a missile of high velocity, you would expect more of an explosive type of exit wound, with more tissue destruction than this appeared to have on superficial examination. (55)

And with the advantage of hindsight, one can only wonder if the answer to his next question served only to deepen the evidence hole in which Specter found himself:

Q. Would it be consistent, then, with an exit wound, but of low velocity, as you put it?

A. Yes; of very low velocity to the point that you might think that this bullet barely made it through the soft tissues and just enough to drop out of the skin on the opposite side.

COMMENT: II.

1. When it is remembered that Specter's schedule for March 25 called for depositions from Parkland Drs. Carrico and Dr.

Perry, it is a reasonable presumption that his first objective was to get agreement from them with the March 15 conclusion of the autopsy doctors that the anterior throat wound was an exit wound. If such were so—and indeed that objective was at least partially secured (as will be demonstrated below) on March 25—the phenomenon of the "**TOP SECRET**" classification of Dr. Jones's November 22 statement becomes more understandable. It was a prudential move either by or on behalf of Arlen Specter in the development of his Single-Bullet Theory. Stated differently, Arlen Specter did not need any more Parkland doctors (following Dr. Jones) concerning themselves with matters of ballistics, when all that was really needed from them was corroboration of Dr. Humes's trajectory conclusion.

2. There remain several curiosity questions relating to that classified statement of Dr. Jones:

- Who decided, and on what basis, that Dr. Jones's statement was not included in the Warren *Report*'s Appendix VIII, which included the statements of eight doctors who had attended President Kennedy?
- Who had authority to assign security classification to a Warren Commission document?
- Who had authority to declassify Warren Commission documents?

Those questions of security classification are prompted by the presumption that a document written/signed/classified on/near November 22/23, 1963 must have been declassified by September, 1964 for its inclusion in Volume XX of the documents which accompanied release of the Warren *Report* to the public. Strangely, however, there is no notice of declassification on the document. Apparently whatever apprehensions warranted the classification had disappeared within six months.

*   *   *

Senator Specter's skill as a wordsmith is demonstrated no better than in the paragraph immediately following his account of that puzzling report of Dr. Jones. He wrote:

> Questions and charges have sprouted over apparent inconsistencies between the Parkland doctors' observations and the autopsy surgeons' findings. If the Parkland doctors had turned Kennedy over and seen the entrance wound, those questions would never have been raised. Once the Parkland doctors were informed of the wounds on the back of the president's head and neck, their findings were consistent with the autopsy report. They all independently concluded that the wound on the front of the president's neck could have been caused by a high-velocity *exiting* bullet. Why, then, did the Parkland doctors not turn the president over when he was in Trauma Room 1 and see for themselves?

COMMENT:

1. Without examples, it is virtually impossible to distinguish "apparent inconsistencies" from whatever else is / may be meant by unqualified "inconsistencies".
2. Without examples, If "findings" is understood to be "the acts of one who finds," it is virtually impossible to know whether there were inconsistencies between the two sets of doctors.
3. Regarding "If the Parkland doctors had turned Kennedy over and seen the entrance wound, those questions would never have been raised.": It depends on what are the questions that would never have been raised. "If" and "never" are not necessarily complementary necessities.

4. Regarding "Once the Parkland doctors were informed of the wounds on the back of the president's head and neck, their findings were consistent with the autopsy report.": This is misleading for two reasons:

    *   It implies that "the Parkland doctors" knew nothing about a wound on the back of the president's head, whereas the statements of Drs. Carrico/Perry/Baxter/ Clark/McClelland/Jenkins, which appear in Commission Exhibit 392, indicate their awareness of a head wound at the time emergency treatment was given Kennedy in Parkland Hospital.
    *   Whatever may be meant by "their findings", the consistency of the Parkland doctors with the autopsy report was generated in their March 30 Commission testimony by way of Arlen Specter's compound assumptions, one of which—the trajectory angle of the "Magic Bullet"—was later abandoned by way of the FBI's May 24 reenactment of the assassination.
    *   Regarding "They [the Parkland doctors] all independently concluded that the wound on the front of the president's neck could have been caused by a high-velocity *exiting* bullet.": Not *all* the Parkland doctors so concluded. Dr. Ronald Jones's March 24 deposition testimony is recalled:

    If this were an exit wound, you would think that it exited at a very low velocity to produce no more damage than this had done, and if this were a missile of high velocity, you would expect more of an explosive type of exit wound, with more tissue destruction than this appeared to have on superficial examination.

5. The last sentence in the paragraph is puzzling: "Why, then, did the Parkland doctors not turn the president over when he was in Trauma Room 1 and see for themselves?"

- If understood as a genuine question that might reasonably be raised by some one unfamiliar with the reason, Specter's answer conveys a sympathetic stance:

    After the president died, the Parkland doctors felt they had no business making any further examination, especially given the official aura that engulfed Trauma Room 1. The [Secret Service] agents asked the Parkland crew to wrap up as quickly as possible and clear the room. (101)

- If understood as conveying a tone of criticism for a step not taken, Specter's answer is equally sympathetic on grounds of professionalism: "The Parkland doctors had every right to expect that an autopsy would include the thorough examination that was beyond the scope of their work." (102)

*   *   *

The last section in this chapter of Specter's memoir account focuses on the press conferences that followed the assassination. It is unlikely that any aspect of the literature of the John F. Kennedy assassination has generated more frustrating debate than the claims and counterclaims of what was said and not said in the press conference held at Parkland Hospital in mid-afternoon on Friday, November 22.

From the perspective of Senator Specter, writing in his memoir, *Passion for Truth*, published in 2000, we are told:

    Reporters stormed Parkland. At the first press conference, Perry and Clark fielded questions. Before one could be answered, another would be fired. Many of the questions called for the doctors to speculate on the direction of the bullets, the number of bullets, and the exact cause of death. (102)

Somewhat more specifically, he adds that in the first Friday press conference,

> Perry told reporters it was possible that the president's wounds were caused by one bullet. Pressed, Perry said it was conceivable that a bullet had entered Kennedy's throat, hit the spine, changed course, and exited out the top of his skull. (103)

And his account provides further details:

> Perry told reporters that it was 'conceivable or possible' that the wound on the front of the president's neck could have been an entry wound. He made it plain to reporters that he was merely speculating, His caveat drew little interest. (103)

From my perspective, I feel, and I hope that future historians will think, it a matter of disturbing disappointment that Senator Specter did not provide reference and citation for those descriptive accounts attributed to Dr. Perry.

Senator Specter did include on pages 102-103 an excerpt from Dr. Perry's Commission testimony given on March 30:

> There were microphones cameras and the whole bit, as you know, and during the course of it a lot of these hypothetical situations and questions that were asked of us would often be asked by someone on this side and recorded by someone on this, and I don't know who was recorded and whether they were broadcasting it directly.
>
> There were tape recorders there and there were television cameras with their microphones. I know there were recordings made but who made them I don't know

and, of course, portions of it would be given to this group
and questions answered here and, as a result, considerable
questions were not answered in their entirety and even
some of them that were asked, I am sure were
misunderstood.

It was bedlam. (3H 375)

*   *   *

I submit this observations for the consideration of the
future historians: The major problem concerning the debate
over what was and what was not said in the press conferences
is trying to understand the failure of the Warren Commission
to insure that there should not be such a debate. For there can
be little doubt that there is a record of at least the first of
those press conferences.[1] Whether Specter had a copy of a
transcript is not clear, but he assured his memoir readers that
he was familiar with its contents:

> The first Friday press conference at Parkland was held
> shortly after the president's death, before the doctors there
> knew about the entrance wounds of Kennedy's back and
> head and before Perry had spoken with Humes and sorted
> out the facts. Perry told reporters it was possible that the
> president's wounds were caused by one bullet. Pressed,
> Perry said it was conceivable that a bullet had entered
> Kennedy's throat, hit the spine, changed course, and
> exited out the top of his skull. 'I expressed it as a matter
> of speculation that this was conceivable.' Perry later
> testified. 'But again, Dr. Clark and I emphasized that we
> had no way of knowing.'
>
> Perry told reporters that it was 'conceivable or possible'
> that the wound on the front of the president's neck could
> have been an entry wound. He made it plain to the
> reporters that he was merely speculating. His caveat drew
> little interest. (103)

Note! It is possible that Specter was familiar with Perry's press conference by way of his interview with Perry in 1997. In the paragraph *following* the account quoted immediately above, there is an endnote numbered "3", which reads as follows: "Dr. Malcolm Perry, interview with the author, 8 July 1997." If such be so, it is an unacceptable style of noting outside the limits of acceptable methodology.

On another plane of understanding, it will be remembered as beyond dispute that the Warren Commission possessed the power to compel persons to produce such records. The language of Appendix III of the Warren *Report* is very clear:

Public Law 88-202
88th Congress, S. J. Res. 137
December 16, 1963

Joint Resolution

Authorizing the Commission established to report upon the assassination of President John F. Kennedy to compel the attendance and testimony of witnesses and the production of evidence.

Resolved by the Senate and House of Representatives of the United States of America in Congress assembled, That (a) for the purposes of this joint resolution, the term 'Commission' means the Commission appointed by the President by Executive Order 11130, dated November 29, 1963.

(b) The Commission, or any member of the Commission when so authorized by the Commission, shall have power to issue subpenas requiring the attendance and testimony of witnesses and the production of any evidence that relates to the matter under investigation by the Commission. The Commission, or any member

of the Commission or any agent or agency designated
by the Commission for such purpose, may administer
oaths and affirmations, examine witnesses, and receive
evidence. Such attendance of witnesses and the
production of such evidence my be required from any
place within the United States at any designated place
of hearing.

(c) In came of contumacy or refusal to obey a subpena
issued to any person under subsection (b), any court of
the United States within the jurisdiction of which the
inquiry is carried on or within the jurisdiction of which
said person guilty of contumacy or refusal to obey is found
or resides or transacts business, upon application by the
Commission shall have jurisdiction to issue to such person
an order requiring such person to appear before the
Commission, its member, agent, or agency, there to
produce evidence if so ordered, or there to give testimony
touching the matter under investigation or in question;
and any failure to obey such order of the court may be
punished by said court as a contempt thereof.

. . . .

(e) No person shall be excused from attending and
testifying or from producing books, records,
correspondence, documents, or other evidence in
obedience to a subpena, on the ground that the testimony
or evidence required of him may tend to incriminate him
or subject him to a penalty or forfeiture; but no
individual may be prosecuted or subjected to any penalty
or forfeiture (except demotion or removal from office)
for or on account of any transaction, matter or thing
concerning which he is compelled, after having claimed
his privilege against self-incrimination, to testify or
produce evidence, except that such individual so testifying
shall not be exempt from prosecution and punishment
for perjury committed in so testifying.

. . . . (WR 473-474)

Given that power as of December 13, it is not easy to understand the problem of nonavailability of documentation as is recorded in the March 30 testimony of Dr. Malcolm Perry. The context is a newspaper article in a French paper, *La Expres.* The commentator is Mr. Specter:

> . . . And I questioned the doctors quoted therein and developed for the record what was true and what was false on the statements attributed to them, so we have undertaken that in some circles but not as extensively as you suggest as to Dr. Perry, because we have been trying diligently to get the tape records of the television interviews, and we were unsuccessful. I discussed this with Dr. Perry in Dallas last Wednesday [on the occasion of his deposition on March 25], and he expressed an interest in seeing them, and I told him we would make them available to him prior to his appearance, before deposition [sic] or before the Commission, except our efforts at CBS and NBC, ABC and everywhere including New York, Dallas and other cities were to no avail.
>
> The problem is that they have not yet cataloged all of the footage which they have, and I have been advised by the Secret Service, by Agent John Howlett, that they have an excess of 200 hours of transcripts among all of the events and they just have not cataloged them and could not make them available. (3H 378)

Whether Specter's recollection of Secret Service Agent John Howlett's advice was accurate is somewhat beside the point made in a March 25 letter from James J. Rowley, Chief of the Secret Service, to General Counsel J. Lee Rankin. It reads in part:

> Reference is made to your letter of March 18, 1964, requesting certain documents for the examination of the Commission.

The video tape and transcript of November 22, 1963, of the television interview of Doctor Malcolm Perry mentioned in your letter has not been located.

After a review of the material and information available at the Dallas television and radio news stations, and the records of NBC, ABC and CBS networks in New York City, no video or transcript could be found of a television interview with Doctor Malcolm Perry. CBS located in its New York office a television news clip on video tape of a broadcast by Walter Cronkite on November 22, 1963, in which he comments upon an interview with Doctor Perry by newsmen in Dallas. This, however, was not a television interview of the doctor. . . . [Deleted material relates to Governor Connally's wounds.]

The available material was transmitted by wire from CBS, New York to the Secret Service office in Dallas on March 25. The material was furnished to Mr. Specter on the same day.

.... (CD 678)

So, whether the problem was "has not been located" as per Rowley to Rankin, on March 25, with "furnished to Specter" on the same day, or whether the problem was "they have not yet cataloged all of the footage which they have . . . an excess of 200 hours of transcripts" as per Howlett to Specter, date unknown, is a missing piece of the puzzle. What seems reasonable to assume is that a Commission command to the corporate persons to produce the desired records following either a due diligence search for the misplaced transcripts, or a speedup of the cataloging process, could have easily resolved the debates over what was said when by whom.

*   *   *

If Dr. Humes's testimony was crucial for establishing the anterior throat wound as an exit wound, Dr. Perry's testimony was equally crucial for his acquiescence in Humes's testimony. There are two dimensions involved in that acquiescence: Trajectory and telephone conversations.

Trajectory

The following data is recalled:

1. During the course of Arlen Specter's interview of Drs. Humes and Boswell on March 13, Admiral Galloway gave Specter, with fingers on his body, a pointed demonstration of the path of the "Magic Bullet." Unmentioned at that time was any estimate of the angle of that bullet path.
2. In his testimony on March 16, Dr. Humes estimated the angle of that bullet path as being "approximately 45°" downward from back to front.

   • It is a puzzlement to understand how Dr. Humes could give that approximate measurement in the same testimony session as he is using the Naval illustrator's drawing—Commission Exhibit 385— which shows the bullet path at any angle that could not possibly be mistaken for "approximately 45°". Indeed, imprecise measurement by way of a protractor will show an angle much closer to the eventual 17°43'30" eventually established by the FBI in the reenactment of May 24.
   • It is most unfortunate that there is no numerical measurement for the angle established by way of Dr. Humes's superior, Admiral Galloway, in his March 13 demonstration of the angle on Mr. Specter's body in the Admiral's office.

   It is recalled from Specter's Memorandum of that session that in the demonstration the Admiral placed one finger on Specter's "back" and one finger on Specter's "chest". IF the

Admiral's finger placement for the "back" wound correlated with the autopsy report's placement of that entry wound, it is not difficult to imagine something approximating a 45°angle established by the Admiral's placement of his other finger on Specter's "chest." And inasmuch as there is no record of *Commander* Humes objecting to *Admiral* Galloway's angle on March 13, there is no reason to expect that Humes's testimony will be at variance with it on March 16.

3. It is difficult to dismiss the elements of a bizarre reality:

(1) Between March 13 and March 16 Drs. Humes and Boswell tutored the Naval illustrator's drawing of the bullet path for Commission Exhibit 385;

(2) Commission Exhibit 385 approximates the eventual 17°43'30" angle established by the FBI reenactment of May 24;

(3) The autopsy doctors' testimony on March 16 established the angle as "approximately "45°".

*   *   *

In his deposition of Dr. Malcolm Perry on March 25, Mr. Specter asked, and Dr. Perry answered:

Q. Were there sufficient facts available for you to reach a conclusion as to the cause of the wound on the front side of the President's neck?

A. No, sir, there was not. I could not determine whether or how this was inflicted, per se, *since it would require tracing the trajectory.* [Emphases added] (6H 11)

Further along, there was this exchange:

Q. Dr. Perry, have contents of the autopsy report conducted at Bethesda Naval Hospital been made available to you?

230 RODGER A. REMINGTON

A. They have.
Q. And are the findings in the autopsy report consistent with your observations and conclusions concerning the source and nature of the President's wounds?
A. Yes; they are. I think there are no discrepancies at all. I did not have that information initially, and as a result was somewhat confused about the nature of the wounds, as I noted—I could not tell whether there was one or two bullets, or from whence they came, but *the findings of the autopsy report are quite compatible with those findings which I noted at the time that I saw the President.* [Emphases added] (6H 14]

[Note! Left unexplained is how the "findings of the autopsy report"—not all of which were not based on the autopsy—could be "quite compatible" with Dr. Perry's *"since it would require tracing the trajectory"*, which was not undertaken in the autopsy.]

Having established "consistency" between the autopsy report and Dr. Perry's "observations and conclusions", it but remained for Mr. Specter to fit Dr. Humes's angle into the critical exchange that took place in Dr. Perry's testimony before the Warren Commission on March 30:

Mr. Specter. Based on the appearance of the neck wound alone, could it have been either an entrance or an exit wound?
Dr. Perry. It could have been either.
S: Permit me to supply some additional facts, Dr. Perry, which I shall ask you to assume as being true for purposes of having you express an opinion.
　　Assuming first of all that the President was struck by a 6.5-mm. copper-jacketed bullet fired from a gun having a muzzle velocity of approximately 2,000 feet per second, with the weapon being approximately 160 to 250 feet from the president, *with the bullet*

striking him at an angle of declination of approximately 45 degrees, striking the President on the upper right posterior thorax just above the upper border of the scapula, being 14 cm. from the tip of the right acromion process and 14 cm. below the tip of the right mastoid process, passing through the President's body striking no bones, traversing the neck and sliding between the large muscles in the posterior portion of the President's body through a fascia channel without violating the pleural cavity, but bruising the apex of the right pleural cavity, and bruising the most apical portion of the right lung, inflicting a hematoma to the right side of the larynx, which you have just described, and striking the trachea causing the injury which you described, and then exiting from the hole that you have described in the midline of the neck.

Now assuming those facts to be true, would the hole which you observed in the neck of the President be consistent with an exit wound under those circumstances?

P.   Certainly would be consistent with an exit wound.

With Dr. Perry's response, the first leg of the "Magic Bullet" became a trajectory "fact" in the evolution of the Single-Bullet Theory. In that theory, the successive legs of the bullet's journey were concerned only with matters of ballistics, a subject of divided opinion among the experts who gave testimony.

Telephone Conversations

This topic addresses a question of chronology: When did Dr. Humes learn of the anterior throat wound? The official account is that found in the Warren *Report* on page 89:

Commander Humes, who believed that a tracheotomy had been performed from his observations at the autopsy, talked by telephone with Dr. Perry early on the morning of November 23, and learned that his assumption was correct and that Dr. Perry had used the missile wound in the neck as the point to make the incision.[172]

Endnote [172] reads: 2H 361-362 (Humes). From that citation, the relevant testimony reads:

> Mr. Specter. Did you have occasion to discuss that wound on the front side of the President with Dr. Malcolm Perry of Parkland Hospital in Dallas?
> Commander Humes. Yes, sir; I did. I had the impression from seeing the wound that it represented a surgical tracheotomy wound, a wound frequently made by surgeons when people are in respiratory distress to give them a free airway.
>   To ascertain that point, I called on the telephone Dr. Malcolm Perry and discussed with him the situation of the President's neck when he first examined the President, and asked if he had in fact done a tracheotomy which was somewhat redundant because I was somewhat certain he had.
>   He said, yes; he had done a tracheotomy and that as the point to perform his tracheotomy he used a wound which he had interpreted as a missile wound in the low neck, as the point through which to make the tracheotomy incision.
> S.   When did you have that conversation with him, Dr. Humes?
> H.   I had that conversation early on Saturday morning, sir.
> S.   On Saturday morning, November 23d?
> H.   That is correct, sir.

It is unfortunate that Mr. Specter did not request a more specific time for the telephone call he made to Dr. Perry "early on Saturday morning". And it is instructive to learn that Dr. Perry's first recollection of the time frame differed from that of Dr. Humes.

The following exchange is from Dr. Perry's deposition on March 25:

> Mr. Specter. Now, did you have occasion to talk via the telephone with Dr. James J. Humes of the Bethesda Naval Hospital?
>
> Dr. Perry. I did.
>
> S. And will you relate the circumstances of the calls indicating first the time when they occurred.
>
> P. Dr. Humes called me twice on Friday afternoon, separated by about 30-minute intervals, as I recall. The first one, I somehow think I recall the first one must have been around 1500 hours, but I'm not real sure about that; I'm not positive of that at all, actually.
>
> S. Could it have been Saturday morning?
>
> P. Saturday morning—was it? It's possible. I remember talking with him twice. I was thinking it was shortly thereafter.
>
> S. Well, the record will show.
>
> P. Oh, sure, it was Saturday morning—yes.
>
> S. What made you change your view of that?
>
> P. You mean Friday?
>
> S. Did some specific recollection occur to you which changed your view from Friday to Saturday?
>
> P. No, I was trying to place where I was at that time— Friday afternoon, and at that particular time, when I paused to think about it, I was actually up in the operating suite at that time, when I thought that he called initially. I seem to remember it being Friday, for some reason.
>
> S. Where were you when you received those calls?
>
> P. I was in the Administrator's office here when he called.

It is unfortunate that Dr. Perry was not asked what time he received the telephone call(s) on Saturday morning.

COMMENT

It is a puzzlement to understand the apparent time confusion of Dr. Perry regarding when the telephone call(s) conversations occurred. The puzzlement flows from this exchange in the deposition testimony:

> Mr. Specter. And did you and I sit down and talk about the purpose of this deposition and the questions I would be asking you on the record, before this deposition started?
> Dr. Perry. Yes; we did.
> S. And did you give me the same information which you provided on the record here today?
> P. I have.

Absent my understanding, I leave to the future historians whether this exchange means that Mr. Specter asked—in the "preparation" preceding the deposition—Dr. Perry about the telephone call from Dr. Humes and was given then the same confused answer as was repeated in the recorded deposition.

Without impugning unattractive motives, it nevertheless is a reasonable criticism to fault the failure of Mr. Specter to determine by telephone logs—exactly when the telephone conversation(s) took place. I submit for the consideration of the historians that from the perspective of prudential common sense, Dr. Humes, as an inexperienced autopsy surgeon, would have been well self-advised to place his call(s) on Friday, prior to the autopsy proceedings.

NOTE

[1] James H. Fetzer (Editor), *Assassination Science: Experts Speak Out on the Death of JFK*, 1998, includes an Appendix C at pages 419-427, which is titled Transcript of Parkland Press Conference, 3:16 p.m., 22 November 1963.

CHAPTER IX

THE SHERIFF'S KITCHEN

The ninth chapter in Senator Specter's Part Two of his memoir, *Passion for Truth* is thirteen printed pages long. It takes its title from the setting of the Dallas County Jail, in which Jack Ruby, the convicted killer of Lee Harvey Oswald, gave his testimony to the Warren Commission, on June 7.

I am more interested in another event that day in Dallas's Dealey Plaza, where Arlen Specter gave Chief Justice Earl Warren a lecture delivered from the vantage point of the so-called "Sniper's nest" window used by the assassin of President Kennedy. As Specter described the scene:

> But it was strictly business at about 11:00 a.m. Central Standard Time, as Warren stood with his arms folded across his chest and studied Dealey Plaza. The chief justice and I stood by the sixth-floor window at the *southwest* [sic; read "southeast"; emphases added] corner of the Texas School Book Depository Building, where Lee Harvey Oswald had fired three shots from his Mannlicher-Carcano rifle at President Kennedy. Except for the cheering crowds and the presidential motorcade, our view of Dealey Plaza, Elm Street, and the Triple Underpass matched what Oswald had seen as he crouched at that window six and a half months before. Tall buildings flanked three sides of the small park, and highways rolled under a railroad trestle on the fourth side.

. . . For about eight minutes the chief justice didn't say a word as I summarized the Single Bullet Conclusion. I opened with the incontrovertible physical evidence: The Mannlicher-Carcano rifle had been found on the sixth floor of the Book Depository Building, not far from the *southwest* [sic; emphases added] corner window. The evidence proved that the rifle belonged to Lee Harvey Oswald. A bullet, recovered in Parkland Hospital from *Connally's* stretcher, was proved through ballistics tests to have been fired from the Mannlicher-Carcano. The autopsy showed that a bullet had struck Kennedy near the base of his neck on the right side and passed between two large strap muscles in his neck, striking only soft tissue as it continued in a slightly right-to left, downward, and forward path, exiting through the president's throat, nicking the left side of the knot of his tie. (103)

COMMENT

1. Regarding (a) "The chief justice and I stood by the sixth-floor window at the *southwest* corner of the Texas School Book Depository Building, where Lee Harvey Oswald had fired three shots from his Mannlicher-Carcano rifle at President Kennedy" and (b) "The Mannlicher-Carcano rifle had been found on the sixth floor of the Book Depository Building, not far from the *southwest* corner window: This is clearly a repeated inadvertent error immediately recognized as such by anyone even slightly familiar with the geographical layout of the assassination scene. And Senator Specter's writing may not be held to a higher standard of accuracy beyond that of every other human being. But when a simple and obvious error is twice repeated in a second edition of a book, a critic can but wonder concerning the quality of the editing process in that professional publication.

2. Sometimes, however, blameworthy error—of either commission or omission—is intermixed with inadvertent

error in this memoir writing virtually devoid of meaningful references and citations. There are at least three such errors in the same two paragraphs involving inadvertent error:

- Regarding "The evidence *proved* that the rifle belonged to Lee Harvey Oswald", there is no proof that such was the evidence as of the time of the assassination. There is evidence that Oswald's name and signature was on the purchase order form dated eight months earlier. But there is no proof that he was in possession of it on the day of the assassination. Reasonable speculation/conjecture perhaps, but no evidence that establishes proof.

- Regarding "a bullet, recovered in Parkland Memorial Hospital from Connally's stretcher, was proved through ballistics tests to have been fired from the Mannlicher-Carcano" involves two problems of proof: (1) Despite the confusion generated by Arlen Specter's style of prosecutorial interrogation of Darrell Tomlinson, his best result was Tomlinson's concession that he could not take an oath (which means to tell "the truth, the whole truth, and nothing but the truth, so help me God") that he was positive the bullet came from Connally's stretcher; and (2) There is no ballistic test that can prove *when* a given bullet was fired from a given rifle. Moreover, neither spectrographic tests nor neutron activation analysis of bullet fragments can prove when their matched bullet was fired.

- Regarding "the autopsy showed that a bullet had struck Kennedy near the base of the neck . . . exiting from the president's throat . . ." that *proof* exists only by way of a mental exercise in logical inferences drawn from the autopsy report of an autopsy which failed to undertake dissection of the bullet path.

*   *   *

Senator Specter's memoir then recounts his lecture to the Commission chairman on the significance of ballistics analysis:

> The bullet's speed, I explained to Warren, was critical, for the missile to have done all the damage we theorized. Tests showed that the muzzle velocity of the Mannlicher-Carcano was 2,200 feet per second. After a flight of 275 feet, the approximate distance between the rifle and Kennedy's neck when the first shot was fired, the muzzle velocity was about 1,975 feet per second. Tests performed on a simulation of the president's neck showed that the velocity of the bullet as it sped past the nicked tie was about 1,875 feet per second.

COMMENT

Conceding, for the purpose of present criticism, the numbers selected by Specter for muzzle velocities [ballistics], there is a problem with his use of a 275 feet measurement as "the approximate distance [a trajectory matter] between the rifle and Kennedy's neck when the first shot was fired." Resolution of the problem involves acceptance or rejection of a critical assumption: If Specter's ballistics lecture to Warren assumes "the first shot was fired" between frames 210-225 on the Zapruder film, either his trajectory—"flight of 275 feet"—or the Warren *Report* is in substantial error. This datum—275 feet—however, has nothing to do with ballistics, but the its usage serves as a good example of the ease with which Specter is inclined to mix ballistics and trajectory data to no good purpose. The *Report* data includes the following:

- Commission Exhibit 893 is concerned with data for Frame 210. It indicates: "Distance to Rifle in Window 176.9 Ft." and "Angle to Rifle in Window 21°34' (WR 102)

- Commission Exhibit 895 is concerned with data for Frame 225. It indicates: "Distance to Rifle in Window 190.8 Ft." and "Angle to Rifle in Window 20°11' (WR 103)
- Inasmuch as the Presidential limousine was hidden from Zapruder's camera lens between Frames 210-225, the calculation for the angle of the bullet hit used the mean between the known angles, the answer being 20°52'30" (WR 106)
- Allowing for a downward grade of 3°9', "the probable angle through the President's body was calculated at 17°43'30", assuming he was sitting in a vertical position." (WR 106)
- In emulation of the calculation for the probable angle, the mean distance to Rifle in Window between Frames 210-225—176.9 and 190.8—establish that the distance to rifle from the President's neck "at the time the first shot was fired" was *183.85* feet.

But all that trajectory data is beside the issue at hand, which was stated very clearly by Mr. Specter: "The bullet's speed [a calculation of ballistics], I explained to Warren, was critical, for the missile to have done all the damage we theorized." Passing mention of damage, however, resolves nothing in the absence of identification of the damage. Specter neatly sidestepped the real issue: How could the "magic bullet" cause seven wounds, including fractures of two bones, and escape with virtually no damage to itself? Specter spent considerable effort trying to extract supportive ballistics testimony from Connally's Parkland Hospital surgeons, and from the Army's Edgewood Arsenal Ballistics experts, but that effort floundered upon their insistence in linking damage with "line of flight"—trajectory—qualifications. And there is understandably no mention of this issue indicated in Senator Specter's eight-minute lecture to Chief Justice Warren on June 7.

*   *   *

Senator Specter's memoir then turns its attention to the subject of trajectory:

> Where Oswald had pointed his rifle, I pointed my finger to show the bullet's trajectory. Standing at the window, it was clear that the assassin had neither a long shot nor a hard shot, especially with a four-power scope. It was also clear that the assassin could maintain the same line of fire as the president's open limousine rolled along the slightly dipping road before easing to the right and heading for the Triple Underpass.
>
> Quickly, but in as much detail as possible, I drew the picture that emerged from the Zapruder film, backed by our on-site tests, on the positions and reactions of the president and the governor to one of the shots. Like the rest of us, the chief justice had been entranced and horrified by the amateur movie that just happened to catch the critical seconds of the assassination as Abraham Zapruder watched the motorcade through the lens of his camera. (109)

COMMENT

1. Regarding "Where Oswald had pointed his rifle, I pointed my finger to show the bullet's trajectory.": Appendix V of the Warren *Report* lists on pages 483-500 "the 552 witnesses whose testimony has been presented to the Commission." Not *one* among those 552 witnesses ever gave positive testimony to having seen Lee Harvey Oswald point a rifle from that or any window in the Texas School Book Depository Building.

2. Regarding "Standing at the window, it was clear that the assassin had neither a long shot nor a hard shot, especially with a four-power scope.": While it may indeed have been

"clear" to Arlen Specter for purpose of his lecture to Warren on June 7, any objective analysis of his claim introduces ignored problems.

- There is no agreement on the position the assassin assumed for the shooting. What is known is that none of the attempts to duplicate the accuracy and timing of the shots has used the location alleged to have been used by Oswald, the designated assassin.
- If Specter's language—"Standing at the window"— means that while standing at the window, it was clear to Specter, etc." he may use whatever language he chooses to use in reflecting a personal perception. If, however, his "Standing at the window" implies that the assassin *shot* from a standing position, he ignores the necessity for the bullet to have been fired through a closed window.
- Given the assassin's presumed awareness of a timing problem for firing a bolt-action rifle, there is no evidence that the four-power scope was used for aiming. Realistically, re-sighting a moving target involved realignment of the scope's crosshairs.

3. Regarding "It was also clear that the assassin could maintain the same line of fire as the president's open limousine rolled along the slightly dipping road before easing to the right and heading for the Triple Underpass.": Absent any indication what Specter means by "the same line of fire", his claim is questionable. Ignored in the account are two additional factors:

- In addition to "the slightly dipping road"—a banked decline—the street was also curved.
- The direction in which the limousine was moving required a left to right lead for hitting the target, but the demands placed upon the bullet in the Single-Bullet Theory required a right to left angle of exit

from Kennedy to Connally's chest. Resolution of this apparent contradiction remains a major obstacle for moving the theory into a provable conclusion.

*   *   *

Following the trajectory section of the lecture, Specter ventured briefly into the positional alignment of the victims:

> Quickly, but in as much detail as possible, I drew the picture that emerged from the Zapruder film, backed by our on-site tests, on the positions and reactions of the president and the governor to one of the shots. Like the rest of us, the chief justice had been entranced and horrified by the amateur movie that just happened to catch the critical seconds of the assassination as Abraham Zapruder watched the motorcade through the lens of his camera.
>
> I reminded the chief justice of the sequence in which Kennedy had suddenly raised both hands to his throat, showing an unmistakable reaction to the shot that pierced his neck. I also reviewed Connally's movements, as shown on the film, immediately after the president raised his arms. . . . (109)

COMMENT

1. Presuming that Specter's "drew the picture" means he described in words what "emerged from the Zapruder film", a reader can but wonder what he described as happened in frames 210-225, which were hidden from the lens of the camera by a highway sign. That sign was subsequently removed from Dealey Plaza. Never explained was either the time or the circumstance under which it was removed. That point aside, this much is certain: The missing sign in no way contributes to the problem of positioning in the "on-site

tests"—the reenactment of May 24—the stand-in limousine for the one involved in the assassination. And it is noted that the basic flaw in that May 24 reenactment was the decision to use a different limousine from the one in which the assassination had taken place six months earlier. The simple fact is that the substitution phenomenon involved variances in basic math specifications that doomed any sense of anticipated accuracy from the tests.

2. Expanding that theme, "I drew the picture that emerged from the Zapruder film, backed by our on-site tests, on the positions and reactions of the president and the governor to one of the shots," we witness an example of a circular argument at work on behalf of the Single-Bullet Theory.

- "One of the shots" necessarily refers to the shot which fired the "Magic Bullet". In the Warren *Report* version of things, either the first or the second of the three bullets fired had to be a miss, so either one could be the "Magic Bullet". Which shot fired that bullet is irrelevant to the point at hand.
- On June 4, the Commission took testimony from FBI agents Lyndal Shaneyfelt and Robert Frazier, both of whom were prominent participants in the May 24 reenactment. Both witnesses were examined by Arlen Specter.

(Note Carefully! The following account of the FBI's professionalism in the calculation of the trajectory necessary for the Single-Bullet Theory is indisputably impressive. Essential to those calculations, however, is the awareness that early on in Shaneyfelt's testimony—which covers pages 5H 143-165) a tell-tale observation established a crucial parameter for any evaluation of its credibility. The observation flowed from a question asked in the context of distances from the sixth floor window of the TSBD to the limousine on Elm Street. The exchanges read on pages 145-146:

Senator Cooper. May I ask a question there? How did you establish the location of the rifle in making those calculations?

Mr. Shaneyfelt. The location of the rifle was established *on the basis of other testimony and information furnished to us by the Commission, photographs taken by the Dallas Police Department immediately after the assassination, and the known opening of the window.* [Emphases added]

It was an estimation of where the rifle most likely was based on the knowledge that the Commission has through testimony.

Mr. Specter. Senator Cooper, Mr. Frazier is present and has been sworn, and he is going to identify that. He could do it at this time, to pinpoint that issue.

Cooper: I think we can just make a note of that, and go ahead with this witness. (145-146)

*   *   *

On page 99 of the Warren *Report* is a photograph of Shaneyfelt. This is Commission Exhibit 887, the caption for which reads: "Photograph taken during reenactment showing C2766 rifle with camera attached."

In Shaneyfelt's testimony, the following exchange occurred:

Mr. Specter. Mr. Shaneyfelt, for purposes of illustration would you produce the photograph [CE 887] at this time showing the mounting of the motion picture camera on the weapon found on the sixth floor?

. . . .

Mr. Shaneyfelt. . . . My location was in the sixth floor window of the Texas School Book Depository that we have designated as our control point. I have a rifle that is the assassination rifle mounted on a tripod, and on the rifle is mounted an Arriflex 16-mm. motion picture camera, that is aligned to take photographs through the telescopic sight.

. . . .

Sp. Was the view as recorded on the film as shown on Exhibit No. 886 the actual view which would have been seen if you had been looking through the telescopic sight of the Mannlicher-Carcano itself?

Sh. Yes.

Sp. How did you determine the level and angle at which to hold the rifle?

Sh. I placed the rifle in the approximate position based on prior knowledge of where the boxes were stacked and the elevation of the window and other information that was furnished to me by representatives of the Commission.

Mr. Dulles. You used the same boxes [as a rifle barrel rest], did you, that the assassin had used?

Sh. No; I did not.

Sp. Were those boxes used by Mr. Frazier?

Sh. They were used by Mr. Frazier and used in making the measurements. ["the measurements" refers to Frazier previously positioning the limousine.] I had to use a tripod because of the weight of the camera and placed the elevation of the rifle at an approximate height in a position as though the boxes were there.

Sp. Was Mr. Frazier present at the time you positioned the rifle on the tripod?

Sh. Yes; he was.

Sp. Did he assist in describing for you or did you have an opportunity to observe the way he held a rifle to ascertain the approximate position of the rifle at that time?

Sh. That is correct.

Sp: May it please the Commission, we will, with Mr. Frazier, indicate the reasons he held the rifle in the way he did to approximate the way we believe it was held at the time of the assassination. (5H 147)

(I interrupt this exchange to point out one of the serious consequences of not using the Kennedy limousine in the reenactment of May 24.

> Sp: Was there any difference between the position of President Kennedy's stand-in and the position of President Kennedy on the day of the assassination by virtue of the difference in the automobiles in which each rode?
> Sh: Yes; because of the difference in the automobiles there was a variation of 10 inches, a vertical distance of 10 inches that had to be considered. The stand-in for President Kennedy was sitting 10 inches higher and the stand-in for Governor Connally was sitting 10 inches higher than the President and Governor Connally were sitting and we took this into account in our calculations. (5H 148)

Whether the manner in which the reenactment "took this into account"—as described on pages 5H 148-149—may be accepted as a valid methodology is a decision the future historians will have to make,)

The next step is to review FBI agent Robert Frazier's testimony as specification of the reasons for the selected angle of the rifle:

> Mr. Specter. What was your position during most of the time of those onsite tests?
> Mr. Frazier. I was stationed at the window on the sixth floor of the Texas School Book Depository Building at the southeast corner of the building.
> S.   How far was that window open at the time the tests were being conducted?

F. I estimated it as approximately one-third. *It was somewhat less than halfway open.*

. . . .

S: Is the distance open on that window about the same as that which you had it open at the time these tests were run?

F. Yes; I would say that this is very close. *The window was placed according to information already furnished to the Commission as to how much it had been opened at that time.* [Emphases added] (5H 165)

COMMENT

Page 66 of the Warren *Report* depicts a photograph taken by a Dallas newsman. Titled Dillard Exhibit C, it is captioned: "Enlargement of photograph taken by Thomas C. Dillard on November 22, 1963." The picture shows clearly that the window in question was a double-hung window in which the bottom frame of the lower half of the window was aligned exactly with the lower 1/4 of the window immediately adjacent to it. Stated differently, Frazier's answer end-runs the more accurate specification that during the reenactment the window in question was open more than ¼ its total length.

Returning to the question raised earlier by Commissioner Cooper during the testimony of FBI Agent Shaneyfelt: "How did you establish the location of the rifle in making those calculations?", the answer given then by Shaneyfelt was really two answers: (1) "The location of the rifle was established on the basis of other testimony and information furnished to us by the Commission, photographs taken by the Dallas Police Department immediately after the assassination, and the known opening of the window." and (2) "It was an estimation of where the rifle most likely was based on the knowledge that the Commission has through testimony." And it will recalled that at that point

Mr. Specter indicated FBI agent Frazier would answer Cooper's question in follow-up testimony.

Turning to Frazier's testimony, the relevant exchange reads:

S: Did you handle the Mannlicher-Carcano rifle during the course of the onsite tests?

F. Yes, sir.

. . . .

S. At what position—what was the basis for your positioning that rifle during those tests?

F. To position the rifle, we selected boxes of the same size and contour as boxes shown in a photograph or rather in two photographs, reportedly taken by the police department at Dallas shortly after the assassination.

We placed these boxes in their relative position in front of the window spacing them from left to right, according to the photographs which were furnished to us, and also placing them up against the window, with one of them resting on the window ledge as it as shown in the photographs.

S. In addition to the placement of the boxes, were there any other guides which you had for reconstructing the position of the rifle to the way which you believed it to have been held on November 22, 1963?

F. Yes, sir; there was one physical obstruction in the building which could not be moved consisting of two vertical pipes just at the left side of the sixth floor window. These prevented me or anyone who was shooting from that window from moving any further to the left.

The position of the rifle, of course, had to be such that it could be sighted out through the window, using the telescopic sight high enough above the window ledge so that the muzzle of the weapon would clear the window ledge, and low enough in position so that the bottom of the window, which was only partly raised, would not interfere with a view through the telescopic sight, which is approximately 2 inches higher than the actual bore of the weapon.

S. Did you position the rifle further, based on information provided you concerning the testimony of certain eyewitnesses of the assassination scene concerning what they observed?

F. Yes, sir; we attempted to put the muzzle of the weapon sufficiently far out the window so it would have been visible from below. (5H 165-166)

It can only be wondered whether Senator Cooper was satisfied with Frazier's testimony as answer for his rifle question he asked Shaneyfelt. But is amusing to speculate whether he had much confidence that it would be answered by way of Specter's deflection to that upcoming testimony of Frazier. Regardless of such amusement, Cooper himself returned to the question 16 pages following the deflection, when he resumed the original exchange with Shaneyfelt:

Senator Cooper. Just one other question. *Assuming that there might have been some variation in the location of the rifle, length of the window, the breadth of the window, or that the rifle was held higher than the rifle might have been, would it have made—how much variation would it have made, in your judgement in these calculations you made?*

Mr. Shaneyfelt. *I don't believe that any movement of the rifle in that specific window would alter our calculations to any appreciable degree if you stay within that window, because our reenactment and*

*our repositioning of the bodies in the car based on
the photographs is subject to some variation, too, so
we have variations throughout.* [Emphases added]
(5H 163)

One can but wonder whether Arlen Specter ever came to
realize that his "historical lens" was badly out of focus if he never
realized the impossibility of replication in history. And if he did
realize that, one can but wonder what were his motivation and
expectation in masterminding the reenactment of May 24.
Measurement "variations throughout" do little to encourage
confidence in the data generated by the Arlen Specter-produced
"reenactment" of May 24, 1964.

*   *   *

I submit for the consideration of the future historians that the
testimony of FBI Agent Lyndal Shaneyfelt on June 4 was the death
knell of Arlen Specter's Single-Bullet Theory because in one concise
exchange, the theory's dependent trajectory was destroyed:

Senator Cooper. *You had to establish the position of the
President at the time the bullet struck him and the
position of the rifle to make a determination about
the degree of the angle of the direction?*
Mr. Shaneyfelt. *That is correct. The positions in the car,
their positions in the car, were based on the
Zapruder film.* [Emphases added]

And given the obstruction to the Zapruder camera lens by
the Stemmons Freeway sign in Dealey Plaza, that precise data
was simply unavailable. Game/Set/Match to Senator Cooper!

It is nevertheless instructive to read Senator Specter's account
of the structure of his famous Single-Bullet Theory, which appears
on page 110 of *Passion for Truth*:

It all boiled down to one key fact: ***When the bullet exited the president's neck, the limousine was in such a position that the bullet had to strike the car's interior or someone in it.*** Our exhaustive examination of the limousine had shown that no bullet struck the car's interior. Then there was Connally, sitting right in the line of fire, directly in front of Kennedy, about to collapse from gunshot wounds. Could the president's neck wound and all of the governor's wounds have been caused by a single bullet? Could the whole bullet found on Connally's stretcher have first passed through Kennedy's neck, then penetrated Connally's chest, wrist, and thigh, leaving a trail of metallic fragments? That's where the facts led.

COMMENT

1. I suggest the future historians should be interested in considering whether the "one key fact" is not "when" the bullet exited the president's neck, but rather "if" the bullet exited the president's neck. Though I am not inclined to pursue them in this writing, there are other possibilities that could explain the frontal neck wound.
2. Those historians should also be interested in whether or not Governor Connally's body was in a turned position from his sitting alignment "directly in front of Kennedy."
3. And they should also be interested in determining whether or not Arlen Specter proved that the whole bullet was indeed "found on Governor Connally's stretcher.
4. As for "That's where the facts led": The future historians will determine whether Arlen Specter's "facts" are statements he has established as empirically verifiable.

*   *   *

From my perspective, the weakest link in the chain of "facts" in the Single-Bullet Theory/Conclusion/Fact/Whatever is the claim that the there is no incompatibility between the placement of the holes in President Kennedy's suit jacket and shirt and the hole in his back/neck. Specter addresses that problem in these words:

> The other major argument against the Single-Bullet Conclusion was that the holes in the president's shirt were so low that the bullet would have had to zig and zag—descend, rise, and then descend again—to cause the wounds. That overlooks the fact that the real issue is where the bullet hit the president, as opposed to the location of the bullet holes in the president's clothing. The lower holes in the clothing were accounted for by the shirt and jacket riding up from Kennedy's back brace, by his getting up and down during the ride, and his constant waving. (112)

COMMENT

1. Regarding "The lower holes in the clothing were accounted for by the shirt and jacket riding up from Kennedy's back brace, by his getting up and down during the ride, and his constant waving,": It has been pointed out by other critics that

   - The exact alignment of the jack and shirt holes is an amazing coincidence inasmuch as the expectation is that a belt would tend to inhibit movement of the shirt to a much greater degree than that of the jacket.
   - There is no evidence that the president was either getting up or sitting down at the time he was struck by the bullet, or that his waving was done without the elbow resting on the door frame.

2. If Arlen Specter had been genuinely concerned with convincing critics that this "bunching" argument was credible, he could easily have included in the May 24 "reenactment" a

simple sequence. In the sequence, the location of the bullet entry hole—as determined by the autopsy report—would be marked on an unclothed "neck" of the stand-in, and aligned with a mark designating the hole in the stand-in's jacket. A photograph could then be taken to demonstrate the phenomenon of the "bunching" argument. But, it may be argued, criticism of the bunching argument was not made until after the May 24 reenactment. True enough, but it is no less true that *no* argunent against the findings published in the Warren *Report* could be made until after the publishing of that report in September 1964. Obviously that simple demonstration could have been made anytime in the past forty years, and could still be made at any time and any place. The failure to have done so, or to do so at this late date, merely reinforces the conviction of critics who dismiss the bunching argument as a ridiculous absurdity.

CHAPTER X

TRUTH AND LIES

The tenth chapter in Part Two of Arlen Specter's memoir, *Passion for Truth*, is titled "Truth and Lies." The chapter is 6+ printed pages of entertaining potpourri reminiscences by a key participant in the happenings that produced the Warren Commission *Report* issued in September 1964. It is not clear why he chose that title for this chapter, because, excluding the title, the words "truth" and "lies" are each used but twice:

- As for "truth", it appears in the first and last sentences in a three-sentence paragraph on page 122:

    The Warren Commission reported the ***truth*** in as much detail as precisely as we could. The watchword was integrity. We followed the chief justice's order, at that initial staff meeting, that the ***truth*** be our client.

Recalling that "Truth Is the Client" was the title of the second chapter on his memoir, perhaps Senator Specter felt that those two mentions had exhausted the topic for one writing. One thing is certain. Nowhere in *Passion for Truth*'s Part II does he undertake to apprise his readers of the meaning of "truth" as he perceives it, or even as he would have them perceive it.

- As for "lies", it appears in several forms (once as an epithet, and once each as the singular and plural noun) on page

121 in a paragraph trashing Oliver Stone's controversial movie, *JFK*. Senator Specter wrote:

I almost sued Oliver Stone after his 1991 pseudodocumentary movie *JFK*, which libeled me by name, calling me a *liar* in reference to the Single-Bullet Conclusion. Stone's movie has done more than any other single effort to distort history and the commission's work. In grainy black and white, Stone filmed scenes conveying his own account of the assassination, then inserted them into his Technicolor movie as though they had been lifted from actual newsreel footage. *JFK* reached a whole generation of Americans who rely on the screen, whether television or cinema, for information. And the film, depicting a vast government conspiracy to kill Kennedy, was such a big *lie* that it almost defied belief. But the *lies* will be corrected in time. Eventually, Stone's movie will fall largely on its own weight, with help from responses like Walter Cronkite's vehement denunciation of *JFK* and his affirmation of the Warren Commission, David Belin's books and later generations' study of the twenty-six volume, 17,000-page record.

COMMENT

1. Absent any evidence of Stone's advertising his movie as a documentary, it is difficult to understand Senator Specter's description of it as a "pseudodocumentary."
2. Absent his selection of which meaning he attaches to "distort", it may be difficult for Senator Specter's readers to understand exactly what is either the history or the Warren Commission's work that is being distorted in the movie.

QUESTIONS

1. When Senator Specter speaks reprovingly of an unidentified generation which sought information by way of the screen,

does he intend to include the generation of the 1960s/1970s which was so misled by the government-endorsed television spectacle known as the Vietnam War?

2. As for the phenomenon of Oliver Stone's "lie" that was the movie, *JFK*, what is the measuring device used by Senator Specter to decide when a lie becomes "such a big lie that it almost defies belief"?

3. When Senator Specter assures his readers that ". . . the lies will be corrected in time" does he imply that further writings in the genre of his political memoir will materially assist the corrective process?

*   *   *

Recalling again the theme around which Senator Specter developed his chapter, "Truth Is the Client," it is instructive to note a subtle shift in reorientation of that theme. He writes on page 124:

> For a while after we finished the investigation, I did not talk about the Warren Commission. I felt bound by a sense of lawyer-client relationship between commission staff and the commission itself. We had done our talking in the report. It seemed inappropriate for us to talk further. I also had a sense that Chief Justice Warren, whom I deeply respected, would not want us to talk about our work. The best thing to do, when in doubt, was to keep quiet.

COMMENT

Clearly something has happened, the result of which has been to substitute a lawyer-client relationship between lawyers and the *commission* to replace Warren's initial charge to regard the lawyer-client relationship as being between lawyers and *the Truth*. Whether this trilateral phenomenon can be manipulated into a syllogistic conclusion that *the Truth* is identifiable with *the Commission* is a logical morass I choose not to explore.

QUESTIONS

1. If the lawyers had in fact remained faithful to Warren's initial charge, why would it be inappropriate for them to talk in a manner which would demonstrate that fidelity?
2. More specifically, if Arlen Specter had remained faithful to Warren's initial charge, why would he feel that Chief Justice Warren would not want him to talk about his work?

Senator Specter then recounts how he changed his mind in 1966 and undertook to talk with writers in defense of the work of the Warren Commission against its critics. In his words,

> I did appear with Bill Coleman [a colleague Assistant Counsel for the Warren Commission] at a Philadelphia Bar Association program shortly after the commission filed its report, but that was the exception. Then Edward Jay Epstein came along. Epstein was doing a master's thesis when he came to see me on a Sunday in the summer of 1965, while my family picnicked in our back yard. I talked to Epstein about our work in a removed, almost academic way, sticking to what was in the report.
>
> Epstein published his book *Inquest* in 1966, challenging our findings. Soon after, I got a call from Fletcher Knebel, who was writing an article for *Look*. I didn't realize that Knebel was the acclaimed author of *Seven Days in May*, and other political novels. I declined his request for an interview. Then Knebel came back to me and said, 'Nobody will talk to me, and I'm not going to have any choice but to give credence to everything Epstein has said.'
>
> I thought it over. I decided that as an elected official— I was then in my first year as Philadelphia DA—I was accountable to the public and should not refuse comment.

I decided to talk to Knebel. He quoted me extensively in his *Look* piece, which turned out to be accurate and fair. Then I received a request from *U.S. News and World Report*. I gave them a three-to four-hour interview in September 1966. They also did a decent job, reporting a lengthy verbatim transcript. David Belin and I traveled to London in January 1967 to debate Mark Lane on the BBC. The program, scheduled from seven to eleven on a Sunday night, was extended until almost midnight.

All of us who played roles in the Warren Commission have been questioned about it all our lives. I get questions about the Warren Commission at almost every open-house town meeting, high school speech, and political forum I hold.

When will the mania ebb? . . . (124)

COMMENT: I.

Regarding "I decided to talk to Knebel. He quoted me extensively in his *Look* piece, which turned out to be accurate and fair.": The article appeared in the July 12, 1966 issue of *Look* Magazine, under the title, "The Warren Commission Report on the assassination is struck by A NEW WAVE OF DOUBT." In the main, the article was a critical review of Edward Jay Epstein's book, *Inquest*. My present interest is not concerned with either the book, or the critical review of it.

There are, however, some relevant numbers that speak to Arlen Specter's comment in his memoir:

- In 6+ pages, Knebel wrote 489 lines of text, broken down into 61 paragraphs;
- In paragraph 55, there are seven lines which read:

Arlen Specter, the key lawyer on this phase [the autopsy findings and report] of the Warren Commission's investigation, says: 'It is ridiculous to indicate that the autopsy findings were changed after November 24, when Commander Humes finished the report. I saw both the [undated] longhand and the typewritten reports when I came to work for the Commission in mid-January. They were identical, and neither was changed from the original in any way at any time.'

•   That is the only quote attributed to Arlen Specter. That is the only place his name is mentioned in Knebel's *Look* article.

COMMENT: II.

Regarding "I decided to talk to Knebel. He quoted me extensively in his *Look* piece": A seven-line quote in a 489-line article lends new meaning to "He quoted me extensively."

COMMENT: III.

Regarding "Then I received a request from *U.S. News and World Report.* I gave them a three-to four-hour interview in September 1966. They also did a decent job, reporting a lengthy verbatim transcript.":

That interview transcript appeared as 12 pages of a 16-page article in the October 10 issue of the magazine. The interview consisted of 71 far-ranging questions asked by an unidentified person, and Arlen Specter's answers with appropriate contextual materials in brackets.

The article is titled "Truth About Kennedy Assassination," and the internal Specter interview is titled "Overwhelming Evidence Oswald Was Assassin."

There is an introductory statement identified as an explanation why Arlen Specter granted the interview:

When I was asked if I would agree to talk to 'U.S. News and World Report' on the subject of the Warren

Commission's investigation of the Kennedy assassination, I decided, after considerable thought, that my answer would be 'Yes'—in view of the public concern that has arisen in the wake of books on the Commission.

I am willing to answer questions which may shed light on the subject and clear up areas of misunderstanding that may exist in the public mind as a result of what has been written and widely published.

In this regard, I believe that the Commission Report itself, and certainly the 26 volumes of evidence, contain within their covers the comprehensive answers to all substantive questions. However, it is not easy for those answers to be available to the average person, who may have read the buckshot attacks which have been forthcoming against the Commission Report.

To put some of the criticism into proper focus, I am willing to respond to questions and point out parts of the Report and areas of evidence which I consider complete answers to the so-called critics. (49)

For any interested person who has access to a copy of the October 10, 1966 article published in *U.S. News & World Report*, a careful reading of it is an educational experience not quickly forgotten.

At the outset, two points seem important to make: (1) It is disappointing that the author of the questions is unknown; and (2) The introduction to the interview is enticingly promising when it reads:

Is there more to the assassination than appears in the mass of testimony and findings made public by the Warren Commission? In this exclusive interview with the lawyer who investigated the physical facts, you get in precise detail what the evidence proves about that fateful day in Dallas three years ago.

Very quickly, however, an unfortunate reality surfaces as it becomes obvious that there is no quick access to the "mass of testimony and findings made public by the Warren Commission." The reason is simple: There is no index for either the 800+ page Warren *Report* or the 26 volumes of data which is the foundation for that report. Add to those absences the fact that Mr. Specter does not include references/ citations for the "precise detail . . . the evidence proves".

An example is in order. Question 4 reads:

> How do you explain the difference between the autopsy report and the FBI's report of December 9 on President Kennedy's wounds—the FBI reported that one bullet went in only to a finger's length, whereas the autopsy report said it went through the President's neck?

The answer is given in seven unreferenced/uncited paragraphs, concerned mainly with early hypotheses generated during the autopsy. The thrust of the answer was to establish that "when the whole picture was presented later, it was apparent that the preliminary conversations reported in the FBI document were only tentative." When Mr. Specter alludes to the "preliminary conversations reported in the FBI document" it will be remembered that the source for the conversations is the Sibert-O'Neill report, a report not included in either the Warren *Report* or the 26 accompanying volumes of evidence upon which the report was ostensibly based.

Regardless of that oversight, Specter's answer in the sixth and seventh paragraphs reads:

> In fact, Dr. Humes had formulated a different conclusion, tentative as it might have been, the very next day when he had a chance to talk to Dr. Perry by telephone in Dallas [Dr. Malcolm O. Perry of Parkland Hospital, one of the doctors attending President Kennedy]. That was when he found that there had been a bullet hole on the front of the neck, before the tracheotomy was performed.
>
> As the autopsy had gone along, Dr. Humes had found the bullet path through the body, and that led to the

phone call to Dr. Perry for more information. (49)
[Bracketed material in original]

COMMENT

1. Regarding Question 4's ". . . whereas the autopsy report said
    it went through the President's neck?", and Answer 4's "As
    the autopsy had gone along, Dr. Humes had found the bullet
    path through the body," the absence of a citation for the
    question, and the absence of both reference and citation for
    the answer, combine to create a distortion difficult to excuse
    as harmlessly inadvertent.

2. As for "whereas the autopsy report said it went through the
    President's neck": There is a distinction that must be
    recognized and remembered. Commission Exhibit 387 is
    titled "Autopsy Report," and is included in the Warren *Report*
    at pages 538-543. It is undated, and is divided into two
    sections: Pathological Examination Report and Summary.

    •   The Examination Report indicates on page 541:

        2. The second wound presumably of entry is that
            described above in the upper right posterior
            thorax. Beneath the skin there is ecchymosis
            of subcutaneous tissue and musculature.
            The missile path through the fascia and
            musculature cannot be easily probed. The
            wound presumably of exit was that described
            by Dr. Malcolm Perry of Dallas in the low
            anterior cervical region.

    •   Inasmuch as Mr. Specter claimed in his Answer to
        Question 4 that Dr. Humes had not talked with Dr.
        Perry until "the very next day" following the autopsy,
        and that was "when he found that there had been a
        bullet hole on the front of the neck," it is not clear

how Specter can reasonably conclude his answer to Question 4 with the unqualified claim: "As the autopsy had gone along, Dr. Humes had found the bullet path through the body, and that led to the phone call to Dr. Perry for more information."

• And the Summary makes no mention of "a bullet path through the body" when it says:

> The other missile entered the right posterior thorax above the scapula and traversed the soft tissues of the supra-scapular and supra-clavicular portions of the right side of the neck. This missile produced contusions of the right apical parietal pleura and of the apical portion of the right upper lobe of the lung. The missile contused the strap muscles of the right side of the neck, damaged the trachea and made its exit through the anterior surface of the neck.

It may of course be argued that this constitutes description of "a bullet path through the body". Perhaps so. But that data was not discovered until the "Y-shaped incision from the shoulders over the lower portion of the breastbone and over to the opposite shoulder . . . reflected the skin and tissues from the anterior portion of the chest". (2H 363 (Dr. Humes) *That* access is what provided by inference the damage report found in the Summary. And the same inference may be just as easily claimed for a path from the anterior throat to the posterior neck. Moreover, if the "path" ends with an exit, and the exit was unknown at the time of the autopsy, it is difficult to understand how there could be "a bullet path *through* the body" established by way of the autopsy. Certainly Arlen Specter never explained that in his answer to Question 4.

* * *

Among the fascinating Questions in the 1966 Arlen Specter interview printed in the October 10 issue of *U. S. News & World*

Report is the ninth question, which reads: "Were there any preliminary autopsy reports or memoranda of any kind that were destroyed?" If the question is uncomplicated, the Answer is not:

> Yes, the record is plain that there had been a series of notes taken by Dr. Humes at the time of the actual performance of the autopsy [on the night of Friday, November 22] when he made a written—handwritten— autopsy report on Sunday, November 24.
>
> Bear in mind, on that point, that, when Dr. Humes was called upon to conduct an autopsy of the President of the President and then retired to his home on Sunday to make a formal report which he knew was important, he did not quite have the perspective of a historian who is culling the premises with a fine-tooth comb.
>
> He had never performed an autopsy on a President, and he was using his best judgment under the circumstances, never dreaming that loose, handwritten notes would become a subject of some concern.
>
> That matter was of concern immediately to his superiors, and he was questioned on it. He made a formal report on it, and he explained his reasons before the Commission.

COMMENT: I

The Question asked about "preliminary autopsy reports or memoranda" that were destroyed, and the Answer speaks to "a series of notes taken by Dr. Humes" which he destroyed "when he made a written—handwritten—autopsy report on Sunday, November 24."

- Unanswered is whether Dr. Humes destroyed a "preliminary autopsy report."
- Unmentioned is whether the other autopsy doctors, Boswell and Finck, had made notes which had been destroyed.

- Also unmentioned is that part of the question as to whether any "memoranda" were destroyed.

COMMENT: II

Regarding ". . . the record is plain that there had been a series of notes taken by Dr. Humes . . . which had been destroyed when he made a written . . . autopsy report on Sunday, November 24.": The following is taken from the testimony of Dr. Humes:

> In privacy of my own home, early in the morning of Sunday, November 24th, *I made a draft of this report* which I later revised, and of which this represents the revision, *That draft I personally burned* in the fireplace of my recreation room. (2H 373) [Emphases added]

COMMENT: III

In 1977 Harold Weisberg published his book, *Post Mortem*, and included on page 524 a copy of the following certificate, dated 24 November 1963:

> I, James J. Humes, certify that I have destroyed by burning certain preliminary draft notes relating to Naval Medical Autopsy Report A63-272 and have officially transmitted all other papers related to this report to higher authority.
>
> s/J. J. Humes
J. J. HUMES
CDR, MC. USN

[Handwritten] Accepted and approved this date

[Handwritten]   George G. Burkley
                   Rear Adm MCUSN
                   Physician to the President

Weisberg writes:

> This is the original of Humes' certificate that he
> burned a draft of the autopsy report. It is *not* the same
> copy printed by the Commission, 17H48, which does
> not include the handwritten approval of Dr. Burkley.
> Indeed, what can be said when the President's physician
> certifies that he accepts and approves the burning of
> evidence in the crime! . . .
>
> This certificate has led to the myth, propagated by Arlen
> Specter, that Humes burned his autopsy notes. 'The record
> is plain,' Specter told *U.S. News and World Report*, 10/1066,
> 'that there had been a series of notes taken by Dr. Humes at
> the time of the actual performance of the autopsy which
> had been destroyed.' Specter knew better, since he put this
> certificate (absent the Burkley endorsement) into evidence
> and had it confirmed by Humes (2H373) As the certificate
> on the next page makes clear, the 'autopsy notes' were
> preserved. What Humes burned he alternately described as
> 'preliminary draft notes (above) and 'that draft' of the
> autopsy report later revised (2H373).
>
> Having been assured by Humes that the first draft of
> the autopsy report had been destroyed forever by burning,
> Specter asked not a single question, not even the simple,
> indispensable question: Why? On this the Commission's
> record is barren. Specter, however, would like the public
> to believe otherwise. He now claims Humes 'explained'
> his reasons (for burning) fully before the Commission'—
> in his testimony.

(Note! Weisberg refers to 2H373, which is Dr. Humes's
testimony, for verification of Humes's usage: "a draft of the autopsy
report" as being what he burned. His testimony reads at 2H 373:

> In privacy of my own home, early in the morning of
> Sunday, November 24th, I made a draft of this report

which I later revised, and of which this represents the revision, That draft I personally burned in the fireplace of my recreation room.

It is difficult to reconcile that 1964 testimony with Arlen Specter's answer to Question 9 in his 1966 interview:

> . . . the record is plain that there had been a series of notes taken by Dr. Humes at the time of the actual performance of the autopsy . . . which had been destroyed when he had made a written—handwritten—autopsy report on Sunday, November 24." (50)

COMMENT: IV

Recalling Weisberg's "as the certificate on the next page makes clear, the 'autopsy notes' were preserved.'", that certificate, under date of 24 November 1964, reads on page 525 of *Post Mortem*:

> I, James J. Humes, certify that all working papers associated with Naval Medical School Autopsy Report A63-272 have remained in my personal custody at all times. Autopsy notes and the holograph draft of the final report were handed to Commanding Officer, U.S. Naval Hospital School, at 1700, 24 November 1963. No papers relating to this case remain in my possession.
>
> s/ J. J. Humes
> J. J. HUMES CDR, MC, USN

Received above working papers this date.

> s/ J. H/ STOVER, JR.
> CAPT, MC, USN
> Commanding Officer, U.S. Naval Medical School,
> National Naval Medical Center

[Handwritten]   Accepted and approved this date
[Handwritten]   George G. Burkley
                   Read Adm MCUSN
                   Physician to the President

Weisberg writes:

This, an original, copy, also bears the endorsement
of Dr. Burkley absent from the copy published by the
Commission. Here Humes makes explicit that he never
burned any notes made during the autopsy. 'Autopsy notes
and the holograph draft of the final report' were preserved
and given to Capt. Stover on November 24. Stover must
have received *all* autopsy notes because Humes specifies
'*all* working papers' of the autopsy were in his possession
until the transfer to Stover, after which 'no papers relating
to this case remain in my possession.' With this
transmittal, the mysterious story of the missing autopsy
notes begins. . . .

*   *   *

The 42nd Question and Answer exchange offers an
explanation that is difficult to accept without reservation. It reads:

How do you explain the apparent conflict between
Oswald's record as a poor marksman and the
extraordinarily excellent marksmanship that he displayed
on the day of Mr. Kennedy's assassination?
It is not true that Oswald was a poor marksman.
The commission examined the details of his record as a
marksman with the Marine Corps, going over the records
of his training. . . .
The experts in Marine training appeared before the
Commission . . . who characterized his ability as a
marksman, and they said that he was a reasonably good

shot and, compared to civilian standards, would be classified as a very good shot, perhaps even better.

What must be borne in mind on that subject is the nature of the shot which was presented by the situation. Bear in mind that as *the assassin stood in the sixth-floor window*, with the rifle pointing out, as described by several eyewitnesses at the scene—the angle of pointing—that it was practically a straight line with Elm Street, . . . so that there was no necessity for an abrupt shifting of the line of aim of the marksman as he fired multiple shots.

It was only a matter of working the bolt action and keeping it in the same line. And, at a shot under 100 yards with a four-power scope, the experts concluded that it was not an extraordinarily difficult shot.

COMMENT: I

There a number of problems within these declarations of Mr. Specter:

1. When the Marine training experts "characterized his ability as a marksman, and they said that he was a reasonably good shot . . .", the presumption must be that he was a reasonably good shot when judged by Marine Corps standards using the same type weapon used in firing for record. A further presumption is that his firing for record used the M-1 semi-automatic rifle that was standard issue in the 1950s. Such being so, it is simply unrealistic to accept any claims for his marksmanship outside those presumptions.

2. Absent specifications for comparative categories of both Marine and civilian shooters, it is absurd to compare a minimal Marine Sharpshooter—the average category for Marines—with *every* category of civilian shooters.

3. Depending upon what is meant by a "marksman with the Marine Corps" it may or may not be impressive that he was judged a "reasonably good shot". It is assumed that the Marine Corps categories were the same as those of the other service branches—Expert/Sharpshooter/Marksman.

   If, on the basis of two record firings, his better performance placed him the lower middle category, it is difficult to interpret the judgment that Oswald was a "reasonably good shot".

4. Mr. Specter simply avoids problems by not considering dependent variables such as the quality and condition of the weapon and scope.

5. A reputation for good marksmanship is not enhanced when some of Oswald's fellow Marines dismissed his marksmanship.

COMMENT: II

The most absurd claim in Arlen Specter's 1966 interview was that "the assassin stood in the sixth-floor window, with the rifle pointing out . . . ." Photographic evidence—Dillard Exhibit C, on page 66 of the Warren *Report*—clearly establishes that the window was only ¼ open during the assassination sequence.

*   *   *

I submit that the most extraordinary feature in this chapter of Senator Specter's memoir of his experience on the Warren Commission is calling readers' attention to this interview published in the October 10, 1966 issue of *U.S. News and World Report*. Recalling from his "Prologue" of *Passion for Truth* his awareness that ". . . every effort must be made to make this book totally accurate . . ." (xii), I urge every serious student of the John F. Kennedy assassination—defenders/neutrals/critics of the Warren Commission and its *Report*—to read that interview and Senator

Specter's evaluation of it: "They . . . did a decent job, reporting a lengthy verbatim transcript." I particularly recommend its reading to the future historians who, after all is said and done, will render the historical judgments on the quality of the Warren Commission's work and the validity of the conclusions in its *Report*.

It is difficult for me to escape the feeling that Senator Specter's style of writing, particularly in this chapter, "Truth and Lies", does in reality define those terms without writing them out to be read. I incline to believe that he subscribes to a simple dichotomy: That which the Warren Commission, its staff, and its *Report* say, is the Truth; that which the critics of the Warren Commission, its staff, and its *Report* say, are the Lies.

•

AFTERWORD

From my perspective as an academic historian, I was disappointed with Part Two of Senator Arlen Specter's book, *Passion for Truth*. The disappointment flows from the absence of an identification of the term "truth" as he uses it in that Part of the book. And I note carefully that I am not criticizing Arlen Specter's concept of truth—which I cannot do because I don't know what it is—but merely his failure to identify it so that his readers might have some reasonable basis for judging the values expressed in his writing. Given the intensity conveyed by the term, *Passion*, it would be educative to know to what it alludes. However, I also note that I have not read the other four parts of the book. So it is of course possible that he includes a working identification of the term, "truth", elsewhere in *Passion for Truth*. But inasmuch as "truth" does not appear as a topical entry in the book's index, my presumption is that he does not provide any working identification of it in the book as a whole. This seems a strange omission, particularly so when reading the chapters, "Truth Is the Client" and "Truth and Lies."

I did read the "Prologue" in the book. And I had high, very high, expectations when I read the following paragraphs on pages 3-4:

> I believe it is particularly important for staff counsel of the Warren Commission to tell their experiences, especially as to the procedures and integrity of the investigation. We have seen, in the thirty-five years since the assassination, an almost morbid obsession about it. The assassination of John Kennedy is the single most investigated event in world history, with the possible

exception of the crucifixion of Christ. And the challenges, the skepticism, and the questions only seem to grow. As soon as the commission legal staff was hired, the chief justice called us together and stressed our mission was to find the truth and report it. That is what we tried to do. 'Your client is the truth,' he told us.

During my extensive travel throughout Pennsylvania and the nation, in, open-house town meetings and in high school auditoriums, hardly a gathering occurs without questions about the Warren Commission, the Single-Bullet Theory, and my role in the investigation. I often answer that truth is stranger than fiction. Generally, I get nods of agreement.

I also often point out that questions still linger about the assassination of Abraham Lincoln.

My former law partner Mark Klugheit once said that my career has been marked by my believing a theory most people doubted (the Single Bullet) and doubting a woman most people believed (Anita Hill). The Bible says, 'The Truth shall make you free.' Keats said, 'Beauty is truth, truth beauty.' Everyone is entitled to his own opinion, but not his own facts. At the very least, truth is the indisputable foundation for a decent, just, and civilized society.

(Note! Anita Hill will be remembered as the recipient of a grueling examination by Senator Arlen Specter in the 1991 Senate confirmation hearings for Supreme Court nominee, Clarence Thomas. That account is found in four chapters of *Passion for Truth*.)

COMMENT

Beyond the problem of an unidentified meaning of "truth" as used in Senator Specter's memoir, there is an allied problem with the meaning of "facts." Thus, when he says "Everyone is entitled to his own opinion, but not his own facts," the not so subtle reality is that there is a tacitly understood meaning of "facts" as they relate to "truth". The result is a circular problem: "fact" means "a thing that has actually happened or that is really true" (*Webster's New World Collegiate Dictionary*, Fourth Edition, 1999, 508) but there is nothing to identify that which has really happened or which is really true independently of the claims of a speaker. The flaw is a matter of illogical reasoning in that facts are merely statements about something that must be interpreted. Stated differently, a "thing" is itself mute. In history, which is what the Kennedy assassination is all about, a person gives meaning to a "thing" by identifying what it is by way of empirical measurement in a conceptual scheme.

*   *   *

From my perspective, the most interesting part of Senator Specter's accounts in the ten chapters of his *Passion for Truth*'s Part Two occurs in the tenth chapter—"Truth and Lies"—where he makes passing reference to his interview given *U.S. News and World Report* in October 1966. Unfamiliar with the interview until I read his mention of it, I located a copy of the article and studied it very carefully. Though it lacked the desired definitions— "Truth" and "Lies"—it was a virtual gold mine for developing an understanding of Arlen Specter's version of the methodology utilized within the work of the Warren Commission. Particularly illuminating were Specter's responses to the eleventh, twelfth and thirteenth questions as they appeared in the October 10 issue.

Q & A 11 on Page 50:

Mr. Specter—going now to the crucial point of whether the wound in the neck was caused by a bullet coming from the front or rear—can you say how it was determined that the exit point for the bullet was in the front, rather than the rear?

Yes. I can tell you how the evidence was analyzed to determine which conclusion was accurate.

The President was found with a series of bullet wounds when examined both at Parkland Hospital and by the autopsy surgeons. At each place, they had only limited access.

First, at Parkland, the President's body was not turned over—for a number of reasons—most specifically because they dealt with the very grave problems of trying to restore his breathing, which was impaired by a hole in his throat, and, secondarily, to try to get circulation through his body, which was impaired by a massive head wound.

So he was gone before they could cope with the problems on his front side.

The autopsy surgeons were limited, to some extent, because they did not see the original hole in the front of the neck, to make observations on what it might have been.

The hole on the front of the neck was visible only for a relatively short period of time by the doctors at Dallas—from the time they removed his shirt and cut away his tie until the time Dr. Perry performed the tracheotomy.

The hole on the back of the President's back was visible for a protracted period of time by the autopsy surgeons who worked on him at the Bethesda Naval Hospital.

The autopsy surgeons described, in detail, the characteristics of the wound on the back of the President's neck, and there was no doubt but what those characteristics showed it to be a wound of entry—a round regular hole, which showed it to be a point of entry.

COMMENT

1. Of the eight paragraphs in the answer, only the first paragraph—Yes, I can tell you how the evidence was analyzed to determine which conclusion was accurate—is relevant to the question.
2. Paragraphs two through seven are *contextually* relevant but not essential for a direct answer.
3. Paragraph eight does not answer the "crucial point" question:

Can you say how it was determined that the exit point for the bullet was in the front . . . ? Instead, it focuses on "the characteristics of the wound on the back of the President's neck".

4. Effectively, The result is a non-answer to an important question:

> Yes, I can tell how the evidence was analyzed to determine which conclusion was correct, but I am not going to do so.
>
> Instead of that, let me inform you of some other things you really ought to know.

Q & A 12 on Pages 50-53

Were pictures taken of these wounds?

Yes, they were. But before we get into that, I want to develop this business of exit and entry wounds. The question is a very complex one, so let me continue to tell you what the characteristics were which indicated what was on the back and what was on the front of the President.

Besides the characteristics of the wound on the back of the President's neck, as testified to under oath by the autopsy surgeons, indicating it to be a point of entry, the fibers of the shirt on the back of the President and the fibers of the suit jacket on the back of the President were both pushed inward, and both indicated that the hole in the back of the President's neck was an entry hole.

The fiber on the front of the shirt was inconclusive—it was a slit. You could not determine in which direction the fiber was pushed, nor could the nick on the tie be used to determine what was the direction of the shot.

The hole on the front of the president's neck was such that, by its physical characteristics alone, it could have been either a wound of entry or a wound of exit.

The reason that such a hole would be inconclusive turns on the consideration that the bullet which passed through the President's neck met virtually no resistance in the President's body—it struck no bone, it struck no substantial muscle. It passed, in fact, between two large strap muscles. It did cut the trachea, and it passed over the pleural cavity. It exited through the soft tissue—or it passed through, without showing whether it entered or exited—the soft tissue on the front of the throat.

Tests were performed by wound-ballistics experts at Edgewood, Md., where the composition of the President's neck was duplicated, through a gelatinous solution in one sample, [53] through a goat-meat mixture in another, and through a third of, I believe, horse-meat composition. And goatskin was placed on each side of the substance to duplicate the President's neck.

The Mannlicher-Carcano rifle, which was found on the sixth floor of the Texas School Book Depository Building, was used in the experiments, as was the same type of bullet found on the stretcher in Parkland Hospital. The distance of approximately 180 feet was used, so as to set the stage as closely approximating the actual conditions as possible.

The characteristics of the entry and exit marks on the goatskin show that it is not possible to tell conclusively whether the point of entry on the goatskin, from a bullet that had traveled through the simulated neck, would be a wound of entry or a wound of exit, because of the factors involved in a high-powered missile which is stable when it passes through a relatively porous material.

Now when Dr. Perry answered questions at a news conference called in Dallas on the afternoon of November 22, as reported in the Commission work and as referred to in a "New York Herald Tribune" report of the same day, he was asked a series of hypothetical questions based on what was known at that time—for example, the fact that there was a wound on the front of the throat and a big wound in the top of the head.

And Dr. Perry said that those wounds could have been accounted for by having a bullet come through the neck, strike the vertebrae in back, and glance up through the top of the head—which would be an extraordinary combination, but one which was conceivable in the light of the limited information available to the Dallas doctors at that time.

But when all the factors I have described here were studied *in the context of the "overlay"—that is, all the things we had good reason to believe occurred*—when they were all put together, the Commission concluded that the wound in the front of the neck, whose characteristics were not determinative, was actually a wound of exit. [Emphases added]

COMMENT

1. Again, the first observation is that Mr. Specter chose not to answer the question beyond saying that pictures had been taken of the wounds.
2. Paragraph two of Specter's answer introduces a puzzlement which has never been satisfactorily explained. The puzzlement is generated by the introductory clauses in that complex sentence:

> **Because of the characteristics of the wound on the back of the President's neck, as testified to under oath by the autopsy surgeons, indicating it to be a point of entry, ...**

It is recalled that FBI agents James Sibert and Francis O'Neill were observers at the autopsy. It is also recalled that neither of their reports—of November 23 and 26—were published by the Warren Commission. However, Harold Weisberg included those reports in his 1975 book, *Post Mortem*. The November 23 report includes this entry:

> A total body X-ray and autopsy revealed one bullet hole located just below shoulders to right of spinal

column and hand-probing indicated trajectory at angle of 45 to 60 degrees downward and hole of short depth with no point of exit. No bullet located in body. (531)

And the November 26 report included a slightly more detailed account:

> During the latter stages of the autopsy Dr. HUMES located an opening which appeared to be a bullet hole which was below the shoulders and two inches to the right of the middle line of the spinal column.
> This opening was probed by Dr. HUMES with the finger, at which time it was determined that the trajectory of the missile entering at this point had entered at a downward position of 45 to 60 degrees. Further probing determined that the distance travelled by this missile was a short distance inasmuch as the end of the opening could be felt with the finger. (535)

The finger-probing account in the Sibert O'Neill report(s) is confirmed by Dr. Humes's March 16 testimony in a very brief exchange sandwiched between a discussion of a nick on Kennedy's tie and a discussion of a telephone call concerning the magic bullet. It reads:

> Mr. Specter. Now, Doctor Humes, at one point in your examination of the President, did you make an effort to probe the point of entry with your finger?
> Commander Humes. Yes, sir. I did. (2H 367)

The size of the back/neck wound was measured by Dr. Humes to be 7x4 millimeters (3H 351), which is the same measurement given in the Warren *Report* on page 88. Those numbers compare reasonably well with the size of the "magic bullet" fired from the 6.5 mm. Mannlicher-Carcano. But there is something baffling when those numbers are considered alongside the account of Dr. Humes's probing the bullet *entry* with his finger. And it becomes increasingly problematical when that data is considered in relation to Arlen Specter's passing mention of Dr. Humes's physical size in 1998. Writing in his memoir account in 2000, he states of Dr. Humes:

> He, Dr. Boswell, and I spoke over lunch in Washington in May, 1998. Retired at seventy-five and teaching part-time in Jacksonville, Florida, Humes had grown frail in his six-foot four frame, but he still spoke with gusto. (78)

While I can personally understand the frailty phenomenon for a man of seventy-five, I find it difficult to believe that as a six-foot four, 40-year-old naval officer in 1963 would have had even his *little* finger fit in a hole caused by the *entry* of a 6.5 millimeter bullet. It may of course be argued that a finger larger than the size of the bullet hole could be forced into it. Were that the reality in this case, however, I submit for the historians' judgment that such could not be done and simultaneously maintain the integrity of the "characteristics of the wound on the back of the President's neck." And if such was indeed the case, one can but wonder how that violation could be undertaken within the constraints imposed upon an autopsy surgeon who gave testimony "under oath" concerning the "the truth, the whole truth and nothing but the truth."

3. Paragraphs 3-10 purport to detail Arlen Specter's answer to what he describes as "this business of exit and entry wounds." Each of them provides an opportunity to argue what he refers to as "the characteristics . . . which indicated what was on the back and what was on the front of the President." I choose to forego the opportunity in favor of moving to consideration of Paragraph 11.

*   *   *

I urge the future historians to pay particular attention to the language of Paragraph 11 In Arlen Specter's answer to Question 12, which is repeated with emphases from above:

> **But when all the factors I have described here were studied *in the context of the "overlay"—that is, all the things we had good reason to believe occurred*—when they were all put together, the Commission concluded that the wound in the front of the neck, whose characteristics were not determinative, was actually a wound of exit.**

And the key word is "overlay". One can but wonder what would have been Arlen Specter's answer to a follow-up question, "What does the term 'overlay' mean?" And if he were to answer by way of repeating, "all the things we had good reason to believe occurred," the next question should be "And who are the 'we' who had good reason to so believe, and what was their standard for belief or disbelief?" But inasmuch as those questions have not been asked, it is really pointless to pursue such musings.

It is not pointless, however, to consider what may be understood by the term "overlay". It is a commonly used term in cartography, where it is appears in glossary style as a "printing or drawing on a transparent or translucent medium intended to be placed in register on a map or other graphic and which shows details not appearing or requiring special emphasis on the base material." In lay terms, I suggest to the historians that it means successive layers of data superimposed on the basic data used in construction of a detail map. (And if it means something else to Senator Specter, I urge him to undertake correction for the edification of the historians.)

More specific in *his* contextual usage, Q&A 13 in the Specter interview reads:

*When Dr. Humes called from Bethesda Naval Hospital
to Parkland Hospital in Dallas, in connection with the
autopsy, were the doctors in Dallas able to shed any light
on the wound, in the front of the throat, that had been
obscured by the tracheotomy?*

As I recollect it, the best information that could
be provided by the Dallas doctors involved the location
of the wound and its general characteristics, without
any definite statement as to the entry or exit.

You must bear in mind that as each individual, in
many contexts in this investigation, saw the evidence,
he saw only a limited amount of the evidence.

And the *overlay*, as the Commission saw it, with
literally thousands of pieces of information, is
something quite different from the way any individual
saw one incident or parts of the evidence.

And if it should happen—and I sincerely hope that it will—
that Senator Specter will indeed undertake to clarify matters for
the *future* historians, I hope that he will make clear his meaning
of the caution: "**You must bear in mind that as each individual,
in many contexts in this investigation, saw the evidence, he
saw only a limited amount of the evidence.**" For there are at
least two possible constructions that come to mind for his
allusion: (1) **Each individual** refers to **each witness**, who saw only
a limited amount of the evidence; or (2) **Each individual** refers to
each investigator who saw only a limited amount of the evidence?
Inasmuch as the first option—**each individual means each
witness**—seems an obvious truism: Each witness saw only a limited
amount of the evidence, logic suggests he means the second option—
each individual means each investigator. And that would normally
be an equally obvious truism. But in this case—the work of the
Warren Commission—for several reasons this is not obvious
because it was not a normal investigation.

*   *   *

Among the factors that detract from the phenomena of the work of the Warren Commission as a "normal investigation" are the following:

1. The Warren *Report* does not include biographical data indicating any of the lawyers appointed to or by the Commission had investigative experience in a homicide case.

   It may be argued from inference that two of the Assistant Counsel, Francis Adams and Arlen Specter had investigative experience; Adams by way of having served as Police Commissioner for New York City, and Specter for having served two years in the Office of Special Investigations in the United States Air Force. Absent relevant data, the possibility—but not evidence—exists that each *was* involved in the investigative dimensions of homicide cases.

   Adams, however, by way of claims from both Specter and his colleague, David Belin, disassociated himself the work of the Commission within two months of his appointment. Inasmuch as he had been paired as Senior Counsel with Specter, as Junior Counsel, in the work of Area I, Adams abandoned the most important part of the "investigation" to the then 34-year-old Assistant Counsel Arlen Specter, then on leave as an Assistant Prosecutor in the Office of the Philadelphia District Attorney.

2. A hint toward understanding the role of Arlen Specter in the work of the Warren Commission may be gleaned from the first Q&A in the 1966 interview given the *U.S. News & World Report*:

Mr. Specter, were you the Warren Commission's chief investigator on the facts about the assassination of President John F. Kennedy— how many shots, where the shots came from, other facts?

I would not describe my role at all beyond what appears in the work of the Warren Commission. It is possible from the notes of testimony to observe that I was responsible for taking the testimony of Governor Connally, Mrs. Connally, the autopsy surgeons, the doctors from Dallas, the wound-ballistics experts— so that it is apparent from that area what my role was. But I think, as an assistant counsel for the Commission, it would be presumptuous for me to characterize my role as that of the "chief investigator" on a key part of the assassination investigation.

What is apparent to me is that Arlen Specter took the testimony of virtually every key witness who gave testimony to the Warren Commission. What is equally apparent is that every one of Specter's witnesses was required to take an oath to "tell the truth, the whole truth, and nothing but the truth" while he, as the interrogator, was not under any sworn obligation to ask all the obvious questions in pursuit of that elusive commodity.

Applying that methodology to the device of the "overlay," the first question following the appearance of that term should have been: "Mr. Specter, what was the *base data* in the context of the 'overlay'—that is, all the things we had good reason to believe occurred?" It is difficult for me to believe the answer to that question could have been anything other than the FBI Report given the Commission on December 9: (1) Oswald was the lone assassin; and (2) There were three shots. And when Mr. Specter alludes to the "literally thousands of pieces of information" that were accommodated in the "overlay" methodology, it is simply astonishing that the overlay could accommodate the impossible contradictions required of it, while simultaneously maintaining fidelity to the base data that were the essential conclusions published in the Warren *Report* in September 1964: (1) Oswald was the lone assassin and (2) There were three shots.

Specific attention is directed to the following problems in the 38 years since Arlen Specter introduced his "overlay" context— "all the things we had good reason to believe occurred":

• *Eyewitness Identification of Assassin*

The Warren *Report* declares on pages 143-145:

> Howard L. Brennan was an eyewitness to the shooting. (143)
> Although Brennan testified that the man in the window was standing when he fired the shots, . . . most probably he was either sitting or kneeling. The half-open window, . . . the arrangement of the boxes, . . . and the angle of the shots virtually preclude a standing position. . . . It is understandable, however, for Brennan to have believed that the man with the rifle was standing. A photograph of the building taken seconds after the assassination shows three employees looking out of the fifth-floor window directly below the window from which the shots were fired. Brennan testified that they were standing, which is their apparent position in the photograph. . . . (144) But the testimony of these employees, . . . together with photographs subsequently taken of them at the scene of the assassination, . . . establishes that they were either squatting or kneeling. . . .
> Brennan could have seen enough of the body of a kneeling or squatting person to estimate his height. (145)

In Arlen Specter's overlay, this constitutes an eyewitness identification of the assassin, and is therefore one of the things the Commission "had good reason to believe occurred."

• *Throat wound of exit*

The Warren *Report* declares on pages 88-89:

> At that time [during the autopsy] they [the autopsy surgeons] did not know that there had been a bullet hole in the front of the President's neck when he arrived at Parkland Hospital . . . . (88)

Commander Humes, who believed that a tracheotomy had been performed from his observations at the autopsy, talked by telephone with Dr. Perry early on the morning of November 23, and learned that his assumption had been correct and that Dr. Perry had used the missile wound in the neck as the point to make the incision. . . . This confirmed the Bethesda surgeons' conclusion that the bullet had exited from the front part of the neck.

In Arlen Specter's overlay, this constitutes the first premise—the neck wound was a bullet exit wound—in his Single-Bullet Theory, which is a centerpiece in his investigation, and as such is another of the things the Commission "had good reason to believe occurred."

- *The downward angle of the "magic bullet"*

Autopsy surgeon Dr. Humes testimony on March 16 states "approximately 45° (2H 370)

Parkland surgeons Drs. Shaw/Gregory measurement on Governor Connally on April 21 is 25° (4H 137)

"Allowing for a downward street grade of 3°9', the probable angle through the President's body was calculated at 17°43'30", assuming that he was sitting in a vertical position." (Warren *Report* 106)

In Arlen Specter's overlay, this is the definitive measurement by the FBI in the May 24 reenactment commissioned by the Warren Commission, and as such is another of the things the Commission "had good reason to believe."

- *Rejection of Governor Connally's testimony*

Perhaps the most extraordinary of the decisions reached by the Warren Commission is that which appears as Conclusion 3. in the 12 Conclusions listed in its *Report*. It reads on page 19:

Although it is not necessary to any essential findings of the Commission to determine just which shot hit Governor Connally, there is very persuasive evidence from the experts to indicate that the same bullet which pierced the President's throat also caused Governor Connally's wounds. However, Governor Connally's testimony and certain other factors have given rise to some difference of opinion as to this probability but there is no question in the mind of any member of the Commission that all the shots which caused the President's and Governor Connally's wounds were fired from the sixth floor window of the Texas School Book Depository.

Combining two relevant fragments from the two sentences, the issue is joined by the relationship of those fragments:

(1) "There is very persuasive evidence from the experts to indicate that the same bullet which pierced the President's throat also caused Governor Connally's wounds."

(2) "Governor Connally's testimony and certain other factors have given rise to some difference of opinion as to that probability."

*   *   *

Very persuasive evidence from the experts

Chapter III of the Warren *Report* is titled "The Shots From the Texas School Book Depository." Therein, between pages 92-96, there is a section titled "The Governor's Wounds." Other than Governor Connally himself, the only names of persons found on those pages are two Parkland surgeons who rendered emergency services to him on November 22: Doctors Robert Shaw (chest surgery) and Charles Gregory (wrist surgery). The name of the surgeon—Dr. Thomas Shires—who treated the thigh wound ie not mentioned. The summary paragraph of their services includes the following:

> In their testimony, the three doctors who attended Governor Connally at Parkland Hospital expressed independently their opinion that a single bullet had passed through his chest; tumbled through his wrist with very little exit velocity, leaving small metallic fragments from the rear portion of the bullet; punctured his left thigh after the bullet had lost virtually all of its velocity; and had fallen out of the thigh wound.

It is of course possible that those doctors may have expressed their belief that there was "very persuasive evidence that the same bullet which pierced the President's throat also caused Governor Connally's wounds." But I am unable to find that evidence in either the Warren *Report* or the transcripts of their testimony.

Beyond those medical professionals, there is no identification of the experts who provided "very persuasive evidence . . . to indicate that the same bullet which pierced the President's throat also caused Governor Connally's wounds."

Governor Connally's testimony

The following is the concluding paragraph in the Warren *Report* section on "The Governor's Wounds." It reads on Page 96:

> Governor Connally himself thought it likely that all his wounds were caused by a single bullet. In his testimony before the Commission, he repositioned himself as he recalled his position on the jump seat, with his right palm on his left thigh, and said:

> > I . . . wound up the next day realizing I was hit in three places, and I was not conscious of having been hit in three places by the same bullet,

and I merely, I know it penetrated from the back through the chest first.

I assumed that I had turned as I described it a moment ago, placing my right hand on my left leg, that it hit my wrist, went out the center of my wrist, the underside, and then into my leg, but it might not have happened that way at all.

The Governor's posture explained how a single missile through his body would cause all his wounds. His doctors at Parkland Hospital had recreated his position, also, but they placed his right arm somewhat higher than his left thigh although in the same alinement. The wound ballistics experts concurred in the opinion that a single bullet caused all the Governor's wounds.

There is nothing in that extract from Governor Connally's testimony to identify it as a "factor" that has given rise to "some difference of opinion as to the probability that the same bullet which pierced the President's throat also caused Governor Connally's wounds."

There is, however, other Governor Connally testimony which does not appear in the Warren *Report*. It appears at 4H 132-133 in response to a question from Arlen Specter about the turn from Houston Street onto Elm Street:

We had just made the turn, well, when I heard what I thought was a shot. I heard this noise which I immediately took to be a rifle shot. I instinctively turned to my right because the sound appeared to come from over my right shoulder, so I turned to look back over my right shoulder, but I did not catch the President in the corner of my eye, and I was interested, because once I heard the shot in my own mind I identified it as a rifle shot, and I immediately—the only thought that crossed my mind was that this was an assassination attempt.

So I looked, failing to see him. I was turning to
look back over my left shoulder into the back seat,
but I never got that far in my turn. I got about in the
position I am in now facing you, looking a little bit
to the left of center, and then I felt like someone had
hit me in the back.

The exchange then took a different focus concerned with
Connally's reaction to being shot. Specter resumed the original
inquiry on page 135:

Mr. Specter. In your view, which bullet caused the injury
    to your chest, Governor Connally?
Governor Connally. The second one.
S. And what is your reason for that conclusion, sir?
C. Well, in my judgment, it just couldn't conceivably
    have been the first one because I heard the sound of
    the shot. In the first place, I don't know anything
    about the velocity of this particular bullet, but any
    rifle has a velocity that exceeds the speed of sound,
    and when I heard the sound of that first shot, the
    bullet had already reached where I was, or it had
    reached that far, and after I heard that shot, I had the
    time to turn to my right, and start to turn to my left
    before I felt anything.

      It is not conceivable that I could have been hit by
    the first bullet, and then I felt the blow from
    something that was obviously a bullet, which I
    assumed was a bullet, and I never heard the second
    shot, didn't hear it. I didn't hear but two shots. I
    think I heard the first shot and the third shot.
S. Do you have any idea as to why you did not hear the
    second shot?
C. Well, first, again I assume the bullet was traveling
    faster than the sound. I was hit by the bullet prior to
    the time the sound reached me, and I was either in a

state of shock or the impact was such that the sound didn't even register on me, but I was never conscious of hearing the second shot at all.

Obviously, at least the major wound that I took in the shoulder through the chest couldn't have been anything but the second shot. Obviously, it couldn't have been the third, because when the third shot was fired I was in a reclining position, and heard it, saw it and the effects of it, rather—I didn't see it, I saw the effects of it—so it obviously could not have been the third, and couldn't have been the first, in my judgment.

Clearly, as of the April 21 testimony of Texas Governor John Connally, a close personal friend of President Lyndon B. Johnson, with whom he had had lunch just hours before he gave his testimony, Arlen Specter's emerging Single-Bullet Theory has not been corroborated by a formidable on-the-scene witness of unimpeachable credentials.

Undaunted by what might have discouraged a less resourceful man, Arlen Specter impressively mastered the situation as explained in his answers to Questions 28 and 29 in his 1966 interview for *U.S. News & World Report*:

Yet the Governor was in opposition to the theory that that's the same bullet that went through the President—
Not precisely. The Governor is of the opinion that he was struck by the second shot—by a shot subsequent to the first shot which he heard—which conclusion was based on the factors of the speed of sound from a shot, as opposed to the speed of a bullet.

But the Governor's testimony was weighed with great care, as was the testimony of every single witness, and the Commission concluded that the *overlay of the evidence* was such that the Governor's opinions were not followed. But every one of his opinions was fully published and set forth for every reading American to see.

And you talked to the Governor, as counsel for the Commission— is that correct?

Better than talk; I questioned him in front of a court reporter, where every syllable that he uttered was taken down and preserved for everyone to read—after a very brief preliminary discussion as to the Commission procedure and a brief session where the Governor witnessed the Zapruder films [a tourist's movie of the assassination]. But the details of his testimony were stenographically transcribed.

COMMENT

1. Regarding "the Commission concluded that the overlay of the evidence was such that the Governor's opinions were not followed": it is not clear why the Governor's opinion was not followed in this instance.

    *   If his "opinion" was a conclusion based on the factor of the speed of sound in relation to the speed of a bullet, and that factor is empirically verifiable, why is the conclusion an opinion as opposed to a historical fact?
    *   If that factor—the speed of sound in relation to the speed of a bullet—was not accurate, all the Commission had to do was demonstrate the error as the basis for not believing the Governor's claim being made in his testimony. Absent a disclaimer on ground of either accuracy or credibility, there must be some other, unidentified, reason why the Commission rejected the claim.

2. What was the evidence that went into/onto (however the system works in Arlen Specter's investigative scheme) the

"overlay" from which the Commission concluded that the "evidence was such that the Governor's opinions were not followed." Noting the plural—opinions—what else besides the sound speed/bullet speed factor did the Commission reject in its dismissal of Governor Connally's claim that he was not hit by a bullet that hit President Kennedy?

*   *   *

I submit this proposition for the evaluation of the future historians: From the perspective of utility, it is difficult to imagine a more effective methodology than the overlay system employed by the Warren Commission. Its beauty lies in its simplistic dichotomy:

(1) When useful selective data—evidentiary or speculative—was needed for corroboration, it was found and inserted at whichever layer of overlay could effectively accommodate the desired result.

When unwelcome, credible, authentic data could not be denied, it was either isolated by way of a superimposition of irrelevant comment, or just ignored.

Either way the fixed focus in effective defense of the data must be maintained by answering only the questions that do not disturb the finished product of the overlay's conceptual scheme.

*   *   *

Perhaps the most extraordinary phenomenon of the great debate between the defenders of the Warren *Report* and the critics of that report, is the defenders' indifference to forty years' evidence, by way of public opinion polls, that has consistently supported the claims of the critics that the Warren *Report* is wrong. And there is no obvious reason to believe that reality will soon change. But if and when the defenders abandon their conviction it can only follow upon both the future historians' condemnation of that *Report*, and its unequivocal disavowal by the United States Government which created and maintains it.

This much, at last, seems certain: Writing in the genre of Senator Arlen Specter's *Passion for Truth*—insofar as the work of the Warren Commission is concerned—does little to hasten the day when the future historians will be inclined to disturb either the focus of Arlen Specter or his historical lens, or the determination of the United States Government to maintain that focus he created forty years ago.

Conversely, I incline to believe that critics of the Warren *Report* would do well to consider the futility of continuing the enervating electronic combat exercises with the *Report*'s defenders.

Rather, I would urge them to refocus their own intellectual energy by way of publication of conventional books which focus on defensible suggestions for the future historians. Should they be inclined to do so, they could discard the chronic problem of name-calling in the battle between "Truth" and "Lies", by embracing the exacting historical methodology of informed common sense and intellectual honesty in a manner which converts data into historical facts: Statements that are empirically verifiable within the framework of a conceptual scheme. And I submit that the best conceptual scheme for destruction of the Warren *Report* is the data found in the Warren *Report* itself. That would indeed ensure that the falling chips would land in a credible, authentic pattern.

INDEX OF NAMES